Hunters in the Shallows

Hunters in the Shallows

A History
of the PT Boat

Curtis L. Nelson

BRASSEY'S
Washington

First paperback edition 2003

Copyright © 1998 by Curtis L. Nelson

Editorial Offices: Order Department:
22841 Quicksilver Drive   P.O. Box 960
Dulles, VA 20166   Herndon, VA 20172

Brassey's books are available at special discounts for bulk purchases for sales promotions, premiums, fund-raising, or educational use.

Library of Congress Cataloging-in-Publication Data

Nelson, Curtis L.
    Hunters in the shallows : a history of the PT boat / by Curtis L. Nelson.
       p.   cm.
    Includes index.
    ISBN 1-57488-167-1(alk. paper) — ISBN 1-57488-601-0 (pbk. : alk. paper)
    1. Torpedo-boats—United States—History.   2. United States—
History, Naval. I. Title.
V833.N45 1998
359.8′358—dc21   98-15797
                                                CIP

First Edition

10 9 8 7 6 5 4 3 2
Printed in the United States of America

For Those

Who Served

Contents

Contents

Preface

I am a baby boomer, born to the generation that fought in World War II. My earliest inkling of "the war" came when my parents, both United States Navy veterans, showed me some service mementos they kept in a small box. Fascinated, I sifted through chevrons, brass buttons, black-and-white photos, and even bullets with little holes drilled in them. I don't remember anything else my mother and father might have done to encourage my interest in naval history; I only knew they had served and were proud of it. Perhaps that was enough.

PT boats always fascinated me, too. As a kid I saw the movie *PT 109*, devoured Robert J. Donovan's book *PT 109: John F. Kennedy in World War II*, and built cardboard mock-ups of the 109 in my basement. In 1995, while a graduate student in naval warfare studies, I decided to write a term paper on the origins of the famous boats. Why had the navy built PTs? What role had it expected them to play in the upcoming war? No one really seemed to know, so I decided to find out. The result is this book.

I am indebted to a number of people for their assistance in making this labor of love a reality. I want to thank my instructors at American Military University, Michael Palmer, Rod Paschall, and Paul Braim, for convincing me I could actually write academic prose; and William Morrison, in whose American naval history class I began this project, for letting me ask more questions than I answered in that paper, encouraging me to expand it into book form, and critiquing an early draft. Don Shannon of the PT Boat Museum and Library in Fall River, Massachusetts, and Alyce Mary Guthrie of P.T. Boats, Inc., of Memphis, were both very helpful in steering my initial research efforts. I would also like to thank Alyce Mary, and Cyndy Gilley of Do You Graphics, for the considerable photo research they performed on my behalf.

At the National Archives, where inevitably I landed, I had the valuable assistance of Vernon and Sandy Smith, Richard Peuser, and Kathy

O'Connor, whose diligence in attempting to track down some especially hard-to-find documents I greatly admire. My thanks also goes out to Lorena Lalicata of the Charles Edison Fund, Ray Teichman of the Franklin D. Roosevelt Library, and James Zobel of the MacArthur Archives, who spared no effort in keeping me supplied with information on PTs and Q-boats in the Philippines and General MacArthur's role in their development. I also want to thank Paul Stillwell of the United States Naval Institute for putting me in contact with the family of John Bulkeley, and James Cheevers of the Naval Academy Museum for details on picket boat *No. 1.*

Mike Walker and Kathleen Lloyd of the Operational Archives Branch of the Naval Historical Center were of considerable assistance, and I would like to give special thanks to Robert Cressman of the NHC for his invaluable critique of the manuscript. His comments and advice on everything from proper naval terminology to where to find sources I had given up hope of finding—or had not known existed—saved me from a lot of potential embarrassment. I hope the finished product meets with his approval. It would mean a lot.

I also wish to give heartfelt thanks to my editor, Don McKeon of Brassey's, for his interest and continuing faith in the book and my ability to see it through. Last but certainly not least I want to acknowledge my wife, Wendi, and our two daughters, Karlina and Linnea, for their patience and understanding throughout the long months Dad worked on his "project." I hope they will look back one day and be proud, too.

Curtis L. Nelson
Eden Prairie, Minnesota

Introduction

March 11, 1942—Luzon, Philippines

Darkness fell hard over Corregidor. A pall of death shrouded the twisted, war-torn landscape, settling like a heavy hand over the men and women gathered on the beleaguered island's North Dock. The stench of filth and destruction filled their nostrils. Stung by the humiliation of impending defeat at the hands of the Japanese, they hoped to escape an even greater ignominy: capture—possibly even death.

Dockside lay their shadowy means of flight, its engines idling impatiently: a United States Navy motor torpedo boat, or MTB. One by one the passengers boarded the small, battle-scarred man-of-war, threading their way between torpedo tubes and 50-gallon drums of gasoline lashed to the deck. With luck, they would not need the torpedoes on the long trip ahead; the extra gas they would need.

Soon only one passenger remained on the dock, Gen. Douglas MacArthur. He looked gaunt and dejected. Yet with characteristic aplomb the general paused and raised his gold-braided cap in farewell salute to his doomed island command. He then replaced his cap and stepped on board. "You may cast off, Buck, when you are ready,"[1] he told the MTB's skipper, thirty-year-old Lt. (jg) John D. "Buck" Bulkeley. Bulkeley's boat slipped its moorings, joining the three remaining MTBs of Motor Torpedo Boat Squadron Three in the inky blackness of Manila Bay. They had one chance to run the Japanese gauntlet. Tonight there would be no turning back.

The next thirty-six hours became the stuff of naval legend. Bulkeley pierced the Japanese blockade, reached the island of Mindanao 560 miles south of Corregidor, and delivered the wet—but grateful—MacArthur for subsequent evacuation by B-17 to Australia. For this

1

Bulkeley became a national hero. MacArthur, of course, went on to prominence as commander in chief of the Southwest Pacific Area. The two men, however, were not the only beneficiaries of this daring naval exploit. MacArthur's rescue also catapulted the American MTB itself into the headlines.

Given the nature of the boats and the circumstances surrounding the event, it is easy to see why. By the spring of 1942, the United States Navy's motor torpedo boats were hardly a secret weapon. The press on the eastern seaboard had followed the sometimes contentious story of their development in the years immediately before the war. They were called PT boats, with "PT" designating a "motor torpedo boat" in the navy's nomenclature system; the PT was not, as is popularly assumed, a *P*atrol *T*orpedo boat.[2] Even so, "PTs" were untested in battle, and they were small, measuring a mere 77 feet. They were built of little more than mahogany, plywood, and lots of glue, like throwbacks to the bygone days of wood ships and iron men, which only heightened their romantic appeal. MacArthur's popularity also contributed to their public luster, his rescue being the first good news to come out of the Philippines since the Japanese attack the previous December.

Predictably, the national press enthusiastically hyped the spunky little boats. A book quickly followed: *They Were Expendable*, by W. L. White, an American war correspondent who earlier had written *Journey for Margaret*, describing his adoption of a three-and-a-half-year-old girl made an orphan by the London blitz. Based entirely on interviews with Bulkeley and three of his officers, *They Were Expendable* overdramatized MTB Squadron Three's role in the futile defense of the Philippines and MacArthur's forced flight. Despite heavy censorship, it became a runaway best seller. For the rest of World War II the public firmly associated PT boats with heroic feats of derring-do. This largely merited but excessively propagandized reputation endures in popular culture to this day.

More than wartime hype was at work here. There is a solid conceptual basis for the PT's appeal, one deeply rooted in the boats' characteristics and the jobs the navy expected them to perform. It is a concept based on twin elements, both of which play an integral role in explaining the PT phenomenon: risk and reward.

Without risk there are no heroics. By that measure, the wartime public must have considered just being on board a PT boat the epitome of romantic heroism. PTs were, of course, tiny compared to other war vessels. One naval writer, for example, affectionately described the PT as a "barnacle-encrusted plywood motorboat hardly bigger than a stockbroker's cabin cruiser."[3] They were unarmored, and defensively equipped with little more than light infantry weapons. Even a single rifle bullet, if luckily placed, could shut down a PT's formidable engine array, rendering the normally fast, highly maneuverable craft all but defenseless. A well-placed bomb or shell could, in a single hellish instant, reduce the boat to matchwood. Since this left them highly vulnerable to air attack, PTs, and similar craft employed by other warring powers, rarely ventured out in daytime without assured air superiority. They were, in effect, nocturnal hunters, and one false move—or sheer bad luck—could turn them into the hunted instead. On a PT boat there was little room for error.

The second element explaining the PT's fame is its potential for bringing a daring commander great reward. Because of their small size in relation to the torpedoes they carried, MTBs packed more lethal punch pound for pound than any other warship afloat during World War II. They attacked warships and merchant vessels far larger and more heavily armed than they were, and often sank them. This gave many PT operations a distinctive High-Noon, David-vs.-Goliath quality, naturally lending a Hollywoodish air to everything they did.

However exciting such wartime hype and tales of genuine heroism, one of the most fascinating—and largely unexplored—aspects of America's celebrated motor torpedo boat is the story of the navy's belated development of the type. It has been popular to suggest that PT boats were "not wanted" by the prewar navy. This is not true; it simply took the navy a while to see the need for them. Once the navy did, it built them. There is, of course, far more to the story than this. As we will see, controversy stalked their hastened development every step of the way.

The United States Navy's early negative reaction to MTBs is easy to fathom. They were simply seen as irrelevant. The MTB evolved from the Civil War spar torpedo boat, essentially a small, mechanically driven launch designed to deliver an underwater explosive charge against the side of a ship. In the late 1800s, however, the United States was slow to adopt the new naval technologies—the self-propelled torpedo, internal combustion engine, and planing hull—that were to define such small craft in their twentieth-century prime. In the early 1900s, when the Europeans, and private American boat builders, successfully combined these technologies and began experimenting in earnest with MTBs, the United States refused to tag along. This refusal reflected dramatic changes then taking place in American naval thinking.

Up to the end of the nineteenth century, the United States, in the face of overwhelming European naval superiority, of necessity followed a wartime naval strategy the French termed *guerre de course*. This age-old strategy called for using a few strong, fast ships for coastal defense and commerce raiding. When, in the aftermath of the Spanish-American War in 1898, the United States emerged as a world power, the navy became free to discard this modest, and institutionally debilitating, outlook. Passive coastal defense was discredited; sea control became the policy of choice. In war, the battle fleet was now to seek out the enemy in decisive fleet actions (*guerre d'escadre*). MTBs, considered passive coastal defense vessels because of their short range and poor seakeeping abilities, were ignored.

In early 1937, spurred by the successful record of MTBs in the World War and fears of another war, America's naval bureaucracy got behind a modest experimental MTB program. With the enthusiastic support of Assistant Secretary of the Navy Charles Edison, the son of noted inventor Thomas A. Edison, the program received funding in 1938. Later Edison, assisted by President Franklin D. Roosevelt, took bold, controversial steps to accelerate the pace of development, moving the program out of its experimental phase into the operational well before anyone thought possible. That General MacArthur, himself an early proponent of "torpedo-throwing" boats, was able to hitch a ride on one of America's first operational MTBs is testimony to Charles Edison's perseverance.

PT boats flourished during World War II. The first operational boat (PT-9) joined the fleet in June 1940. By 7 December 1941, eighteen of the newly minted craft suddenly found themselves in the combat zone. A dozen boats were at Pearl Harbor on that fateful day, six of which awaited transshipment to join the six boats of John Bulkeley's squadron in the Philippines. There poor maintenance facilities, bad gas, and nonexistent air support hampered the boats' effectiveness. They nevertheless fought the Japanese steamroller as best they could before all were destroyed.

From their experiences, and others in the Solomon Islands and New Guinea later on, formal PT doctrine began to emerge. Formality, however, counted for little when it came to PT boats. Wartime doctrine can be said to have consisted of "sneakin' in, hittin' hard, and runnin' like hell." This is what made PT surface actions so colorful. They were more reminiscent of sharp, close-action skirmishes in the age of sail than long-range fleet engagements in the age of steam.

After the war, most navies discarded their MTBs. They were old and battle-worn, in many cases rotten from exposure to seawater. Absent the unique strategic and tactical conditions under which they fought, they no longer served an operational purpose. Despite their obsolescence, though, they have not been forgotten. With such a dramatic reputation, and given the popular interest in World War II naval operations as a whole, MTBs, and PTs in particular, have continued to attract attention.

The problem is that this attention has included very little in the way of serious scholarship. Perhaps it is because stories of PT operations make such exciting reading and because the PTs themselves, being little more than oversized speedboats, are of such intriguing design that virtually everything written about them has been either operational or technical in nature. However fascinating, or simply informative, these works are, they take an uncritical view of PT operations and do nothing to place the PT within the overall context of American naval history.

What strategic and tactical rationales, for example, kept the navy from early on appreciating the value of MTBs? Why were they finally built? What were their anticipated uses? One would expect serious naval scholars to have addressed these, and many other, questions over the past half century. One is hard pressed, though, to find much of substance about PTs in scholarly naval works. Like the prewar navy, naval historians have taken their time warming up to the tiny PT.

There are several reasons for this neglect. One is that during their prewar development PTs existed on the periphery of the navy's institutional aspirations. They cost relatively little and involved few diversions of badly needed manpower from larger ships and shore installations. Most examinations of the pre–World War II navy can therefore overlook PTs and not be compromised. The same is true of studies of the wartime navy. PT boats were generally not an integral part of the war-winning blue-water fleet. Nor in their ancillary role did they contribute decisively toward victory.

The foregoing does not mean they should be neglected, of course. The reasons for this nevertheless do give rise to a vital question: Were PT boats worth the prewar navy's investment in them?

It is easy to see why nations developed aircraft carriers, submarines, and destroyers. Further, in light of the decisive role all played in World War II, it requires little effort to convince people their development was justified. This is not so in the case of PT boats. Had they not been built, could their wartime role have been adequately taken over by other small combatants? Or could their role have been eliminated altogether by tactical innovation or strategic sidestepping?

This work is intended to answer this and other intriguing questions about the American MTB, thereby helping fill the gap between uncritical adulation and neglect. Part I will examine the forces that created the PT boat. Part II will offer a critical analysis of the PT's operational value during the whole of its existence in World War II. The purpose is to gain a deeper understanding of these remarkable little ships and provide a springboard for future critical studies.

Fortunately, there are a number of vital navigational aids along the route. First and foremost is the acknowledged "bible," the official history of PT boats entitled *At Close Quarters: PT Boats in the United States Navy*.[4] A former PT officer, Capt. Robert J. Bulkley, Jr., wrote the manuscript immediately after the war. In 1962 the Naval History Division published Bulkley's work in book form, because of the tremendous interest in PT boats occasioned by another former PT officer's rise to the presidency—John F. Kennedy. Though *At Close Quarters* gives short shrift to the underlying reasons for the PT's development, it is an absolutely indispensable resource for anyone wishing to study PT boats. Viewing them in the larger context of U.S. naval history and offering critical analysis of their value are simply not within the book's scope.

Actually, in discussing development, *At Close Quarters* is quite exceptional: Other secondary works on PT boats devote only a page or two to their preoperational history, if that. There is one important exception. That part of the book dealing with development is drawn largely from an unpublished administrative study of PT boats, "An Administrative History of PT's [sic] in World War II," written by the Naval History Division in 1946. Though the authors, Frank A. Tredinnick, Jr., and Harrison L. Bennett, again both former PT officers, delve more deeply into the background of the PT boat than any other source, even they avoid detailed discussion of the larger questions about the PT's role in our naval history.

In more recent years there have been a number of commercial works dealing specifically with PT boats. Some are anecdotal; most are technical, concentrating on details of boat design, construction, and deployment—apparently for the benefit of model and weapon enthusiasts. These books do not address aspects of the PT phenomenon much beyond the basic operational level. Again, that is not their purpose.

There are other sources as well, each with its own piece of the puzzle to contribute to the larger analysis of the PT boat in American naval history. Despite them, the seas are largely uncharted, the sailing far from smooth. Therein lies the challenge.

PART I

A Question of Need
(1864–1941)

Lt. William Barker Cushing, USN. *National Archives*

CHAPTER ONE

The First Yankee Torpedo Boats

*A*challenge: Lt. William Barker Cushing, USN, expected nothing less from the Confederate picket aboard the half-submerged wreck of the *Southfield*. Both the sunken Union gunboat and a Confederate schooner loomed directly ahead in the narrowing river. The rainy, bone-chilling night was black—but not black enough. Surely he and his men would be seen. The steam launch's chugging engine, boxed in and further muffled with a tarpaulin, was barely audible in the stillness. Yet how could the rebels not hear the water slapping her bows and those of the cutter he towed behind?

Cushing gave the wheel a quarter turn, steering between the two blackened shapes. A bare twenty-yards separated them from the *Southfield*. The tension mounted; no one dared breathe. He had already signaled the twelve-man assault force in the cutter to make ready to attack the picket at the first sign of trouble. Closer now. So far so good—

Suddenly he heard voices in the night; a match flickered and went out. Still no alarm sounded, no shouts were heard. No hot lead skipped over the cold, blackened waters of the Roanoke toward them. They were past. Better yet, they remained undetected.

Now things were about to get really serious. Another mile upriver, tied to a Plymouth wharf and protected by an unknown number of Confederate troops, lay a veritable mountain of iron, a Goliath to test the mettle of his puny David—the ironclad ram *Albemarle*. Cushing had a personal score to settle with the ram, though he would as soon seize her as sink her. To seize her he had but a handful of heavily armed men; to sink her but a single 100-pound spar torpedo. Either way, he was about to have the distinction of sailing the United States Navy's first small torpedo boat into action against an enemy ship for the first time.[1]

The dramatic story of Lt. William Cushing and his steam launch, an open-deck 45-footer ingloriously named picket boat *No. 1*, is a fitting place to begin an examination of PT boats in the United States Navy, despite the fact that three quarters of a century separates the adventures of the former from the advent of the latter. Picket boat *No. 1*'s short operational history as a torpedo boat is instructional for two reasons. First, it dramatically illustrates the technical hurdles to be overcome before a truly effective small torpedo boat could be built. Second, it demonstrates the necessity of having a courageous, rock-steady hand at the helm of a small combatant. In William Barker Cushing we see, long before the first sailor rode the canting deck of a PT boat, the debut of quintessential PT man.

The tall, twenty-one-year-old lieutenant used picket boat *No. 1* in the fall of 1864 for a specific tactical purpose: to deliver him and crew into the *Albemarle*'s lair, and—if necessary—sink the ram with its crude spar torpedo. It was for Cushing to succeed where all other means, some conventional, some not, had failed. From the beginning, the cards were stacked in grim repose against him.

In January 1863 the Confederates began constructing the *Albemarle* at Edwards Ferry, in the Roanoke River near Halifax, North Carolina. Like so many rebel ironclads, she suffered her share of construction impediments: poor or nonexistent dockyard facilities, lack of skilled workmen, shortages of iron. A lack of secrecy also plagued her, though in the American Civil War, in which the two sides shared a common language, porous borders, and the traditions of a free press, there was nothing unusual in that. Disaffected Southerners, spies, and runaway slaves soon brought the Union blockaders news of the ram taking shape along the riverbank.[2] Unfortunately, the payoff on such intelligence was not as high as it might have been.

As early as the summer of 1863, reports came of the *Albemarle*'s armor plating being laid on. Lt. Comdr. Charles Flusser, commander of the Union blockading squadron in the lower Roanoke, became worried. Two years earlier, Union forces had seized the port town of Plymouth, eight miles inland from Albemarle Sound along the south bank of the Roanoke, in an effort to control the inland waters and deny them to blockade runners. Flusser surmised the ram might be part of an eventual Confederate effort to retake Plymouth. With his gunboats unable to navigate as far upriver as Edwards Ferry, he asked the army for a raid by five hundred cavalry to destroy the ram. The army felt the ram posed no threat as yet, so did nothing in response to his request.[3] Since Union ironclads drew too much water to enter Albemarle Sound, Flusser could only place obstructions in the river above Plymouth, strengthen his wooden blockading force . . . and wait.

On 18 April 1864, with workmen hammering the last rivets into place, the *Albemarle* finally headed downriver to assist in the capture of

Plymouth. She was 158 feet long with a 35-foot beam, and built of 8-by-10-inch timbers of solid yellow pine. Her two powerful 8-inch—actually 6.5-inch—Brooke rifles were encased in an octagonal shield 60 feet long, covered by two 2-inch layers of iron plating. The guns each pivoted between ports, so as to be capable of firing ahead, or behind, or to the sides. Her ironclad ram was strong and deadly sharp. In the early hours of April 19 she got a chance to make good use of it.

The *Albemarle*, after successfully passing over the river obstructions above Plymouth, set upon Flusser and two of his heavily armed side-wheelers, the gunboat *Miami* and the converted ferryboat *Southfield*. In the darkness, the *Albemarle* rammed and sank the *Southfield*. On board the *Miami*, Flusser was killed when a 9-inch shell rebounded off the side of the armored beast and exploded at his feet, almost tearing him to shreds. The *Miami* retreated, leaving the Confederates in control of the lower Roanoke.

For William Cushing, then commander of the screw steamer *Monticello* on blockade duty off Wilmington, North Carolina, Flusser's death came as a tragic blow. Flusser had been one of Cushing's instructors at the Naval Academy before the war. He considered him his closest friend after his brother Alonzo—who had been killed at Gettysburg. When he heard the news about Flusser, Cushing said grimly: "I shall never rest until I have avenged his death."[4]

In the meantime, Flusser's fears were realized. The morning after the *Albemarle* sank the *Southfield*, the undamaged ram helped rout the Union defenders in Plymouth. The Confederates retook the city on the 20th; 1,600 Union soldiers marched into captivity. This was a major victory. With the main Confederate armies stalemating Union forces to the north in Virginia, the ability of the Confederate hinterland to sustain the troops was more important than ever. By retaking Plymouth, the rebels had regained access to two of the richest counties in North Carolina. Something had to be done about the *Albemarle*.

Acting Rear Adm. Samuel Phillips Lee, commander of the North Atlantic Blockading Squadron—and a third cousin of Robert E. Lee—sent for Capt. Melancton Smith. Smith had experience with rams, having fought the *Manassas* in the New Orleans campaign. Lee spelled out for Smith his prescription for success against the *Albemarle*: more ships, more guns loaded with extra-heavy charges, pouring more fire into the ram's weak points—her ports, stern, and roof. As a last resort they were to ram the ram. The Union navy was getting desperate.

On May 5, 1864, Smith had a chance to put Lee's strategy to the test. The *Albemarle*, hoping to add her weight to a planned Confederate assault on the Union garrison 60 miles to the south at New Bern, sallied forth into Albemarle Sound. This time Smith had seven wooden

Sassacus ramming the *Albemarle,* 5 May 1864. *National Archives*

ships to drive home the attack. One, the *Sassacus,* succeeded in ramming the *Albemarle,* but did little damage. The *Miami* exploded a spar torpedo near the *Albemarle*'s hull; that too accomplished little. The Union fleet took a heavy beating, but compelled the *Albemarle* to retire. One of her big guns was damaged, her smokestack was riddled, and her steering mechanism was shot up. Though the ironclad remained basically intact, her condition forced both North and South to reevaluate their respective tactical and strategic situations.

The Confederates resolved never to risk the *Albemarle* in pitched battle again if they could help it. Nor did they fail to appreciate the ram's value in the continuing defense of Plymouth, whose recapture had been the bright spot of the Confederate efforts. The *Albemarle* became, in effect, a fleet in being unto herself, tied to the wharf at Plymouth, protected by pickets and shore batteries and her own still formidable guns.

The federal navy resolved that the ram must be sunk, though Admiral Lee decided he could risk no more wooden ships, and ironclads still drew too much water to break into the sounds. Captain Smith suggested a tug with a spar torpedo to "torpedo the monster in her lair."[5] No one, however, believed the tug would ever get close enough. Finally Lee saw only one option: "a small-boat raid either to cut the vessel out and capture her, or blow her up with powder."[6]

Lee cast about for a senior officer with a reputation for daring to lead such a desperate expedition. The ones on his list either were unavailable, could not be spared, or were unwilling to try. Finally, early in July he sent for William Cushing.

He made an excellent choice. William Barker Cushing, born on 4 November 1842, near Milwaukee, Wisconsin, had a younger sister and four older brothers—two of whom were to have notable military careers of their own. Will's father died when Will was four. Soon after, the family moved to Fredonia, New York, where Will attended Fredonia Academy. He was said to be good at math and English; a born fighter, he was even better with his fists. During his Fredonia childhood, his irrepressible self-confidence and appetite for challenge grew, as did his ambitions. In 1856 he became a page in the United States House of Representatives.

The next year, he traded on political contacts in Washington and back home in Fredonia to land an appointment to the United States Naval Academy in Annapolis. There new challenges awaited him—though not always of the officially prescribed sort. Midshipman Cushing earned more than his fair share of demerits at the Academy. Pranks and exam deficiencies, the latter perhaps blown out of proportion because of personal resentments against him by certain instructors and administrators, finally caused his enforced resignation on 23 March 1861, only three weeks before the South fired on Fort Sumter. Whatever the underlying reasons, Gideon Welles, then secretary of the navy, would write in 1876 that he felt them "insufficient to justify such severe treatment."[7]

To what degree Welles's later opinion was colored by Cushing's stellar war record is a matter of conjecture. He certainly had reason to be impressed. After Sumter, Lieutenant Flusser managed to get Cushing an appointment, backdated to April 1, as a master's mate. It was a relatively junior rank reactivated because of the wartime emergency, but better than no rank at all. Cushing took it from there. Attached to the North Atlantic Blockading Squadron, which covered the coastline from Virginia south to Wilmington, he was subsequently given command of two prize ships and participated in raids ashore, helping burn and capture Confederate ships around Hampton Roads. Promoted to lieutenant in August 1862, he became executive officer of Flusser's *Commodore Perry*. Cushing's coolness under fire during an attack on Franklin, Virginia, in October finally earned him a command of his own, the iron gunboat *Ellis*.

Cushing was assigned to blockade duty off the North Carolina coast, but he was too restless a soul for passive patrolling. He took to his small boats, on "expeditions," burning a schooner here, destroying a saltworks there. He even took to slipping his gunboat over dangerous shallows, at one point capturing the town of Jacksonville for a few hours. His luck ran out in New River Inlet when the *Ellis* grounded within range of some heavy Confederate shore batteries. With five men he returned the rebel fire until the gunboat was pounded to pieces. Afterward he set her afire and slipped away to join the rest of his crew on board a captured schooner.

In April 1863, commanding the *Commodore Barney,* a powerful 512-ton steamer, Cushing fought a series of brisk river actions in the lower Nansemond above Suffolk, Virginia. On the 22nd, to avenge a Confederate misuse of a flag of truce, he led a 90-man expedition ashore, at one point audaciously countercharging a troop of rebel cavalry. The Confederates, unused to such daring, turned and fled. Gideon Welles, who had long followed Cushing's career with interest, wrote a letter of commendation after Suffolk, praising his "gallantry and meritorious services."[8]

Such laudatory reviews paved the way in late summer 1863 for Cushing to command the 655-ton steamer *Monticello,* then undergoing repairs in Philadelphia. She was not ready to sail until February 1864, when she joined the blockading fleet off the Cape Fear River, downstream from Wilmington. Here Cushing led his most daring shore expeditions. On February 29, without permission, he led twenty men in two small boats under the guns of Fort Caswell and stole in the darkness into the riverbank town of Smithville—now Southport—in an attempt to capture Gen. Louis Hebert, who had the effrontery to be absent at the time. Cushing contented himself with the capture of Capt. Patrick Kelly, chief engineer of the defenses of the port, and returned unscratched to his ship.

On the morning of 7 May 1864, the rebel ironclad *Raleigh* appeared at the mouth of the Cape Fear and drove off the blockading squadron. Upon learning of that "mortifying affair"[9] off Wilmington, Cushing wrote to Admiral Lee offering his services to destroy the ram. He proposed two possible courses of action.

> If [the *Raleigh* is] there when I arrive, I shall use the *Monticello* as a ram, and will go over her or to the bottom. If [the ram is] inside, I shall send in a written petition to carry the ram by boarding in the harbor.[10]

The *Raleigh* never showed. Subsequently, on May 21, Welles received Cushing's boarding plan. The letter is instructive in that it gives us a glimpse of Cushing's tactical mind at work, outlining ideas he later hoped to use against the *Albemarle*:

SIR: Deeming it possible to capture the rebel ironclad *Raleigh* at Wilmington, N.C., I submit the following plan, respectfully asking that it may receive your favorable consideration:

Selecting a time when the ram is anchored at Smithville, I can, as I have often done, take boats by the forts and up to the anchorage, and, covered by the darkness, approach to within a short distance of the enemy. The *Raleigh*'s low, flat decks are very favorable to boarders, while there are but two small hatches communicating with the officers' quarters and berth deck. The lookouts can easily be swept away and these hatches guarded, while the main force, rushing through the ports and hatch, will secure the unprotected gun deck, which will give us the engine room and magazine hatch.

Objections have been made that after gaining the deck we could no more get at the lower portion of the vessel and the crew than they could get at us. To settle this point, I propose to take in the boats a dozen long-fuzed shell and a piece of slow match. One shell down each hatch would be likely to bring all hands to terms.

Having captured the ironclad we might bring her out or destroy her, as circumstances dictated.

With my knowledge of the harbor and of the ironclad, I am confident that I would succeed.

I have the honor, sir, to be, very respectfully, your obedient servant,

W. B. CUSHING[11]

Welles enthusiastically approved the plan. After sunset on June 23, Cushing set out in a cutter with seventeen men. He slipped into the river past the forts, foxed the soon alerted defenders into thinking he was running for home, and hid out along the riverbank only seven miles below Wilmington. The next day Cushing captured some fishermen who told them that the *Raleigh* had run aground at high water a few days before, and when the water dropped she had fallen apart under the weight of her own armor. That night, Cushing reconnoitered Wilmington's river defenses and lay in wait along the main turnpike between Wilmington and Fort Fisher—the fort guarding one of the Cape Fear outlets downriver—to see what further information he could obtain. He captured a pilot, among others, who eventually led him to the *Raleigh*, which proved indeed a total wreck.

By more clever boat handling the next night, Cushing succeeded in escaping with several prisoners and valuable information about the state of Wilmington's defenses. "Captain Cushing's Exploits in the Cape Fear River," as they came to be known, caused quite a sensation. "Many Northern newspapers picked up the story, and it was known for thirty years after the war."[12] It was Cushing's reports of these adventures that had prompted Lee in early July to send for him.

Cushing arrived at Hampton Roads on the 5th. When Lee suggested he have a go at the *Albemarle*, Cushing "at first proposed an attack . . . with our gunboats at Plymouth, or a boat expedition, led by himself, with 80 men."[13] Lee instead proposed "a torpedo attack, either by means of [an] India-rubber boat . . . which could be transported across the swamp opposite Plymouth, or a light-draft, rifle-proof, swift steam barge, fitted with a torpedo."[14] The admiral requested Cushing's "mature views" on the subject within a couple of days.

Cushing responded in a July 9 letter to Lee, in which he outlined his intentions:

> SIR: Deeming the capture or destruction of the rebel ram *Albemarle* feasible, I beg leave to state that I am acquainted with the waters held by her, and am willing to undertake the task.
>
> If furnished with three low-pressure tugs, one or more fitted with torpedoes, and all armed with light howitzers, it might be effected, or, if rubber boats were on hand to transport across the swamp to a point immediately abreast of Plymouth. If detailed for this work, I would like to superintend the outfit of the boats. . . .[15]

The above wording used by both Admiral Lee and Lieutenant Cushing is significant from a larger historical perspective. Lee, writing a good forty years before the first modern European MTB dropped into the water and seventy-five before the first American version, was defining the essence of a whole new class of war vessel. It should have a shallow, or light, draft for use in coastal and riverine operations; it should be rifle-proof, suggesting sufficient sturdiness of construction to ward off small-arms fire; it need be swift, to strike quickly and hightail it afterward; and it should be equipped with a torpedo. That the "torpedo" of the time was little more than a canister of guncotton on a long pole is beside the point. Despite the primitive technology, the idea was the same as that of the later self-propelled torpedo: the underwater delivery of a powerful explosive charge against the side or underside of a ship.

While Lee helped presage the MTB, Cushing deserves some credit for anticipating MTB tactics. Even before Assistant Secretary of the Navy Gustavus Fox approved Cushing's overall plan and ordered him to proceed to New York to "purchase suitable vessels," Cushing settled on a torpedo attack as his preferred method of handling the rebel ironclad. As he wrote in his postwar journal, he hoped to employ two

> very small low-pressure steamers, each armed with a torpedo and a howitzer . . . [intending] that one boat should dash in, while the other

Picket Boat No. 1. Engraving from a painting by R. G. Skerrett, 1900. *Naval Historical Center*

stood by to throw canister and renew the attempt if the first should fail.[16]

These tactics bear great resemblance, admittedly in a general, commonsensical way, to those initially developed by the British for use with their MTBs and MGBs—Motor Gun Boats—during World War II. While the MGBs would make feint attacks, firing their guns and distracting the defenders, the MTBs would press home their attacks with torpedoes.[17]

On August 7, in preparation for Cushing's arrival, Gideon Welles telegraphed the general superintendent of the New York Navy Yard, Rear Adm. Francis H. Gregory, to fit out two steam picket launches for his use.[18] There were six such open-deck launches available, in various stages of completion in private yards along the coast, the Navy Department having ordered them earlier that year to assist with the blockade.

Admiral Gregory made available to Cushing the two picket boats farthest along, designated *No. 1* and *No. 2*. Each had a single screw, powered by a double piston reciprocating Root engine. The navy's engineers hoped the Root, which "[took] up in weight and room less than 50 percent of any marine engine [then] in use,"[19] would ease a nagging problem, one that later profoundly affected MTB development: the basic incompatibility between bulky steam technology and small boat hulls.

As to the size of these picket boats, there is continued debate, particularly over *No. 1*, the boat Cushing used against the *Albemarle*. Cushing, in his postwar journal, wrote that it was 30 feet long. The *Official Records of the Union and Confederate Navies in the War of the Rebellion (ORN)* lists her at 40 feet. Chief Engineer William W. W. Wood, who oversaw her outfitting, told the *New York Times* that *No. 1*, built by Lewis Hoagland of New Brunswick, New Jersey, was 45 feet in length, with a 9- or 10-foot beam. Dana Wegner, curator of ship models for the United States Navy, acknowledges that the "documentation is confusing" but believes the 45-foot figure is probably the more accurate.[20]

When Cushing arrived in New York he set about transforming *No. 1* and *No. 2* into spar torpedo boats:

> A 12-pounder howitzer was fitted to the bow of each, and a boom was rigged out, some fourteen feet in length, swinging by a goose-neck hinge to the bluff on the bow. A topping lift, carried to a stanchion inboard, raised or lowered it, and the torpedo was fitted into an iron slide at the end. This was intended to be detached from the boom by means of a heel-jigger [lanyard] leading inboard, and to be exploded by another [trigger] line, connecting with a pin, which held a grape shot over a nipple and cap. The torpedo was the invention of [First Assistant] Engineer [John L.] Lay of the navy, and was introduced by Chief-Engineer [William W. W.] Wood.[21]

As for the complicated Wood-Lay spar torpedo equipment, Cushing "later remarked laconically that it 'had many defects and I would not again attempt its use.'" He nevertheless successfully tested the device several times on the Hudson River, concluding it would work if one "had enough leisure to make sure that the lanyard and trigger line were pulled at exactly the right moments."[22]

Cushing pressed ahead, despite low confidence in his principal weapon. He may have done so out of awareness of Confederate successes with similar spar-mounted devices. On 5 October 1863, a semisubmerged cigar-shaped steamer called the *David* had exploded a torpedo against the ironclad screw steamer *New Ironsides*, causing considerable damage. On 17 February 1864, the Confederate submersible *H. L. Hunley* torpedoed and sank the steam sloop *Housatonic* off Charleston—the first successful submarine attack in history, despite the loss of the attacker. The main explanation for his dogged enthusiasm, however, seems to be his belief that he would not need his unwieldy torpedo. He still hoped to do with the *Albemarle* what he had wanted to do with the *Raleigh:* capture her if possible.

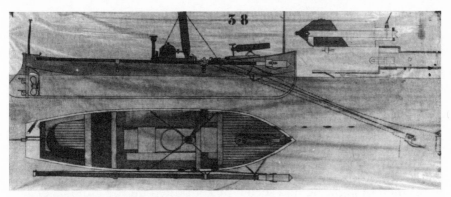

Picket Boat No. 1, profile and deck view, showing the workings of the Wood-Lay spar torpedo equipment. *Naval Historical Center*

On September 8, Welles ordered Admiral Gregory to send Cushing and his picket boats to Hampton Roads. He also requested that the other four picket boats, even then undergoing torpedo conversion under Engineer Wood's direction, be sent there as soon as completed.[23] Not until Thursday, September 22, did both picket boats leave the New York Navy Yard for Hampton Roads. Cushing left the next day to meet them.

Along the way both boats suffered engine trouble and grounded. They finally became separated when Ens. William L. Howorth, in command of *No. 1* and impatient with the delays, left *No. 2* when her engine began acting up again. On October 8, *No. 2* put into the mouth of Reason Creek, in the Great Wicomico Bay on the coast of Virginia, to make repairs. Before they could be finished a Confederate home guard unit—about seventy-five to eighty men—attacked from shore. Acting Ens. Andrew Stockholm, commanding, fought back until he expended his ammunition, then set fire to the launch. They were all taken prisoner, the boat lost.[24]

With his one remaining torpedo boat, Cushing steamed through the Chesapeake and Albemarle Canal, including a thirty-mile stretch still in Confederate hands. Finally, on October 23, he reached the Union stronghold of Roanoke Island. There he learned he had already lost the element of surprise. The rebels apparently had seen, or knew from Northern newspaper accounts, that there was "a steam launch" in the river intending to destroy the ram.[25] He also discovered that five months earlier a coal heaver named Charles Baldwin, with four other enlisted men, had made a swimming raid on the *Albemarle*, attempting to attach two 100-pound torpedoes to the bow. Rifle fire drove them off.[26] The Confederates, it seemed certain, would be expecting him.

Cushing, though angered by the security breach and the loss of one of his boats, remained undaunted. On October 24 he joined the blockading fleet off the entrance to the Roanoke, only twelve miles from the *Albemarle*'s lair, and asked for additional volunteers for the dangerous mission ahead. With his derring-do reputation preceding him, the only problem proved to be whom to turn down. Here he learned of another problem. Acting Ens. Rudolph Sommers had recently completed several small-boat reconnaissances of the Roanoke. He reported there were possibly as many as four thousand soldiers in Plymouth and along the riverbank near the moored ram. Worse, one of his men thought he had seen a picket posted on the gunboat *Southfield*, sunk to her hurricane deck about a mile below the town.[27] To anyone else the whole operation would have looked unthinkable, but not to William Cushing. "Impossibilities are for the timid," he wrote later, and "we determined to overcome all obstacles."[28]

There were obstacles aplenty. At nine in the evening of October 26, Cushing set out for the *Albemarle* with fourteen men in picket boat *No. 1*, but soon ran aground near the entrance to the Roanoke. By early morning they managed to free her. Cushing decided to press on upriver, until they were challenged by a Union army tug—attracted to them, so Cushing believed, by the sound of the picket boat's chugging engine. By the time they explained themselves, it was too late to continue. He would try again the next night.

The abortive attempt, it turned out, proved a blessing in disguise. The tug's challenge alerted Cushing to a potentially fatal defect in his boat, one that would later haunt its twentieth-century progeny: loud engines. Whereas later MTB engineers would try to ensure a stealthy, undetected approach by installing a small auxiliary engine or mufflers, Cushing simply had the whole engine boxed in with wood and covered with a tarpaulin. Had he not seen the need—and taken the unexpected opportunity—to so muffle the noisy engine, he might have been detected far sooner than he was the following night. If so, events could have taken a nasty turn for the worse.

The extra day also made possible another benefit: additional intelligence provided by three escaped Negroes, who reported a picket on board the *Southfield*. A Confederate schooner was also anchored near the wreck. No one knew how many rebels were on board the two ships; even so, Cushing could ill afford to ignore even a handful. When he set out once again toward midnight on October 27, he had twelve eager volunteers from the side-wheel gunboat *Shamrock* in one of that vessel's cutters, towing them behind. Should the picket challenge his passage, the men in the cutter would scramble on board and prevent them from sending up a warning rocket, while he went after the ram.

The night of 27 October 1864 was cloudy, about 65 degrees, with occasional rain and a light wind out of the south. For two hours Cushing and crew made their way silently upriver, fearful of being challenged by sentries along the bank. No talking was allowed. Communication was by hand signal, or by tugging on lines Cushing had attached to his body. The young, lanky lieutenant became, in effect, the lone nerve center upon which the entire fragile enterprise depended.

On the deck at the bow was Ensign [Thomas] Gay. He would handle the boom, swung around to the stern now, on which the torpedo was fixed; around his wrist was a line which Cushing held in his hand; the boom was to be moved forward when he pulled the line. Another line was attached to Engineer [William] Stotesbury's ankle; a pull on it would increase the speed, two pulls would stop the engines altogether. Still another line was attached to the howitzer; if it became necessary to shoot it, [Ens. William L.] Howorth would man the gun, and receive firing orders by means of the line, which he would attach to his person at the last moment. Lieutenant Cushing held these three lines in his right hand; in his left he held the two lines which controlled the torpedo. He had worked out the manner in which he would, in an emergency, distinguish between the five different lines, and had no doubt that his mind would, at the last moment, be absolutely clear.[29]

Around 2 a.m. they reached the schooner and the wreck of the *Southfield*. As previously related, they passed by without being detected, one Confederate newspaper later reporting the six-man picket to have been asleep.[30] A mile and ten anxious minutes later, they reached Plymouth. Rounding a bend, they saw the *Albemarle*, her ominous silhouette outlined against the riverbank. The town was dark and silent.

That decided it. Cushing gave the wheel a sharp turn and headed for a nearby wharf. He still hoped to land and dash aboard the ram from the bank. That he believed himself outnumbered 10 to 1 by the ram's crew, and that thousands of enemy troops were close by, did not faze him a bit. As he wrote later,

. . . a surprise is everything, and I thought if her fasts were cut at the instant of boarding, we might overcome those on board, take her into the stream, and use her iron sides to protect us afterwards from the forts. . . . but just as I was sheering in close to the wharf, a hail came, sharp and quick, from the ironclad, and in an instant was repeated. I at once directed the cutter to cast off, and go down to capture the guard left at our rear, and, ordering all steam, went at the dark mountain of iron in front of us.[31]

The silent night erupted in violence. Heavy small-arms fire opened on the Yankee torpedo boat from troops on shore and on board the ram itself. Not having such a thing as star shell, the Confederates lit a large fire on the bank to expose their attacker. It exposed something else. ". . . by its light," Cushing related, "I discovered the unfortunate fact that there was a circle of [cypress] logs around the *Albemarle*, boomed well out from her side, with the very intention of preventing the action of torpedoes."[32]

Cushing ran alongside the torpedo boom until amidships, braving the unrelenting hail of fire to examine the logs more closely. He turned away and sped off—at all of 7½ miles an hour, the torpedo boat's rated top speed—intending to describe a wide arc in the river and go at the boom bows-on. His one hope for success lay in the logs being so slimy, from being long in the water, that under a full head of steam his bow would ride up over them and slip into the ram's pen. So what if he never got out again—with the firing "very severe," he would probably never get in to begin with. Even as he turned away, the back of his coat was torn out by buckshot and a bullet carried away the sole of his left shoe. Miraculously, he remained unhurt.

Cushing headed a hundred yards out into the river, circled, then came charging back. He dropped the three lines he used to control boat movement, taking up the torpedo lanyard ("heel-jigger") in his right hand and the trigger, or exploding, line in his left. He ordered the torpedo boom swung around, facing the bow. As the boat drew nearer, there came a lull in the firing. Cushing reports that

> the [*Albemarle*'s] captain hailed us, again demanding what boat it was. All of my men gave comical answers, and mine was a dose of canister from the howitzer. In another instant we had struck the logs and [the bow rose and hung up on them], with headway nearly gone, slowly forging up under the enemy's quarter-port. Ten feet from us the muzzle of a rifle gun looked into our faces, and every word of command on board was distinctly heard.[33]

Standing at the bow, Cushing ordered the boom lowered and angled forward until the torpedo disappeared into the water beneath the ram's armored overhang. As bullets "perforated" his clothing, he gave "a strong pull on the detaching-line, [waited] for the torpedo to rise under the hull, and hauled in [his] left hand [holding the trigger line], just cut by a bullet."[34]

Cushing's attack on the *Albemarle*, 27 October 1864. *National Archives*

Just as the torpedo exploded, sending a tower of water crashing down on the frail boat, the *Albemarle*'s 8-inch rifle spoke, unleashing 100 pounds of grape. Most of it flew harmlessly overhead, but the combined effect was to flatten the torpedo boat against the logs, forcing her down into the water. Believing his boat doomed, Cushing twice refused requests to surrender and shouted for his men to save themselves. He threw off his sword, revolver, shoes, and coat and dove into the frigid Roanoke. Several of his men followed suit, bullets everywhere filling the night air and smacking the water's surface.

Cushing's subsequent escape reads like a Hollywood script. In the minutes after the attack, he managed to elude Confederate picket boats sent to capture him and the other waterlogged swimmers. After failing to save one of his crewmen from drowning, he crawled spent from the river, some way downstream on the town side, and passed out on the bank. The next day, after several near-brushes with rebel sentries, he learned from a Negro that his mission had been successful: he had indeed sunk the *Albemarle*. He stole a small skiff from seven careless Confederate pickets and made his way downstream, reaching the picket vessel *Valley City* that night after ten hours of continuous paddling. When he told the fleet of the ram's demise, "rockets were thrown up and all hands were called to cheer ship."[35]

So ended the first completely successful small torpedo boat attack in history, an earlier attempt by a 23-foot cigar-shaped Confederate "torpedo launch" on the steam frigate *Minnesota* having damaged, but not sunk, the huge warship.[36]

The results of William Cushing's exploit were nothing less than spectacular. According to the *Albemarle*'s captain, Lt. Alexander F. Warley, the torpedo blew "a hole in her bottom big enough to drive a wagon in." The ship sank immediately, though no one was killed, settling on the river bottom in eight feet of water, her casemate the only part showing above the lapping Roanoke.[37] With the ram out of the way, the Union squadron bombarded Plymouth on October 31. When a shell blew up the defenders' magazine, the rebels hastily withdrew, leaving the town—and the now worthless ram—in Union hands. The sinking also opened all of Albemarle Sound to Union assault and freed the blockading squadron for employment elsewhere. The *Albemarle* herself was raised, towed to Norfolk, and ingloriously sold for scrap in 1867.

Of the fifteen men in picket boat *No. 1*, eleven were captured, two drowned. Only one other man, an ordinary seaman named Edward Horton, made it back to the fleet besides Cushing.

The torpedo launch remained afloat, used as a picket boat by the Confederates until later recaptured during the general Southern collapse. Sent to the Naval Academy after the war, it was rerigged, called the "Steam Brig *Albemarle*," and used by Adm. David Dixon Porter, superintendent of the Academy from 1865 to 1869, as his barge. In the fall of 1867 it was modified with a new steam engine, but on 19 October 1867 its boiler exploded, killing the engineer, Even Hoyt, and three sailors. Admiral Porter was luckily too sick to use the boat that day. The launch apparently "lasted a good while longer" at the Academy, then was sold to someone in Baltimore.[38]

As expected, Lieutenant Cushing, whose exploits were already legendary, became a national hero. He received a letter of commendation from Gideon Welles, a letter of thanks from Congress, and promotion to lieutenant commander, and was eventually awarded $56,000 in prize money.[39] He never again participated in any "torpedo boat" raids, probably because of a lack of suitable tactical opportunities worthy of his stature in the closing months of the war. He remained in the U.S. Navy, but, sadly, after a long, painful illness—of still unknown origins—that left him delirious in his final days, he died in the Government Hospital for the Insane in Washington, D.C., on 17 December 1874. He was only thirty-two. His early death was a sad ending for a man whom the no less venerated Adm. David Farragut would call "*the* hero of the [Civil] War."[40]

Though Cushing moved on, torpedo boat fever swept the Union navy after the *Albemarle* sinking. On November 5, Rear Adm. David Dixon Porter, having relieved Lee as commander of the North Atlantic Blockading Squadron on October 12, read General Orders No. 34 to the crews assembled on the quarterdecks of the squadron's ships in Hampton Roads. He paid homage to Cushing's gallantry and offered

> opportunities . . . to all those who have the energy and skill to under-take like enterprises; and 20 volunteers are wanted at this moment to perform a like service. The chances are death, capture, glory, and promotion.[41]

Due to Cushing's infectious example, 77 officers, 149 enlisted men, and the entire ship's company of the steamer *Tuscarora* volunteered. On November 26, an old friend of Cushing's, Lt. Roswell H. Lamson, offered to take a "like torpedo boat" and destroy two rebel steamers, the *Tallahassee* and *Chickamauga*, near Wilmington. Nothing came of Lamson's request.[42] On December 2, Porter revealed what he meant by "like service" when he wrote to the commander of the James River Squadron that "the picket boats must always be kept in readiness at night, with their torpedoes ready for service, and if an ironclad should come down they must destroy her, even if they are all sunk."[43] Fortunately for the crews likely to be involved, such an opportunity never presented itself.

However, there remained few important targets, like the *Albemarle*, the Union torpedo boat men could reasonably be expected to sneak up on in the middle of the night. Even had the war continued another year or two, it seems unlikely the circumstances producing the *Albemarle* victory would have been reproduced. Although picket boat *No. 5* later captured several Confederate steamers near Halifax on the Roanoke, the Union navy mostly employed the boats on reconnaissance, or in running mail—service similar to that of the first operational PT boats in the Philippines in the winter of 1941.[44] Indeed, the surviving picket boats, grandiosely dubbed "The New Steam Picket-Boat Fleet" by the Northern press, made no more torpedo attacks at all during the few remaining months of the war.[45]

It was probably just as well. When one considers the spectacular raid on the *Albemarle* in retrospect, an inescapable truth hits home: Picket boat *No. 1* was a poor torpedo boat. Her success came in spite of severe technical deficiencies, most notably her complicated torpedo device, and a tactical situation verging on disaster at every turn. The boat lucked out, achieving tactical surprise because of the inattentiveness of the *Southfield* picket. As a result, Confederate small-arms fire was confused and largely ineffective. It is to poor Confederate leadership, however, that we may attribute the first of *No. 1*'s two greatest pieces of good fortune.

Lieutenant Warley, the *Albemarle*'s captain, reported that he had doubled the guard on board the ram and "took extra precaution," having heard of a steam launch in the river gunning for his command. He further reported that after small-arms fire was opened on the small steamer, the "officers and men were at their quarters in as quick time as was possible, but the vessel was so near that we could not bring our [8-inch] guns to bear. . . ."[46] Certainly by the time Cushing hung the launch up on the boom he was too close. The gun crew was unable to sufficiently depress the ram's after gun, so the 100 pounds of grape it eventually fired slashed harmlessly over the launch. But what was that gun crew doing during the minute or two (or three?) it took Cushing to make that long, slow arc a hundred yards out into the Roanoke, preparatory to hitting the log boom head-on? Was the gun even manned yet, despite Warley's possibly blame-shifting assertion that the men quickly reached their stations? Especially when the launch was on her final straight-on approach, she represented a nearly stationary target well out into the river. Blame surprise, the night, poor visibility from the ram's gunport, general confusion, or overconfidence, or wrap all of the above up in the "fog of war." Whatever the reason, the rebels failed to take advantage of this unexpected last-minute opportunity to blow picket boat *No. 1* out of the water.

The launch's second piece of good fortune was Lt. William Barker Cushing. He was the torpedo boat's single greatest—indeed, indispensable—asset. Without Cushing, or some other unusually fearless, cool-headed man at the controls, it seems doubtful that picket boat *No. 1* could have succeeded in actually blowing up the *Albemarle* despite its good luck in reaching its target. Naval historian James R. Soley, a later assistant secretary of the navy, describes Cushing's merits in overcoming the deficiencies of the "exceedingly complicated" torpedo apparatus he was forced to operate:

> . . . it must be remembered that nothing short of the utmost care in preparation could keep [the torpedo's] mechanism in working order; that in making ready to use it, it was necessary to keep the end of the spar elevated until the boat had surmounted the boom of logs, and to judge accurately the distance in order to stop the boat's headway at the right point; that the spar had then to be lowered with the same precision of judgment; that the detaching lanyard had then to be pulled firmly, but without a jerk; that finally, the position of the torpedo under the knuckle of the ram had to be calculated to a nicety, and that by a very gentle strain on a line some twenty-five or thirty feet long the trigger-pin had to be withdrawn. When it is reflected that Cushing had attached to his person [multiple] lines . . . ; that he was also directing the adjustment of the spar by the halliard; that the management of all these lines, requiring as much exactness and delicacy of touch as a surgical operation, where a single error in their employment, even a pull too much or too little, would render the whole operation abortive, was carried out directly in front of the muzzle of a 100-pounder rifle, under a fire of musketry so hot that several bullets passed through his clothing, and carried out with perfect success, it is safe to say that the naval history of the world affords no other example of such marvelous coolness and professional skill as were shown by Cushing in the destruction of the *Albemarle*.[47]

Though Soley's account differs slightly in the details, the point is easily made: Without Cushing's exceptional steadiness under fire it is doubtful the United States Navy's first small torpedo boat attack would have succeeded. Of course, there is also an element of luck involved: One bullet in Cushing's vitals before he had a chance to launch or explode the torpedo, and things would probably have turned out far differently.

It is purely speculative whether another member of the crew would have, or could have, stepped in to take Cushing's place had he been shot down. Neither Cushing nor his biographers touch on this point. It seems likely someone else was trained, but would he have held up under fire and yanked the lines at precisely the right moment? These questions are unanswerable. One thing is certain, however, even if the Union navy did not realize it at the time. For future small, unarmored torpedo boats to be a viable weapon, they needed two things the converted picket boats did not have: high speed and a less complicated torpedo device, one easily capable of launch far from the deadly muzzles of the enemy's big guns and small arms.

It would be another forty years before both improvements were melded sufficiently by naval engineers to form the first modern MTB. Already, however, even as Cushing sailed up the Roanoke, gingerly fingering the lines of his primitive spar torpedo, others were taking those first tentative steps toward the future. A radically new kind of torpedo was in the offing, one that would not only make possible the modern MTB but change the nature of naval warfare forever. For that story, we need to leave the war-torn United States and turn our attention across the Atlantic.

Chapter Two

The Ship Killer

he exact date of the meeting is lost to history, though not its
fateful consequences. In 1864, a retired Austrian naval officer,
Fregattenkapitän (Commander) Giovanni de Luppis, showed a
British engineer named Robert Whitehead plans for a strange new
ship-destroying weapon. Intrigued, Whitehead rethought and reengineered de Luppis's idea. Eventually the Englishman created a device
that did destroy ships, lots of ships. So many ships, in fact, that navies
the world over bristle with the device to this day. We call it the torpedo.

The impact of this dark, porpoiselike contraption on late-nineteenth
and twentieth-century naval history is very nearly incalculable. In the
decades following the introduction of Whitehead's revolutionary new
device, many navies converted or specially built small, non-oceangoing
surface craft to carry it. These boats did not, however, find lasting favor.
By the end of the nineteenth century, small torpedo boats were out of
vogue in Europe, while the United States built none to begin with. To
fathom this state of affairs, we must examine the naval climate in the
United States, the torpedo's European origins, and America's surprising reaction to it and overseas torpedo boat developments.

The United States Navy, despite its glorious fighting tradition and
seemingly prominent place in America's defense establishment, has not
been a sacred cow. It often twists in the wind, subject to cycles of boom
and bust, tethered to the constitutionally mandated whims of civilian
presidents and partisan leaders in Congress. While we would have it no
other way, it has not been easy on the navy as an institution. Over the
decades our civilian leaders have held widely differing philosophies regarding the size, makeup, professional quality, and proper function (if
any!) of the navy. These philosophies, shaped by a variety of social, economic, political, and personal factors, challenge the navy's institutional
interests at every turn.

Central to this ongoing philosophical debate is the question of how large and technically advanced the United States Navy should be compared to potential overseas rivals. During the nineteenth century, before America became a major world power, this debate was a luxury of sorts. The United States' relative geographic isolation from Europe, combined with a lack of strong enemies sharing the North American continent, meant vital national interests rarely demanded a particular, self-evident naval strategic response. Presuming ourselves reasonably safe behind our watery moat, we felt free to pick and choose the kind of navy we wanted.

While some political leaders sought to build the navy up, others pushed to have little or no navy at all. These small-navy people, collectively called anti-navalists, proceeded from a variety of motives. Those from inland agrarian states resented footing the bill for naval ships whose presence seemed to only benefit merchants—and their congressmen—from the seaboard states. Others simply saw large, autocratic institutions such as Britain's Royal Navy—and, by extension, the United States Navy—as affronts to democratic peoples. Since the young nation could ill afford a big fleet anyway, anti-navalists frequently held sway in both the White House and Congress. They debated to keep the navy small and unobtrusive, hoping to keep America from becoming sucked into the morass of European power politics. To their credit, they succeeded.

Before the Civil War, the federal government was free to employ the navy's few ships chasing pirates and slave traders and protecting American overseas commerce. Fortifications and land militias were to suffice in the unlikely event of an invasion, while the navy's job was to cripple the enemy's seaborne commerce—as it tried, but failed, to do against the British during the War of 1812—and to run at the first sign of serious naval opposition.

The Civil War, 1861–65, temporarily blew away the freedom to debate the navy's proper scope and function. The navy had only 42 ships in April 1861, scattered among its various cruising stations around the world. By the end of 1864 the Union navy listed nearly 700, mounting almost 5,000 guns. In sheer numbers and cutting-edge technology the navy rivaled even Great Britain's.

By 1870, however, the United States Navy had returned to its prewar state—and function. It counted only 52 ships in commission, many of which were obsolete.[1] While the European navies, rivals all, leaped ahead in the 1870s and 1880s with revolutionary improvements in steam, armor, and ordnance, the United States allowed its navy to deteriorate. The relative neglect of the navy during this period, referred to as "the doldrums" by American naval historians, is relatively easy to comprehend.

> A reaction against things military had set in even before the final downfall of the Confederacy. It was widely believed that the American people had probably fought their last war. The United States had no overseas colonies to defend. We had no incentive to interfere in the periodic crises of the Old World. It was then deemed unthinkable that we would ever embark upon a war of conquest. Wide oceans separated us from all potential enemies. And the unstable balance of power in Europe would effectually deter any of the Great Powers from adopting "an aggressive policy towards the United States." All things considered, there seemed to be slight justification for maintaining a powerful navy patterned after those of the European Powers.[2]

Slight justification indeed. America had other things on its mind after 1865: reconstruction; building railroads to connect west with east; settling the vast expanses of the continent in between. To these ends the navy itself was largely irrelevant.

Since Congress, and the conservative naval officers in charge of the navy, only required naval vessels to show the flag and protect the nation's overseas commerce from minor diplomatic nuisances, there seemed no need for armored ships with the latest high-powered ordnance. The officers preferred pristine white—actually gray—canvas to bulky steam engines and dirty coal bunkers. Aesthetics aside, the latter took up space badly needed for the stowing of extra provisions while cruising on distant station—an important concern given the country's lack of overseas colonies. In short, the country rejected the new technologies, so eagerly embraced by foreign navies, as being incompatible with the navy's simple commerce-protecting mission.

As might be imagined, this not unreasonable devotion to finding uniquely American solutions to uniquely American problems did have an adverse effect on the nation's reaction to the Whitehead torpedo—only not in readily imaginable ways.

By the end of the American Civil War, underwater explosive devices were nothing new. Their violent reputation derived from a single, terse hydrodynamic fact: Water concentrates, not dissipates, the force of an underwater explosion. Even a small charge placed against a ship's hull can do tremendous damage, as countless sailors and civilians alike have discovered to their peril.

European experiments with underwater explosives date back to the early 1600s. Later, upstart American colonists got into the act. In 1775,

David Bushnell, looking to name a 150-pound charge he hoped to attach by submersible (the *Turtle*) to the British frigate *Eagle* anchored in New York harbor, coined the term "torpedo," after the electric rays of the Torpedinidae family. Unlike his charge, the name stuck. It soon came to denote all underwater explosive devices.

His and all subsequent "torpedoes," however, had one considerable drawback: They had no independent means of movement. They either had to lie in wait for enemy ships or be maneuvered into contact by daring sailors like Cushing. None were self-propelled, with all the attendant advantages to the attacker, who could simply stand back, set the beast loose, and watch the fireworks. Robert Whitehead changed all that.

It is said that twin passions dominated the genteel Englishman's long, productive life: proving to himself and the rest of the civilized world that he could solve seemingly intractable engineering problems, and making money. By any measure, he proved extremely good at both.[3]

In 1864, at age forty-one, Whitehead managed and served as driving mechanical genius behind the Austrian manufacturing firm Stabilmento Tecnico Fiumano (STF), located a few miles down the Adriatic coast from Trieste, at present-day Rijeka in Croatia. He had a topflight reputation as a marine engineer, supplying the expanding Austrian navy with first-rate, if not exactly revolutionary, steam engines and boilers.

The plans de Luppis showed him, originally inspired by some unknown officer of the Austrian coast artillery, were for a contraption called the *Küstenbrander*—"coastal fire ship." Designed to attack blockading ships close inshore, the "fire ship" was essentially a very small boat filled with explosives and a percussion detonator, powered by a small clockwork engine and screw, and steered from shore by tiller ropes. Intrigued, Whitehead joined de Luppis in producing an experimental prototype. Too many problems doomed the concept to failure, and the partnership lapsed.

Still, Whitehead was bitten. Something about the concept of a robot torpedo challenged his ingenuity, until it became virtually an obsession. Early on, he visualized the basic torpedo as we know it today. He knew it must be sleek and cylindrical, and self-propelled, unhampered by external lines and ropes. It must have a safe and reliable detonator and trigger mechanism. Most important, it must strike ships, especially the new armorclads, below the waterline where they were most vulnerable. And it must *run* underwater to get there, so the crew of the target ship could not see it coming and take evasive action.

Robert Whitehead at Fiume, 1880. *National Maritime Museum, London*

So inspired, he virtually locked himself away in a small hut in an obscure part of his factory for two years, striving to give his vision a nut-and-bolt reality. That he succeeded is proof of his creative genius, for virtually every mechanical aspect of the device had yet to be conceived, let alone built and tested.

Having settled on the torpedo's basic principles and appearance, he tackled the problem of motive power by designing a tiny engine that ran on compressed air. There were, however, two problems that defied easy solution: how to get the torpedo to start and stay on course, and how to set it to a specified running depth and force it to stay there. The need to solve these two basic stability issues and to coax greater speed and range (performance) out of the device were to occupy Whitehead, and other torpedo engineers, for decades.

Whitehead first announced his work-in-progress in the summer of 1866, taking advantage of publicity his powerful marine engines received for their role in helping the Austrian navy win the Battle of Lissa on 20 July 1866. By today's standards, or even those of World War II, the device was crude. It was 11 feet 7 inches long and 14 inches in diameter, and weighed 346 pounds. It could travel 600 to 700 feet at a speed of 8 to 10 knots.[4] Whitehead also produced a 16-inch-diameter model—the diameter measurement becoming the standard means of differentiating torpedo sizes.

In December 1866, the Austrian navy ran trials, but rejected Whitehead's device because of the inventor's failure to find even a rudimentary solution to the depth-keeping problem. Not until October 1868 did he find a viable answer, the "balance chamber"—the form of which remained virtually unchanged until after World War II.[5] Impressed, the Austrians became the Englishman's first buyers.

The Whitehead torpedo should be viewed for what it was: a commercial product designed and manufactured by a civilian engineer out to make a profit. To maximize those profits, Whitehead jealously guarded his torpedo's secrets, in particular the balance chamber—known for years afterward as "the Secret." To that end, oddly enough, he long refused to take out a patent. He had no faith in patents, having had several silk-weaving patents nullified by the Austrian government in the aftermath of the violent 1848 revolution in northern Italy, where he worked at the time. He was also afraid—justifiably so—that desperate governments would lift the secrets of his new device from the patent papers. Anyone therefore wishing to know his secrets either had to physically steal them or buy the rights to the torpedo itself.

Whitehead's attitude toward his new device is another apparent contradiction. He confidently felt the torpedo would become a mainstay of naval arsenals the world over. According to British naval historian and Whitehead biographer Edwyn Gray, however, the soft-spoken engineer abhorred violence and sincerely believed the torpedo would make war too horrible to wage. If so, he was as naive about the motives of men as he was sophisticated about the inner workings of machines. Gray also reports that Whitehead tended to believe everything he read in the newspapers—unwise even in that less cynical day and age.[6]

How Whitehead planned on achieving his quaint nineteenth-century version of Mutual Assured Destruction is unclear, since from the beginning he offered *exclusive* rights to his torpedoes to any power with enough hard currency to buy them. No one ever did purchase

The "Devil's Device"—one of the earliest known pictures of the Whitehead self-propelled torpedo, 1870. *Edwyn Gray*

his untried weapon outright, but in the ten years after the Austrians bought in he did sell plenty of nonexclusive rights, more than enough to make him an extremely wealthy man.

The British Royal Navy came on board next, holding trials for Whitehead's device in the summer and fall of 1870. The committee members had reservations about fitting broadside torpedo tubes—another Whitehead invention—to large ships, and felt bow tubes would interfere with rams, now in vogue after some ramming successes at Lissa. Nevertheless, they enthusiastically endorsed the torpedo itself, agreeing that "any maritime nation failing to provide itself with submarine locomotive torpedoes would be neglecting a great source of power both for offense and defense."[7] The contract the British signed called for the right to manufacture the torpedo in England, the right to be kept fully informed of all improvements as soon as made, and the right to use such improvements.[8]

The sharing of such progress soon became a two-way street. Early in 1872 the British completed their first torpedoes at their Royal Laboratory, or Woolwich, facility. They shared their innovations—such as using twin propellers turning in opposite directions to avoid the heeling effect of a single screw—with Whitehead, who incorporated them into his own designs. These new and improved designs he shared, ironically, with England's rivals on the Continent. With the British navy—the most powerful in the world—on the bandwagon, the rest of Europe had begun to fall in step.

The French purchased manufacturing rights in 1872. Italy and Germany joined the Whitehead club the next year. In 1875, Norway, Sweden, and Denmark signed on. Russia acquired rights in 1876. And the next year, Portugal, Argentina, Belgium, Chile, Greece, and Turkey also became "Torpedo Powers."[9] Though it had yet to best rival torpedo designs in combat and was still in great need of refinement, the Whitehead torpedo—and modified versions built on the same general principles—had definitely arrived on the naval scene.

The Whitehead torpedo did not, however, reach America until 1891. In the meantime the United States Navy succeeded in developing a viable—though ultimately unsuccessful—self-propelled torpedo of its own, but did not complete initial development until 1889. This means that for over a decade after the last Europeans put to sea armed with self-propelled torpedoes, the United States Navy had none and was consequently at a serious disadvantage in case of war. Since without operational torpedoes there were obviously no operational torpedo boats, the reasons for this delayed reaction to European torpedo developments are worth relating.

From the beginning, the United States took active notice of the Whitehead torpedo and its potential to radically alter naval warfare. According to *The Times* of London of 6 September 1869, quoting a report from the British *Army & Navy Gazette*, Rear Adm. William Radford, USN, who had plenty of experience with torpedoes—that is, mines—as commander of the Union navy's James River Squadron, visited Fiume in the summer of 1869. The article states that the Americans (Radford) were even then "greatly interested in these [Whitehead's] torpedoes and entertain a serious idea of making them the base, so to speak, of naval warfare, not only for defense, but for attack." As Edwyn Gray relates, however, the Americans "balked at the asking price . . . and found various reasons for losing interest before finally leaving Fiume without signing a contract."[10]

Whitehead did not give up there. Between Radford's visit and 1873, the Englishman approached the United States on at least one and possibly more occasions, offering "to sell the secret and right to manufacture" the torpedo for £8,800, or $44,000.[11] The Americans just said no.

This reluctance seems mystifying. It might be assumed that the United States Navy's delayed reaction to other revolutionary naval technologies during the 1870s and 1880s extended to the self-propelled torpedo. Ironically, this is not the case. Torpedo research was in fact a relatively high priority within the navy and, to the extent the navy was relevant at all, in Congress during the "doldrums" years. Unfortunately, such research concentrated on American designs that ultimately proved unsatisfactory. If the navy knew about self-propelled torpedoes, appreciated their potential as a future weapon of war, and stood willing to spend money developing them, then why not give the best European entry in the field a fair shot? The answer comes down to one word: pride.

Nothing else adequately explains the American delay in accepting the Whitehead. There are other factors relating to the nation's decision to keep clear, but in the end they do not, either alone or in combination, suffice to explain it. One is the Whitehead torpedo's high initial cost compared to available funding; another is the belief that the Whitehead represented emerging technology more deserving of suspicion than experimentation.

In 1869, the navy's highest-ranking officer, Adm. David Dixon Porter, who was fascinated by the possibilities of underwater explosive devices, established a Bureau of Ordnance torpedo test station and school on Goat Island at Newport, Rhode Island. Porter's "Torpedo Corps," as it came to be called, became the navy's testing center for both defensive torpedoes—stationary mines—and offensive spar and movable, or self-propelled, types.

To run the Newport Torpedo Station, from its inception to the end of the fiscal year ending 30 June 1882, the navy requested Congressional appropriations totaling $1,328,552. Congress responded with

$905,830, an average of $75,485 per year.[12] Most of the money went for basic operating costs, including supplies to build various spar and stationary torpedoes then in operational or experimental use. Judging from a breakdown of Congressional appropriations, an average of no more than a third was spent yearly on testing both defensive and offensive torpedoes and instruction in their use.[13] Even if half of that third went toward self-propelled torpedo experiments (one-sixth of $75,485), that comes to only around $12,580 a year. Recall that Whitehead wanted $44,000 up front for the secret of and manufacturing rights to his torpedo. At 1870s appropriations levels, that figure represents at least three to four years of offensive torpedo development funding.

The cost of the Whitehead may therefore have given the navy and Congress pause, though aside from Gray's assertion that the Americans "balked at the asking price" in 1869, there is little in the way of documentation to support this conclusion. Even if there was, it would prove little. Everyone else during the 1870s was, after all, anteing up. Why not take the same gamble? Certainly the United States could afford to do so—if it really felt the Whitehead was worth it.

Which leads to the argument questioning the need to experiment. *Was* the Whitehead worth it? It was indeed a revolutionary new and untried weapon, not just in concept but in every mechanical aspect. Everyone knew the Whitehead needed work, not least the Europeans. When they rose to the challenge, there were many in the United States perfectly willing to let them foot the experimental bill. After all, the United States was in no hurry. It could always buy in later if necessary.

There is some validity to this second argument. Lance C. Buhl, in his cogent essay challenging the notion of the United States Navy's backwardness compared to the Europeans during the "doldrums" years, supports the essential veracity of this contemporary line of reasoning:

> However linear and inexorable the technological progress of the period appears in hindsight, to contemporaries everywhere, experts and amateurs alike, things were a terrible jumble—a confused jigsaw puzzle of many unknown pieces, being fit together quite unsystematically. Thus, the millions that European navies were lavishing on naval experimentation produced as many, if not more, expensive failures and partial successes as stunning accomplishments.[14]

In other words, Americans at that time saw the Whitehead torpedo as just another European naval experiment, one that still had a lot of expensive bugs to be worked out—or that might even fail altogether. Its universal acceptance in Europe could be put down to the usual competitive jitters European nations always seemed to get whenever their close neighbors obtained a lethal new weapon. All this misses the point: The Americans *were* experimenting with self-propelled torpedoes throughout the same period, spending money on them, trying to solve many of the same emerging technological problems that beset the premier version across the Atlantic. Why not see firsthand what the Whitehead was all about and try to benefit from the progress made? Why not indeed.

Interestingly, instead of buying a Whitehead model, the Newport Torpedo Station between 1871 and 1874 made attempts to copy its gross features. It failed, primarily because of the inability of American industry to construct an equivalent air flask, or air chamber, able to handle the compressed air—370 pounds per square inch in Whitehead's device—needed to propel the torpedo adequately.[15]

Instead of then trying out the Whitehead itself, Newport conducted a long series of tests with mostly controllable torpedoes attached by lines and cables to shore stations. These, termed "Movable Torpedoes Under Control" as opposed to Whitehead-type "Automatic Movable Torpedoes," were all by American inventors, such as John Ericsson, of *Monitor* fame, and John Lay, who had built Cushing's spar torpedo.[16] These designs, some quite exotic, eventually fell by the wayside as being too unwieldy to be used on board ships and too slow to be used for harbor defense.

The nation's persistence in nurturing its own talent and testing questionable designs—despite, by 1878, the total European adoption of the Whitehead and derivatives like the German Schwartzkopff—must remain puzzling if cost and uncertainty over the worthiness of the Whitehead design are the only factors considered. Something else must have been at work. After all, American designs cost money, and were no better performers. That something else, as previously mentioned, is pride. Call it Yankee pride or faith in American ingenuity. Whatever the name, it helped keep the United States from fielding a serviceable torpedo until the 1890s.

An excellent example of this prideful American attitude came from Congress, where such sentiments counted. On 11 June 1878, the year the last Europeans adopted the Whitehead, Congressman Benjamin W. Harris, Republican of Massachusetts, a member of the House Committee on Naval Affairs, submitted a committee report recommending the passage of H.R. 5183. The bill called for $250,000 "to provide for experiments in and the purchase of movable torpedoes (after competitive trials) for military and naval defense." Considering the small amounts of money then being spent on such experiments, this bill represents a stunning reappraisal of the movable torpedo's perceived worth by naval supporters in Congress.

The report says much more, pointing out that $250,000 "is not a large sum when we consider how powerful the torpedo has proven to be, how universally it has been adopted as a means of defense, and how great is the cost of a single vessel of war." These were all sufficiently good reasons to support passage, but the committee's report went further. It asserted that "the torpedo is essentially of American origin"—referring to Robert Fulton, another early pioneer in what were actually *pre*-movable-torpedo days—and that it "is entitled to be regarded as worthy of the best efforts of American genius toward its complete perfection."

Harris's report kept up this line of thought.

> In this country we have the truly ingenious Lay torpedo, which is guided and directed by electricity, and Europe is expending millions upon the Whitehead or fish torpedo, and in adapting ships of war to its use. We believe, however, that invention in this direction is but in its infancy, and that these devices will soon be superseded by others far more certain in their operation, simple of construction, rapid in motion, and destructive in their effects, and that if the government will take the measures requisite to stimulate the inventive genius of its own people, the problem of successful offensive torpedo warfare will soon be fully solved.
>
> No people in the world have shown greater capacity for invention in the mechanic arts than the people of the United States. . . .[17]

This passage is highly revealing. One wonders if the politicians ever asked themselves *why* the Europeans were lavishing all those millions on the Whitehead. There is no indication they did wonder, for they obviously felt Whitehead's fish would soon be left rotting along the wayside. They also clearly believed that movable torpedo research had yet to begin in earnest, and that if the problems were to be "fully solved," it was going to be the Americans, not the Europeans, who would be doing the solving. We will meet up with this prideful attitude again in 1939.

In the meantime, despite this plea, the money was not appropriated, though work on controllable types like the Lay continued at the previously reduced levels—with lots of carping at Newport about lagging Congressional support.[18] Nevertheless, the report gives an excellent indication of the fundamental U.S. reaction to the Whitehead torpedo, which seemed to be "It's okay, but we can do better." In the end, however, the Americans did not do better—though they certainly tried.

As far back as June 1870, Comdr. John A. Howell, USN, submitted plans for a cylindrical "fish" torpedo 4 feet long and 1 foot in diameter, driven by a heavy flywheel. The model had severe stability problems, such as a tendency to surface and coil (describe an arc through the water). Howell continued work throughout the 1870s and 1880s, however, finally producing in 1889 a viable product that rivaled Whitehead's device in size and performance. "It was simpler and cheaper . . . required no [potentially explosive] air flask, and could steer a straighter course, since its heavy flywheel acted as a gyroscope."[19]

Ultimately, though, the Howell's range was limited by its design, i.e., the strength of its flywheel, which had to be revved up in the torpedo tube itself. On the other hand, the Whitehead could utilize improved construction techniques and increase the compressed air pressure feeding its engine, thereby increasing its speed and range. Though the Howell armed many American vessels throughout the 1890s, its fundamental design limitation forced it to begin giving way to the Whitehead as early as 1890, when the United States finally acquired rights.

Many factors contributed to the change in America's attitude toward the Whitehead between 1878 and 1890. In the early 1880s, the United States Navy began to revive. The usual boom-and-bust cycles were responsible. The economy rebounded after slumping in the seventies. Pro-navy Republicans controlled both houses of Congress and the White House for a crucial time. Congressional investigations of the Navy Department in the mid-1870s had pointed out the need for reform, while reform-minded officers were gaining ascendancy within the navy itself. And from overseas came rumors of a new wave of imperialism by the Great Powers. If the Europeans began encroaching on America's own growing economic interests around the globe, the United States Navy would be powerless to stop them.

Having at least gotten Congress's attention, the navy began to push for modernization of the fleet—steel warships instead of wood ones, and rifled, breech-loading ordnance in turrets instead of old smoothbores in broadside. And the Whitehead torpedo. In 1882, the chief of the Bureau of Ordnance, in a report on "auto-mobile" torpedo experiments, recommended its purchase:

> Among the torpedoes of this (auto-mobile) nature which have presented themselves of late years the "Whitehead" is the only type which has met with decided favor among maritime nations, and has shown itself capable of working with any certainty at other than moderate ranges. As it is now adopted by all naval powers of any consequence, the inference is unavoidable that it must possess merit, and the United States should also acquire it.[20]

In 1884, a Torpedo Board convened to run trials on currently developing American designs. Though it recommended continued development of the Howell, the board also reiterated growing navy support for the Whitehead. It noted several deficiencies, nevertheless concluding that the Whitehead "is a commercial success and is used by almost every nation of importance—excellent reasons why the United States should possess it."[21] In 1885, the Naval Advisory Board, first established by the then secretary of the navy in June 1881 to advise him on the navy's badly needed improvements, again pointed out that since everyone else had the Whitehead, the United States should as well. The navy's intention at the time was to purchase the rights—then priced at $50,000—and build the torpedoes at the Newport Torpedo Station.[22]

Congress measured its response to these and other pleas for naval revival, in large part because while recognizing the need to modernize, it still perceived the navy as a commerce-protecting, passive-coast-defense organization best kept out of trouble. But slow ahead was better than all stop. In 1890 the Navy Department finally got the go-ahead to purchase the Whitehead. The department placed its first order for one hundred torpedoes in 1891 with the English Whitehead establishment, though plans eventually called for privately manufacturing them in the United States.

To this end, in 1890 Whitehead's company, in anticipation of the American change of heart, purchased E. W. Bliss & Company, a Brooklyn, New York, manufacturer of presses and sheet metal tools. The American Whitehead versions would be built, and improved on, there. From these first Whitehead-based Bliss weapons, the United States Navy can trace a direct line of heavy torpedo development to at least the Mark 48, first studied in 1957.[23]

By the early 1890s the United States Navy had finally settled on the Whitehead, which eventually bested the Howell in comparative tests, as its self-propelled torpedo of choice. Better late than never, though there is no evidence the nation's security was unduly jeopardized by the delay.[24] The delay *is* significant in how it affected the navy's attitude toward torpedo-boat development. As long as the navy regarded the technology best suited to arm torpedo boats as being in a state of flux, it could hardly be expected to embark on a major building program or even engage in significant design testing. Predictably, the Europeans were not so timid. Beginning in the 1870s, having adopted the Whitehead torpedo early on, they binged on torpedo boats. Their efforts, as we will see, had a profound impact on later American efforts to enter the race.

As soon as Whitehead's self-propelled torpedo arrived on the scene, many innovative Europeans set about examining ways to employ it. There were, in these pre-aviation days, three torpedo-launching solutions: from shore, from large men-of-war, and from specially constructed ships. All were done. Our concern here is with ships specially built to launch torpedoes, of which there were four general types:

1. Experimental (including converted small craft)
2. Oceangoing
3. Non-oceangoing (precursor MTBs)
4. Submersible

Submarines lie outside the scope of this study, though it should be noted that they emerged as the most successful of the four when it came to sinking ships. Their ability to strike unseen from beneath the water, one of Whitehead's early precepts, is responsible for this deadly efficiency.

As for the development of torpedo-launching surface vessels, the late 1800s can be roughly divided into two periods. The first is an experimental period running from the end of the American Civil War to the end of the 1870s. A wide variety of test craft were converted or built during this time, for the Europeans—and Americans—were experimenting not only with self-propelled torpedoes, but with spar torpedoes and "towing" torpedo devices as well. These surface test craft were necessarily small, non-oceangoing types. Edwyn Gray observes:

> Initially built for use with the spar torpedo the first torpedo boats were little more than steam pleasure launches similar in every detail to the smartly painted, brass-funneled craft that cruised the rivers, estuaries, and coasts of Victorian England, but hastily stripped and converted to carry in their bows the lowering gear for an unwieldy 45-foot-long spar. The suicidal range necessary to successfully explode an outrigger torpedo against its victim required a handy, fast-moving attack craft, and these small steam launches were the only vessels immediately suitable for the purpose without the expenditure of vast sums of money in designing a special warship to carry out this one specific task. And, of equal importance, they were expendable.[25]

The first such boats appeared in 1873, the handiwork of two English shipbuilders, Alfred Yarrow and John Thornycroft, both based on the Thames in the London area. Many were sold to minor navies around the Continent. It is not hard to understand the interest of these navies. Small spar torpedo boats had shown potential in the American Civil War. The torpedo—spar or other—for the first time in history made it possible for small ships, boats really, to sink large men-of-war. No weight of broadside considerations here, or questions of staying power in a knock-down, drag-out fight. Just sneak in, deliver your warhead or "fish," and run before the befuddled enemy could bring his guns to bear.

Small torpedo boats had other advantages as well. Besides being stealthy and hard to hit, they were relatively cheap and quick to produce. Unlike larger warships, they could operate in restricted waters. No wonder governments with small navies, not only in Europe but in South America, were excited. They looked upon torpedoes and torpedo-equipped boats as a means of countering the huge, bullying fleets wielded by the Great Powers—ironically, of course, the very powers supplying their small craft needs.

Naturally, huge, bullying navies wanted to stay huge and bullying. In 1876, pestered by John Thornycroft, the Royal Navy finally ordered its first torpedo boat, the *Lightning*. Delivered in May 1877, the *Lightning* was 87 feet long, was narrow-beamed like a dagger, displaced 32.5 tons, and had a 460-horsepower steam engine that drove her along at 19 knots—about 7 knots faster than the average ironclad of the day. Originally equipped as a spar torpedo boat, she was later given two "dropping cages" for Whitehead torpedoes and finally, in 1879, a single bow torpedo tube. Her design was prescient. Nearly every surface craft, including MTBs, later built around the primary purpose of discharging self-propelled torpedoes is descended from this one experimental boat.

In 1877 the Russians and Turks thoughtfully helped bring closure to this experimental small-boat phase when they went to war over the Balkans. The Russians, who possessed nothing resembling a fleet in the Black Sea, conducted a series of steam-launch raids on Turkish naval anchorages between May 1877 and January 1878. The launches, carried on board a mother ship (the *Constantine*) and dropped off a few miles from the target area, were armed with whatever experimental torpedoes the Russians happened to have on hand. The "test" results, while unfortunately far from tidy or bloodless, seemed to vindicate the faith European navies put in Whitehead's self-propelled device.

Of the three types used, towing torpedoes, which rode out behind towing vessels at a consistent 45-degree angle, fared the worse—proving too unwieldy to be tactically useful. Spar torpedoes did better, though despite one heroic sinking they were largely frustrated by the presence of booms around the Turkish ships. Most of the Whitehead torpedoes either failed to hold an accurate course, hit nets, or otherwise failed to explode, but with one spectacular success on the night of 25 January 1878, off Batum, they evened the spar score. Around 2 a.m., the Russians reported, two of their launches crept within eighty yards of the Turkish revenue steamer *Intikbah* and put two Whiteheads into her. The steamer sank within two minutes.

Though the Turks disputed the Russian claim that a ship was sunk, a controversy that continues to this day, the fact remained that the sinking was widely reported, and the reports were believed.[26] While spar torpedoes had achieved equal apparent success, Europeans realized they would never find an antidote for boom defenses. The Whitehead's defects, on the other hand, were internal and could be improved upon.

This sifting out of torpedo designs had tremendous impact, ushering in a new phase of torpedo craft development. From the late 1870s through the 1890s, European navies built hundreds of oceangoing torpedo boats (TBs), all generally having the same narrow beam as the *Lightning*, only larger, in the 100-to-170-foot range. Called "first-class" torpedo boats, they were originally intended for coastal and harbor defense. As they became progressively bigger and faster, more seaworthy, and more heavily armed with multiple torpedo tubes and quick-firing guns, governments came to see them as a threat to their capital ships on the high seas and built torpedo gunboats, called "catchers" or "destroyers," to counter them. In such an escalating fashion these ships evolved, beginning around 1895, into the twentieth-century destroyer, a fleet appendage combining guns and torpedoes and, later, antisubmarine weaponry.

In the meantime, the Russo-Turkish War accelerated the development of small, nonexperimental torpedo craft—types more akin to the later MTB. As early as 1873 the British had converted ships' boats and steam launches to carry spar torpedoes and Whiteheads and placed them on board their larger warships. No doubt influenced by Russian tactics in 1877–78, the Royal Navy bought a merchant vessel then building in England and outfitted her as a mother ship (the *Hecla*) to carry small torpedo boats for offensive use.[27] These first boats were smaller versions of the TB—steel-hulled and 60 to 70 feet long. Many were also placed on board warships, replacing the earlier ships' boats, the idea being to release them from davits to use against enemy ships once in the area of operations.

Note the role reversal here. The larger, oceangoing TBs were first used for coastal defense, while the smaller—precursor MTB—torpedo craft were originally slated for offensive use with the fleet on the high seas. This was by no means universally true, of course. The French, in addition to using small TBs at sea, long adhered to the *jeune école* ("young school"), which stressed the use of small torpedo boats in harbor and coastal defense. These smaller French boats, like the others, later evolved into oceangoing types. By the turn of the century these defensive/offensive roles were at least partially reversed. Several factors contributed.

As previously noted, to compete with foreign boats, first-class TBs became progressively larger and faster, requiring increased seaworthiness to protect torpedo-vulnerable capital ships in the open ocean against the enemy's increasingly seaworthy TBs. They, as did later destroyers, became inseparable components of the fighting fleet.

Small, second-class boats, on the other hand, ultimately proved too fragile for work on the open ocean. Not only that, the very concept of launching small torpedo craft at sea against an adversary's fleet was deeply flawed. Most of the time no one knew when to expect the enemy. If enemy ships should suddenly appear out of the mists, what commander in his right mind wanted to signal all stop in the middle of a hot and heavy fleet engagement just to hoist out some bobbing little boats? So by 1900, the notion of using small torpedo boats offensively on the high seas had gone the way of the ram as a viable tactic of war. For reasons discussed later, though, second-class TBs did not swap coastal defense functions with the first-class TBs. They simply disappeared from the scene.

There were, however, several precedents established during the second-class TB period in the 1880s and 1890s that have later bearing on both European and American MTB development.

By 1883, the British, realizing that their thin-skinned second-class steel boats were too fragile for hoisting on and off their bigger warships and too unseaworthy for high-seas use, turned to slightly slower, but sturdier, wood-hulled boats, similar to traditional ships' boats and steam pinnaces. English boatbuilder J. Samuel White, based on the Isle of Wight near the giant British naval base at Portsmouth, was a leader in the production of these craft. The dimensions of his boats varied, but most were around 56 feet long, with a 9-foot beam. Their 140-to-200-horsepower steam engines drove them at up to 15.5 knots. Armament consisted of two 14-inch torpedoes in dropping gear, or one 14-inch torpedo in a tube—or a spar torpedo—and one or two machine guns. They required a crew of nine.[28]

The 1880s not only presaged the use of wood in the construction of the twentieth-century MTB, but pointed the way to how they would eventually be used. It was perhaps due to their resemblance to traditional ships' boats, or even growing suspicions as to their value on the high seas, that the British in particular began to view them less in terms of torpedo attack and more as "capable of many and varied duties including torpedo attack when required."[29] That they ran messages, scouted, and performed rescue feats is beyond doubt. Little wonder then that later MTBs and PTs were so often called upon to do the same.

The design and manufacture of small torpedo craft by private versus government yards is another precedent. While the British Admiralty produced the designs of nearly all other vessels in the Royal Navy arsenal, it left it to the private yards of such men as Thornycroft, Yarrow, and White to not only draw up the plans for small torpedo boats but perform much of the experimental work on new hulls and machinery. The expertise thus gained by these early strike craft pioneers, imparted to such builders as Hubert Scott-Paine in the 1930s, later proved instrumental in the prewar design and construction of·the PT, in particular the Elco-77s and -80s.

These nineteenth-century developments in torpedo craft, meanwhile, did not go unnoticed by the Americans, though true to form they reached somewhat different conclusions as to the torpedo boat's proper function.

As in Europe, the United States went through an experimental torpedo boat phase in the decade following the Civil War. In the early 1870s, the Newport Torpedo Station trained officers in the use of "fast guard boats to foil both mines and torpedo boat attacks."[30] The station also used several experimental spar torpedo vessels. These included the ponderous 84-foot ironclad *Spuyten Duyvil*, two large, slow, iron-hulled torpedo rams called the *Alarm* (800 tons, 173 feet) and *Intrepid* (1,150 tons, 170 feet), and the 137-foot iron screw steamer *Nina*. While the *Spuyten Duyvil* and *Nina* were laid down during the Civil War, the *Alarm* and *Intrepid* were new vessels, both launched in 1874 for a total cost of $600,000. Even given that the navy was able to use most of the vessels in other capacities, this is a considerable sum given over to torpedo and torpedo boat experimentation—further demonstrating the nation's commitment to this new mode of warfare.

By the end of the experimental period, the United States, while having no small, swift torpedo boats of its own, at least appreciated their potential. In June 1878, Benjamin Harris, in the same report recommending the $250,000 for movable torpedo experimentation, pointed out that the United States "had to-day practically no navy," and that an enemy fleet, while barred from making "near approach" to America's coastal cities by defensive torpedoes and fortifications, could still stand off and blockade the coast. He noted that the offensive use of the torpedo, "by the aid of fast and small vessels," was fast gaining ground overseas, and indicated that by using similar vessels, in lieu of an expensive fleet, the United States could extend the torpedo's value by using it to break such a blockade.[31]

In 1880, the United States Naval Institute, then as today echoing the thoughts of progressive naval officers, published an article in its *Proceedings*, written by a French naval lieutenant, Charles Chabaud Arnault, in the aftermath of the Russo-Turkish War. He advocated the nocturnal use of "torpedo boats of special construction," equipped with both spar and Whitehead torpedoes—depending on the tactical circumstances—for use in active coastal and harbor defense against warships. To counter any suspicions that small TBs were floating death traps, he examined American Civil War and Russo-Turkish War incidents and concluded that "the danger to a torpedo boat attacking a [larger] vessel has been greatly overestimated."[32]

At least the navy listened. The first Naval Advisory Board, called by the secretary of the navy to advise him on badly needed reforms, issued a report in November 1881 calling for massive new construction to lift the navy out of the "doldrums." It recommended, among numerous larger ships, the construction of 5 torpedo gunboats; 10 "cruising" (first-class) torpedo boats, "about 100 feet long, having a maximum speed of not less than 21 knots"; and 10 harbor (second-class) torpedo boats, "about 70 feet long, having a maximum speed of not less than 17 knots."[33]

A February 1883 report by the second Naval Advisory Board, so called as a result of administrative reshuffling following the assassination of President Garfield in 1881, responded to Congressional opposition to such massive expansion plans by dramatically scaling back the request for torpedo boats. It recommended one "cruising torpedo boat to cost $38,000."[34] Also in 1883, the chief of the Bureau of Ordnance recommended, along with the purchase of the Whitehead torpedo, the purchase of one "very light and swift boat" from the best yard abroad, to be used "as a model from which more could be constructed in this country."[35] This was 1883, however, and Congress was in no mood yet for torpedo boats, foreign or otherwise.

The navy, though, kept up the pressure. In October 1885 still another Naval Advisory Board pushed for the purchase of two first-class TBs from England, for use as models for those to be built in American yards. It did, however, reject the Bureau of Ordnance chief's idea of purchasing second-class TBs from the same source. The board, defining such boats as being 40 to 60 feet long, with a 6- or 8-foot beam, and equipped to carry spar torpedoes, submarine rockets, or Whiteheads, asked that two of them, the smaller of wood construction, the larger of steel, be built by an American manufacturer.

The board's plan for the use of these first- and second-class vessels also had a distinctly American slant. It called for using both types exclusively for coastal defense—as opposed to using the smaller ones offensively as the British and French were doing. Though it noted that the use of the second-class boats was being abandoned by European navies, the board pointed out that in Europe the harbors were very small, "and it has been found that practically every torpedo boat for coast defense must be able to go to sea." In the United States, on the other hand, "where we have such large bays as the Chesapeake and Delaware and harbors like New York and San Francisco, the second-class boats would be found exceedingly convenient and abundantly large for sheltered waters." In short, the geographic configuration of the United States coastline made second-class TBs more useful for coastal defense here than in Europe.[36]

Consequently, the board recommended both boat types as the basis for a comprehensive torpedo boat defense of the entire U.S. seaboard, including the Great Lakes and Alaska. The plan's scope, calling in a threatened war for the use of no fewer than "*two hundred* first-class and *sixty* second-class torpedo-boats" (emphasis original), is nothing less than staggering given the fiscal and naval-philosophical realities of the day.[37]

Congress, as might be imagined, balked at such a grandiose scheme. It did, however, finally give the navy a torpedo boat. In the Naval Appropriations Act of 8 March 1886, it authorized the construction of a 140-foot first-class boat to be used for experimental torpedo work. This boat, aptly named the *Cushing*, was laid down in April 1888 at the Herreshoff Manufacturing Company of Bristol, Rhode Island, and launched on 23 January 1890. Assigned to Newport off and on throughout the 1890s, she was instrumental in testing the Whitehead torpedo.[38]

The *Cushing*, however, was not the United States' first torpedo boat. On 3 March 1886, Congress had authorized the purchase of a torpedo boat then under construction as a private speculation by Herreshoff. This 94-foot wood-hulled boat, the *Stiletto*—the name says a lot about its appearance—entered service in July 1887. It was the United States Navy's first torpedo boat capable of launching self-propelled torpedoes. Assigned to Newport, she would spend her entire useful career experimenting primarily with the Howell torpedo.[39]

In all, the United States built only 30 first-class TBs, all between 1887 and the end of the century, with nearly half of them (12) autho-

The *Stiletto* firing her bow torpedo, 1900. *National Archives*

The *Cushing*, TB1. *U.S. Naval Institute*

rized on the eve of war with Spain in April 1898.[40] These small numbers should not be surprising, since the Americans did not join the European race to build first-class boats until that race was almost over. By the mid-1890s, the United States Navy, like its European counterparts, had switched emphasis to the building of larger, faster, oceangoing kinds of multiple-use torpedo boats, namely the destroyer.

We have seen that two decades after the appearance of the first, special-built surface TBs, small non-oceangoing types were fast losing out to their larger oceangoing cousins. The United States built no small torpedo boats at all, despite their proven wartime efficacy, a compatible peacetime naval strategy—passive coastal defense—and plenty of suitable inland waters. War-weariness, naval irrelevancy, the lack of a suitable torpedo, and Congressional reluctance to do more than modernize the navy in the 1880s and 1890s all contributed to this nondevelopment. Europeans showed disfavor toward small torpedo boats for different reasons, primarily their fragility and inability to operate with the fleet on the high seas. They also failed to take them seriously as coastal defense weapons.

There are two basic reasons small torpedo boats died out instead of taking over the coastal defense duties previously held by the larger boats. The first is that the bigger TBs—and the new destroyers—continued to perform their coastal defense function regardless of whether they were in harbor or attached to the fleet at sea. Defending a mother country's coast is, after all, what naval fleets are all about. The second reason for their failure to step in was their slow speed.

Up to the early 1900s all surface vessels used displacement hulls, meaning the hull must push aside, or displace, water when moving through it. This limits the speed of a vessel in a highly formulaic way, the practical effect being that the shorter the hull, the slower the maximum attainable speed, called the hull speed.[41] This is why naval designers made displacement-hull torpedo boats so long and narrow. By decreasing the weight-to-power ratio and improving hull design to reduce drag, they hoped to overcome the theoretical limitations of hull speed by producing a partial planing effect. The dagger shape helped accomplish this to a degree. Since, however, all TBs and destroyers relied on essentially the same bulky, low-efficiency steam technology for their motive power, the smaller, shorter boats remained comparatively slow.

As previously noted, second-class TBs operated in the 15–16-knot range, while longer first-class TBs were capable of speeds in the mid-20s.

Destroyers, larger oceangoing ships still, were correspondingly faster. They were even classed, in those speed-obsessed days in the late 1800s and early 1900s, as "27-knot" or "28-knot" destroyers, and so on up. Small torpedo craft therefore faced serious tactical limitations when compared to their longer TB and destroyer cousins—fatally so, given their inability to withstand gunfire.

With their relative versus intrinsic value thus compromised, it is little wonder they faced such hard times at the turn of the century. If the self-propelled torpedo was to be wedded successfully to small, light coastal craft, a way had to be found to dramatically increase their speed relative to larger boats, without a corresponding increase in what gave them their intrinsic value—their small size. That happy day, as it turned out, was right around the corner.

Chapter Three

They Were Ignorable

*C*all them "tactically challenged." By the beginning of the twentieth century, the fortunes of small coastal torpedo boats were everywhere in decline. Europeans considered them too slow in relation to the larger oceangoing torpedo boats and destroyers in their arsenals. Americans failed to build any to begin with. For the small torpedo boat to become a viable weapon of war, a way had to be found to eliminate its chief tactical liability—slow speed—without eliminating its tactical advantage—small size.

No small order. Nevertheless, between 1904 and 1916, in both peace and war, small-boat designers and engineers on both sides of the Atlantic rose to the challenge. They tossed out the small, steam-driven torpedo boat altogether, producing instead a whole new class of small combatant: the motor torpedo boat. As we will see, the United States ignored the potential of this new weapon, just as it had that of the Whitehead torpedo. For America, at least until 1936, the MTB was the wrong weapon, at the wrong place, at the wrong time.

It is quite common for inventions to appear ahead of their time. Sometimes they must lie hidden for years in the dusty files of a government patent office, or beneath the soiled mattress of some long-suffering genius. Or they must await the arrival of still another revolutionary concoction before they can realize their full potential. The last is true of the planing hull and the internal combustion engine, the two revolutionary advances in hydrodynamics and motive power that made possible the transformation of the small, steam-driven torpedo boat into the modern MTB.

The planing hull reached the naval scene first. In 1870, the Rev. Charles Meade Ramus, an English clergyman, proposed that the Admiralty adopt the planing hull for warships. Its secret was a hard chine—a sharp or abrupt angle between the sides of a boat and the bottom, versus a steady curve. The chine allowed a vessel to rise above, or skim, the water instead of cutting through it. Given enough horsepower, a ship using a planing hull theoretically knew no speed limit, giving the planing hull a considerable advantage over the traditional displacement hull.

It seemed a fine idea, but the Admiralty turned him down. For a planing boat to take advantage of its design, it cannot weigh more than 35 pounds per unit of horsepower in its propulsion unit. Given the heavy, low-efficiency steam machinery of the day, there was no possibility of building a vessel within that limit. Though John Thornycroft patented the planing hull in 1877, it, "like the airplane and the motorcar . . . had to await the development of the [lightweight] gasoline engine to become practical."[1]

The idea of using explosive gases as a propellant dates back to twelfth- and thirteenth-century Asia, though the construction of a safe, practical, self-contained internal combustion, or compression-ignition, engine took just a bit longer. In 1824, the French physicist Sadi Carnot provided the theory; in 1859, Pennsylvania oilmen discovered the seemingly inexhaustible fuel supply; and in 1883, the German engineer Gottlieb Daimler built a working design he used two years later to power the first automobile.

The new engine soon went off-road—*way* off-road. In the 1890s, rich European and American yachtsmen, looking for ways to liven up their sport, introduced the gasoline engine, or "motor," to small-boat racing. Inspired by the increased size and reliability of the engines powering these fast "motorboats," would-be designers and builders of small torpedo craft saw their chance. By 1904 they had taken it.

Credit for the first generally recognized motor torpedo boat goes to the Italians, whose interest in small craft is attributed to their ongoing naval rivalry with Austria-Hungary in the narrow, island-strewn Adriatic. Built as a private design by Comte Recepe, the inaugural MTB—though such boats were not to be called that until the mid-1930s—had a single 14-inch torpedo tube built into the bow.[2]

Less known is the first American entry into the motor torpedo boat field. In August 1904, Flint and Company received an order from the Russian government for ten 90-foot MTBs. Two gasoline engines totaling 600 horsepower drove them at 20 knots. Armament consisted of one 47mm gun, two machine guns, and one 18-inch torpedo tube amidships. They were assembled in Sevastopol in 1905 and transferred to the Baltic fleet. Some served as late as World War II.[3]

The British firms of Yarrow and Thornycroft, not to be outdone, weighed in with their first experimental entries in 1905. Yarrow produced a tiny 15-foot boat, equipped with two torpedoes, said to have made 25 knots.[4] Thornycroft built the *Dragonfly*, a 40-foot, 4.5-ton wood boat capable of launching a single torpedo sideways from a folding discharge chute. A single 120-horsepower engine pushed her at 18 knots.[5]

In 1906 the Italians built a multipurpose motorboat, armed, much like the original American MTB built for Russia, with a 47mm gun, two machine guns, and two 14-inch torpedo tubes. Top speed was 16 knots, provided by twin 80-horsepower gasoline engines. After successful trials, the Italian navy bought her, making her the first MTB to join the fleet of any nation.[6]

So far, however, the new motor torpedo boat showed no appreciable increase in speed over its heavier, steam-driven ancestors. In 1897, the Englishman Charles Parsons had introduced a steam turbine that promised, and delivered, many improvements over the older reciprocating triple-expansion engines. Parsons gave a dramatic demonstration of his turbine's capabilities by installing it on a small yacht, the *Turbina*, and crashing a naval review for Queen Victoria's Diamond Jubilee at Spithead. None of the Royal Navy's steam picket boats sent in pursuit could catch the *Turbina*, which raced before the assembled crowd of foreign naval observers at an astonishing 34.5 knots—a speed virtually unheard-of in those days. So graphic a demonstration, combined with the fact that the turbine had a much higher power-to-weight ratio, took up less room in the engine compartment, was simpler, and vibrated less, virtually assured the adoption of Parson's turbine by the world's navies. In 1899 the turbine pushed the first warship receiving it, the 325-ton destroyer HMS *Viper*, along at an incredible trial speed of over 36 knots.[7]

Not only rival war vessels were getting faster. The period 1904–5 saw the first patented use of "wet" and "dry" heated-air torpedoes, based on the discovery that hot air, or even a warm sea, improved torpedo performance. Speeds jumped overnight, and torpedoes began to perform in the 30-to-40-knot range.[8] Clearly, something more was needed if the MTB was to compete with its rivals in naval arsenals.

That something more was Charles Ramus's planing hull. In 1908 the French wedded the gasoline engine to a stepped—versus another type, the V-shaped—planing hull, producing the *Rapiere III*. Thornycroft followed two years later with the *Miranda IV*, her stepped planing hull allowing her to reach the remarkable speed of 35 knots by reducing drag and the size of the bow wave.[9] All the base components of the MTB were now in place: torpedoes, lightweight motive power, and improved hydrodynamic design. All that remained was the need for them. That came in August 1914.

The Great War did not immediately afford opportunities for navies to use MTBs. By 1915, however, with naval stalemate a reality in the North Sea and Adriatic, the British and Italians—who entered on the side of the Triple Entente on 23 May 1915—began to tap the wealth of their prewar small-craft research.

As early as March 1915 the Italian navy placed an order for two prototype MTBs, the basis for a total of 299 built during the war. Called MAS boats, they came in two principal stripes: *motobarca armata silurante* ("torpedo-armed motorboat") and their submarine-hunting sisters, *motobarche anti-sommergibili*. A typical MAS boat was 52 feet long and weighed from 12 to 16 tons. Depending on their use, MAS boats came equipped with two torpedoes and machine guns or a single larger gun such as a 47mm. Their gasoline engines drove them anywhere from 21 to 30 knots.[10] Many of the torpedo-throwing types were also equipped with 10-horsepower electric motors, capable of 4 knots, for use in silent approaches to their targets—an early twentieth-century solution comparable in intent to William Cushing's wood box and tarpaulin.

During the war the Italians sent these small, relatively slow boats to prowl the coasts and harbors of the Adriatic, where they helped whittle away at the Austrian navy. Probably their most spectacular feat, and indeed one of the most spectacular of the war, took place on 10 June 1918. While on patrol in the early-morning hours off Premude Island, an outer island of the Kvarneric chain about 70 miles due south of Fiume, Capitano di Corvetta (Commander) Luigi Rizzo in *MAS 15* sighted clouds of smoke belching from what could only be a large warship. He immediately raced to the scene. Rizzo, already a national hero in Italy for using a MAS to sink an Austrian battleship in Trieste harbor seven months earlier, slipped undetected to within 350 yards of the smoke-belching giant, the 22,200-ton Austrian dreadnought *Szent Istvan*, and sent her to the bottom of the Adriatic with two torpedoes. Rizzo's feat so impressed his countrymen that on 16 June 1936, they enshrined his boat "in the Museo del Vittoriano at the base of the Victor Emmanuel II monument in Rome," where it remains to this day.[11]

Though their achievements were not strategically decisive, the MAS boats proved well worth their investment. By sinking a total of three Austrian—later Yugoslavian—capital ships, they accounted for 90%, by tonnage, of all Austrian naval losses inflicted by the Italians in World War I.[12]

Of note is how valuable MAS boats were despite their relatively slow speeds. Stealth was their forte. All their major successes came at night, from the Civil War on the small, low-profile torpedo boat's natural habitat, and resulted from their ability to move slowly and silently past enemy pickets. Even Rizzo opted to go slow in his attack on the *Szent Istvan*, fearful his high-speed wake would be noticed by the Austrians.[13] This nocturnal interplay, this nerve-racking coin toss of when to run or stay and fight, would become a regular feature of MTB combat in World War II.

The British employed their own version of the MAS, called CMBs (coastal motor boats), during the Great War, though their exploits were less spectacular. These 40- and 55-foot boats first saw service in 1916, their successful design benefiting, like that of the Italian boats, from extensive prewar testing, especially of John Thornycroft's stepped planing hull.

The Royal Navy ordered the first twelve 40-foot boats in January 1916, the idea being to utilize their light drafts to slip over German minefields and raid their bases in occupied Belgium. Built of wood, they displaced a mere 4.5 to 5 tons, in hopes they could be hoisted, like the second-class boats of old, on and off the davits of light cruisers. The British used only one cruiser, the *Diamond*, for this purpose, so little came of the idea.[14] The typical 40-foot CMB came armed with a single 18-inch torpedo tube in a stern trough and a couple of machine guns. The early boats had a 250-horsepower engine capable of around 25 knots, while later versions had 275-horsepower motors that drove them along at a nice clip of over 35 knots. A 55-foot version was also built, similarly armed with one or two torpedo tubes. It was faster, in the 35-to-40-knot range.

British CMBs laid mines, performed reconnaissance and rescue duties, and took part in the highly publicized blocking raid on Zeebrugge and Ostend on 23 April 1918. Later that year, on August 10 off the Dutch coast, six CMBs prowling for German minesweepers were attacked, in broad daylight, by machine-gunning German seaplanes. The CMBs tried a series of sharp evasive turns and fought back with their Lewis guns, but in the end three were sunk, two disabled.[15] The sunken boats accounted for 60% of all CMB battle losses during the war, teaching a lesson well heeded by future torpedo-boaters: Unlike blood and salt water, daylight, MTBs, and airplanes did not mix.

The British had built sixty-six 40- and 55-foot CMBs by November 1918, as well as a small number of 70-footers. Thirteen had been lost, though only five because of enemy action. Following the Great War, CMBs fought Russian Communists after the Russian Revolution. Several raided Kronstadt in 1919, sinking or disabling two capital ships, a cruiser, two destroyers, and other craft, at a loss of only two boats. As with the small torpedo boats in the nineteenth century, actual losses of CMBs and crews during World War I and the Russian Revolution were "amazingly low."[16] On the other hand, their operations showed that under the right tactical circumstances MTBs could be quite deadly to the enemy if properly handled.

As in the steam torpedo boat era, Americans took ample notice of these developments, including the more celebrated wartime feats. American naval leaders were curious about MTBs, to be sure, but mostly irreverent. Despite the proven worth of the British and Italian boats, despite a vibrant homegrown small-boat industry eager to design and build them, and despite the United States Navy's dramatic growth from sixth place among the world's navies in 1900 to virtual parity with first-ranked Great Britain by 1918, the United States made no serious attempt to keep pace with European MTB development either before or during the war. Not until 1936, when war clouds once again began gathering over Europe, did the Americans begin to take notice.

The reason is simple: The United States Navy deemed motor torpedo boats irrelevant. During the pre–World War I period, when naval technology evolved sufficiently to produce the first MTBs, the navy veered dramatically away from the strategic and tactical rationales compatible with their use. Whereas the navy in the 1880s and early 1890s embraced the notion of using second-class torpedo boats as an integral part of its passive coast defense strategy, its zealous switch by the early 1900s to a strategy of sea control left no room for the second-class boat's tiny, stay-at-home descendant. As far as the brass was concerned, the small torpedo boat belonged in the past—a past they were eager to forget.

This strategic change of heart was a century in the making. From its inception in 1794, the United States Navy played the role of weaker sibling to the dominant European navies, principally Great Britain's. As discussed in Chapter 2, anti-navalist politicians deliberately kept the navy small and unobtrusive, adopting in war a passive coastal defense and commerce-raiding strategy the French call *guerre de course*. There were periodically those who pushed for a larger, sea-control force, but not until the end of the nineteenth century did the country's strategic outlook really inspire one.

In 1890 the frontier officially closed; an ever growing, ever ambitious America looked outward. Building on 1880's reforms, the navy slowly grew and modernized. At the same time, naval leaders came increasingly under the spell of Alfred Thayer Mahan, the American naval officer and theorist who popularized the concept of sea power. Mahan wrote that the function of navies was to control the seas with powerful fleets of capital ships—battleships at the time.[17] In war, the fleet sought out the enemy fleet in decisive battle (*guerre d'escadre*). No more passive coastal defense, Mahan insisted; no more commerce raiding!

A lot of influential people, both in and out of the navy, agreed.

In 1898, American imperialistic tendencies brought on the Spanish-American War. While this war was not especially long or meaningful, it had two profound results. One, a couple of lopsided naval victories against obsolete, poorly led Spanish cruiser squadrons seemed to vindicate Mahan's emphasis on sea control. Two, the United States acquired the trappings of empire, including Guam, Puerto Rico, and the Philippines, and established a naval base at Guantanamo Bay in Cuba.

These acquisitions vastly heightened United States involvement in the Caribbean, Central and South America, and the Far East. This heightened involvement, with its corresponding increase in American naval activity, set America at odds with real and perceived German and Japanese interests in these same areas, thus firmly establishing the strategic rationale for Mahan's strong, world-class navy. It remained only for a strong political leader to help make that navy a reality.

That leader was Theodore Roosevelt. Roosevelt, a naval historian and navalist in his own right, was assistant secretary of the navy up to the beginning of the Spanish-American War. Though far from slavishly devoted to Mahan, with whom he often disagreed on nonstrategic, technical issues, Roosevelt ardently concurred with the naval thinker when it came to questions of the size and purpose of navies.[18] As president from 1901 to 1909, he capitalized on the potential threat from the Germans and Japanese by building a sea-control navy. His obsession with obtaining battleships was equaled only by the navy's desire to use them, if need be, in fleet engagements on the high seas.

Mahan's early "forward reach" philosophy thus became the driving force behind the American navy's actual growth in capital ships. His preachings also shaped the navy's attitude toward its traditional passive coastal defense role. In 1889, he wrote that

> it may safely be said that it is essential to the welfare of the whole country that the conditions of trade and commerce should remain, as far as possible, unaffected by an external war. In order to do this, the enemy must be kept not only out of our ports, but far away from our coasts.[19]

Roosevelt echoed this line of thinking. In December 1907, for example, he spoke out against public demands that fleet units be scattered among West Coast cities in defense against attack by then hostile Japan.

The Navy's true function, he reiterated, was not "to defend harbors and sea-coast cities," but to attack and destroy the enemy's naval forces. In this way, a battle fleet would contribute vitally, if indirectly, to coast defense.[20]

As far as the new sea-control navy was concerned, if the coast needed defending, the battleship fleet would take care of it. In the face of this all-consuming strategic and tactical focus, it is not surprising that MTBs, like the old second-class boats considered passive coastal defense vessels, were overlooked. As for using MTBs offensively, with the fleet, there is no evidence the United States did more than briefly flirt—around 1905—with the idea of equipping battleships with steam torpedo boats. The navy dropped the idea after the boats turned out to be too heavy for the battleships' boat cranes.[21] The Europeans had, of course, already rejected this practice.[22]

Admittedly, the evidence so far presented as to the navy's attitude toward the new MTB is circumstantial, the result of analyzing broad trends in naval strategic thinking. We unfortunately know very little about the navy's specific attitude toward MTBs. Revealing glimpses can, however, be found in the files of the General Board of the Navy.

In March 1900, Secretary of the Navy John D. Long created the General Board to "advise the secretary on strategy, war plans, and ship design."[23] Admiral George Dewey of Manila Bay fame—another ardent Mahanian—was the board's first president. Especially in its first decade, it wielded considerable power.

> Despite its advisory nature, the board served as a focal point for strategic formulation and policy decisions throughout the [prewar] period. The board influenced not only the navy itself, but also in various ways the President and the secretary of state.[24]

Should the navy need to respond to small-craft plans submitted by private designers, or to Navy Department requests for similar development, it was up to the General Board to determine feasibility and make recommendations—a responsibility it assumed until its elimination in 1951.

The board took its first documented look at MTBs on 27 June 1906, when Lewis Nixon of New York submitted a two-page proposal for a 75-foot, 17-ton "vedette" boat (*vedette* is French for motor launch). The boat was steel-hulled and, unlike unarmed vedette boats in England and France, could be equipped with one 15-inch torpedo tube and machine guns. Nixon proposed that vedettes be used offensively, "to accompany the fleet and to act as dispatch and patrol boats and to guard against enemy submarines." He also mentioned they could be carried aboard a battleship. This suggests he was aware of the navy's emphasis on the offensive use of battleships and its interest in experimenting with hoistable torpedo boats.

Like any good businessman, Nixon was also quick to point out the deficiencies of his competitors, criticizing the British for "not having developed a suitable marine engine" for their vedette boats and the French for "ignoring their value." This last point shows that American small-boat manufacturers were fully tuned in to overseas developments and were not afraid to use that knowledge in pitching their own projects. As for this particular proposal, we know only that the board filed the accompanying blueprint of Nixon's vedette boat "in Drawer No 7, Chart Case, GB Room."[25] Apparently that is where it stayed.

In 1908, Nixon, having failed to interest his own government in small torpedo craft, sold ten of them to Russia, though, as we have seen, his was not the first American firm to do so. These boats may be considered something of a hybrid between a true motor torpedo boat and larger, steam-driven, oceangoing types. There are no published figures as to their exact size, though one is said to have cruised under its own power from New York to Sevastopol in moderate seas.[26] This capability is beyond that of the typical World War I–era MTB, which operated primarily in protected waters and only rarely in the open ocean.

Later that year the Navy Department itself got into the act. On 31 December 1908, Assistant Secretary of the Navy Herbert Satterlee asked the General Board for a recommendation on the development of a 150-foot, 300-horsepower "gasoline type of motor boat for use in bays, sounds, and harbors." Though the size of this boat is consistent with oceangoing torpedo boats of the time, the General Board's response is telling from the standpoint of MTB development. On 22 April 1909, Admiral Dewey wrote:

> The General Board does not recommend that the building of small torpedo boats of any type for the defense of harbors and inland waters shall be made a part of the naval policy of the country. The military value of such boats . . . is small and their theater of action would be restricted. The same amount of money expended in torpedo boats capable of keeping the sea and serving at any point within the limits of an area of considerable extent, would be of greater value.[27]

Despite this refusal by the General Board, the same year Congress appropriated $445,000 for the development of an experimental subsurface torpedo boat. This could be construed as a circumvention of the board, or it might simply be further evidence of the navy's interest in submarine technology during the prewar period. From an "unsinkable surface hull hung a submarine hull, equipped with a torpedo tube for firing [torpedoes] underwater." The "46-foot [craft] never got beyond the experimental stage, but its designers learned the hopelessness of a compromise between MTBs and submarines."[28]

In 1911, another small-craft designer, W. Albert Hickman, a native of Nova Scotia, invented a planing-hull boat called a sea sled—the hull, when viewed bows-on, resembling a W. Hickman apparently "offered his boats to the U.S. Navy and to Britain for use as torpedo boats" at the beginning of World War I, but neither expressed interest. The United States Navy did, however, take advantage of the stability offered by the sea-sled design to build a number of his boats as individual sea-plane carriers. The use of this unique design represents the closest the navy came to actually employing a true planing-hull MTB-type vessel during World War I.[29]

When the Great War came to Europe, the United States Navy's attitude toward MTBs changed little. This may seem odd, given the eventual British and Italian use of such boats, until one realizes that despite the wartime emergency, the navy's coastal defense philosophy and sea-control mission remained substantially unchanged. That the German U-boat was the principal naval challenge to the United States is largely beside the point. The U-boat merely temporarily replaced the battleship as the oceangoing contender for sea control.

After the war declaration in April 1917, the navy responded to the submarine menace by employing hundreds of small craft—subchasers, private yachts, motor launches and the like—in U.S. and European coastal waters. These ships, however, represented a compromise solution. While approving a design for a 110-foot subchaser on the eve of war, the General Board reminded Josephus Daniels, the secretary of the navy,

> that the most efficient offensive vessel against submarines is the destroyer, but in an emergency like the present these can not be supplied in sufficient numbers in a short time and the proposed 110-foot boat seems the most valuable emergency vessel for the work now obtainable.[30]

The problem, therefore, was time. Practically overnight, the navy needed all the antisubmarine vessels it could get its hands on as quickly as possible. Despite this anti-U-boat emphasis, however, the navy did perform several experiments with small, fast MTBs. Three are worth noting.

The first came in 1915 when the Navy Department decided it wanted a "high-powered motor boat" for testing. It acquired plans to build a 50-foot boat with machine guns and one 16-inch torpedo tube, but the project died for unknown reasons.[31]

In 1917 the navy tested a 40-foot boat capable of 40 knots. It proved unseaworthy in rough seas and was written off. The navy made another attempt in 1918, testing a 27-foot boat known as "W. Shearer's one-man torpedo boat." It was similar to the subsurface torpedo boat testing in 1909 in that it had a submerged torpedo tube. A navy trial board approved the boat, recommending that "construction of a number of [these] boats be undertaken in Great Britain." Nevertheless, the General Board turned down the recommendation, reporting, "It is thought labor and material for large numbers of such boats can be better employed to win the war in turning out destroyers, submarine chasers, submarines and aircraft."[32] As a direct result of this understandable emphasis on combating the U-boat threat, the navy built no operational MTBs, such as those employed by the British and Italians, during World War I.

Ironically, American small-boat firms built scores of light patrol craft—motor launches, or MLs—for America's allies during the war. Various U.S. companies sent Russia a total of 67 such boats. But by far the most prominent U.S. builder of Allied small craft was the Electric Boat Company (Elco Division) of Bayonne, New Jersey. From April 1915 through July 1917, the British placed orders for 580 of Elco's 75-foot, 34-ton gasoline-powered craft. They proved seaworthy, though ill suited to carry torpedoes. Elco also built 105 80-foot MLs for the Italians in 1917–18. All were shipped without their gun armament to Italy.[33] In making these overseas sales, Elco gained the expertise, in small-boat design and manufacturing, that it later put to good use as the major producer of the American PT.

The United States Navy, meanwhile, while not seeing the need for its own MTBs during the war, at least felt the need to satisfy its curiosity about European boats. In 1920 the secretary of the navy approved a recommendation by the Bureau of Construction and Repair and the General Board for the purchase of one 40-foot and one 55-foot British CMB for testing purposes. The Bureau of Construction and Repair carried out speed trials on both boats in 1922 before interest waned. The 40-foot boat was used for torpedo recovery work until 1928, then used as a crash boat—picking up downed fliers—before being condemned in 1934. Some experiments continued with the 55-foot boat until it was scrapped in 1930.[34]

In accounting for this disinterest, it should be noted that even the British ignored their CMBs in the 1920s and early 1930s. They, like other major navies, with the notable exceptions of the Italians and Germans, sold off what boats they had and entered a period of postwar financial retrenchment. Small craft were seen as a luxury, for although they were relatively cheap to build, they did "require large investments in research and development and large numbers of skilled manpower to operate."[35]

Still, one group of enterprising Americans in the 1920s and early 1930s took a very keen interest in making such investments—and in discarded CMBs at that. Prohibition-era (1919–33) rumrunners bought an unknown number of the British boats for use in running illegal liquor from Canada to sheltered coves and inlets along the Eastern Seaboard. In order to outrun the Coast Guard, first charged with interdicting these shipments in 1923 on behalf of the Customs Department, the rumrunners constantly sought to improve CMB engine performance. Their efforts included a successful attempt at adapting the water-cooled Liberty engine, of World War I aviation fame, to marine use.[36]

Several sources consulted for this work claim that this illicit activity greatly influenced the subsequent development of the PT and the tactical doctrine for its use. Unfortunately, these sources offer little detail as to how or when such engineering or tactical expertise passed from the bootlegger to the naval professional.[37] None cite any documentary evidence of such a connection. And one senses that many PT writers—with an eye toward glamorizing the PT's colorful wartime career—have gleefully reported this influence to help lend a piratical aura to the PT phenomenon.

Did such influence exist? Most certainly, and it took several forms. Coast Guard records show that the navy was aware of the use of high-speed motorboats by rumrunners as early as February 1924, when the Coast Guard ran into a little snag.

When the interdiction patrols began in 1923, coast guardsmen noted how "the foreign vessels engaged in the illicit liquor trade" tended to anchor close together mostly by night. The motorboats used were "comparatively slow and manned by crews that would stop upon a whistle signal or a blank shot for examination." This changed in November of that year, when the foreign vessels began to separate, and "the slow boats [were] replaced by fast motorboats . . . manned by crews of desperate character."

Emboldened by their increased speed, the rumrunners began to operate both at night and in broad daylight, when they could escape "because of the lack of speed of the cutters, thus requiring gun fire to stop them." Not expecting the increased expenditure of ammunition, the Coast Guard ran low. The February letter to the Bureau of Ordnance outlined the above problem with the new fast motorboats and asked the navy for more shells.[38]

There also existed—and still exists—a close, ongoing, and largely amicable relationship between the Coast Guard and its big-sister service. This would have encouraged the exchange of information about bootlegger craft and tactics. During this period the navy often helped recruit men for the Coast Guard and train them in navy facilities, while navy yards routinely reconditioned CG vessels. Personnel transfers between the two services also occurred.

In one documented instance, on 11 June 1924, the Coast Guard requested that a navy aviation machinist's mate first class who had applied for enlistment in the Coast Guard be allowed to enlist. The Coast Guard hoped to use his experience with internal combustion engines on its "high speed motor-boat program."[39] There is every reason to suppose the navy similarly benefited from the technical expertise Coast Guard personnel gained while working on this and other attempts to counter the rumrunners' high-performance boats.

Awareness, however, does not necessarily translate into influence. Rumrunner influence most likely passed to the PT program largely in the form of experience gained by America's small-boat manufacturers. Not only did they design and build most of those high-performance boats for the bootleggers, they also "built for the Government still faster boats to capture [them]." At least one industry official would later claim that "liquor syndicates with unlimited capital challenged American motorboat designers to turn out the fastest cargo motorboats the world has ever seen, and . . . [as a result] hull design of American motorboats advanced twenty years overnight."[40] Two such American small-craft manufacturers, Elco and Higgins Industries, eventually took advantage of that experience to produce the final designs for nearly all the PT boats used in World War II.

The rumrunner experience may have also influenced the PT program in less direct ways. A number of the former CMBs were seized during Prohibition, which may have afforded opportunities to naval officers interested in small craft to inspect their innards. Even as late as 1946 several of these boats were reported to be laid up in East Coast shipyards, "so altered [as to] no longer be recognizable as CMBs."[41]

Even more important may have been the undocumented contributions of the rumrunners themselves, particularly those who reengineered and maintained the boats. After Prohibition some of these men found their way either into private boatyards, such as Elco and Higgins, where they could put their knowledge to more legitimate use, or into the navy itself. Capt. Robert Bulkley, the author of *At Close Quarters*, and himself a serving PT officer during World War II, relates that one unidentified "engineer whose experience and know-how were valuable to the World War II PT program was frequently known to preface his comments on perplexing technical problems with the remark, 'Well, when I was a rummie, we . . .'" Bulkley remarked, too, that it "would be interesting to know how many PT technicians (and others) had such a phrase flash through their minds but failed to utter it."[42]

How many indeed.

While Prohibition ended in 1933, the General Board's reluctance to fund Bureau of Construction and Repair requests for MTB experimentation did not. In 1935, a year after the 40-foot CMB was scrapped, the bureau took an interest in another foreign design, this one for a 28-ton "torpedo carrying speed boat" by J. F. Bogaerts of Brussels, Belgium. The board refused funding.[43] It also passed on a November 1936 proposal by a well-known American designer named J. Starling Burgess, naval architect for the Aluminum Company of America, for a new high-speed aluminum hull.[44]

The General Board's rejection of these designs, primarily on financial and technical grounds, should not be viewed as evidence of implacable hostility toward the MTB. In the spring of 1937, even as Burgess's aluminum hull failed to make the cut,[45] the board gave the go-ahead for a modest experimental MTB program. Why the change of heart? Several factors likely contributed.

One relates to the General Board itself. It is tempting to imagine from the foregoing that the board consisted of crusty traditionalists, totally opposed to anything new. Nothing could be further from the truth. Composed of experienced line officers, the board possessed great prestige within the naval establishment and was generally perceived as having an analytical, or managerial, style described as being "open-minded and innovative."[46]

As for the United States Navy's single-minded determination to possess a sea control force of battleships at the expense of the rest of the fleet (and MTBs), much had changed since the pre–World War I days. Though the navy's sea control and coastal defense philosophy remained constant after the war, the face of the navy changed considerably. Treaties limiting naval armaments, such as those stemming from the Washington Naval Conference in 1921, set strict limits on capital ship tonnage. These limitations, combined with falling peacetime budgets and spending to keep pace with rapid technological changes in naval aviation, submarine warfare, fire control, and propulsion, prompted the navy to scale back on battleships and seek a more balanced fleet.

The "balanced fleet" concept, formulated as early as 1916, made perfect sense. While the battle fleet remained at the core of strategic planning during the 1920s and 1930s, the navy understood that improved land- and sea-based aircraft, submarines, and fire control on smaller ships such as cruisers all heightened the threat to the reduced numbers of battleships. To protect them, the navy added as many aircraft carriers with the latest aircraft types, submarines, cruisers, and destroyers as budgets and treaties would allow. It also increased the numbers of auxiliaries, essential for supplying a thrust across the Pacific against Japan.[47] This receptiveness to new ship types, and technological progress in general, no doubt played a role in the General Board's now favorable disposition toward the MTB.

Another factor is that by 1936, the world was fast becoming a more dangerous place. Japan, having already gobbled up Manchuria, publicly refused in January to go on with naval disarmament and embarked on a big building program. In March, Adolf Hitler denounced the disarmament terms of the Treaty of Versailles and openly began to rearm Germany. With the Washington and 1930 London treaties set to expire on December 31, Great Britain showed every inclination of following suit.[48]

Once again the world readied itself for war. The time had come for the United States to earnestly begin doing the same.

Chapter Four

"A Moderate Experimental Program"

*P*erhaps it was inevitable. In the late 1930s, war clouds darkened the horizon in both Europe and Asia. Few within the American military long believed the United States would stay above the fray. In the North Sea and Mediterranean, both likely to be contested waters in the event of another general European war, motor torpedo boats—modernized versions of a proven weapon in the last one—were beginning to appear in growing numbers. Sooner or later, someone was bound to interest the United States Navy in building its own MTBs, if for no other reason than just to keep pace. As it happened, later came sooner, and that someone was Rear Adm. Emory Scott Land.

Emory S. Land (1879–1971) is the first in a long, illustrious line of men associated with the United States Navy's MTB program who disdained red tape and stuffed shirts. The Naval Academy graduate had a well-deserved reputation for plainspoken pugnaciousness. As the new chief of the Bureau of Construction and Repair in October 1932, he nevertheless knew he had to play by the rules to get the job done. The job, in this case, called for getting the navy's "brass hats" to sign off on something they had previously disdained: motor torpedo boats.

Little in Land's background definitively accounts for his interest in MTBs. Perhaps the idea came from some unheralded subordinate, or perhaps it was just one of those things the bureau felt it should be doing to feather its nest, like pushing for those foreign experimental designs. Speculation aside, it is known Land was a specialist in submarine construction and naval aviation, with an M.S. degree in naval architecture from the Massachusetts Institute of Technology, and therefore no stranger to challenging battleship orthodoxy. His service record indicates that his only direct experience with small craft came for a short period in 1916. While a lieutenant attached to the Industrial Depart-

Rear Adm. Emory S. Land. *National Archives*

ment at the New York Navy Yard, he served on a board inspecting civilian motorboats, apparently as part of a program to assess their convertibility to patrol boats in time of war.[1] Perhaps that was enough.

In any event, in December 1936, despite being only four months away from retirement, Emory Land sized up the prospects for American MTB development. On the one hand, with naval limitations about to expire, the navy was free to ask for whatever it could squeeze out of Congress. On the other, President Franklin D. Roosevelt had pledged in his 1936 reelection campaign to cut the growing federal budget deficit. After winning his second term the month before, FDR moved to keep his promise, directing that "all Navy Department bureaus . . . trim their estimates drastically."[2] The time seemed right to ask—but not for too much.

On December 5, Land submitted his MTB proposal to Adm. William H. Standley, outgoing chief of naval operations (CNO), by way of the Bureau of Engineering to get its views. Land's proposal, here quoted in full, is remarkable in that it represents a departure from previous Bureau of Construction and Repair attempts to get the navy interested in MTBs. Notably, Land is not asking the Navy Department to consider the merits of any particular MTB design—especially a foreign design—but rather to consider the merits of an MTB program as a whole. By not pinning the naval bureaucracy to a specific course of action, he at the very least freed up thinking on the subject. This allowed the naval staff to agree to the program in principle, without anyone having to stick their necks out.

---

5 December 1936

From: The Bureau of Construction and Repair
To: The Chief of Naval Operations
Via: The Bureau of Engineering

1. Developments since the War of the motor-torpedo-boat type, then known as Coastal Motor Boats, have been continuous and marked in most European Navies. There has been considerable interest in the fundamentals of the type among the small boat designers and builders in this country based upon patriotic desire to develop pleasure boats which may be of value for naval use in the event of mobilization.

2. The results being obtained in the foreign services are such as to indicate that vessels of considerable military effectiveness for the defense of local areas, are being built, the possibilities of which should not be allowed to go unexplored in our service. It is, of course, recognized that the general strategic situation in this country is entirely different from that in Europe, so that motor torpedo boats could not in all probability be used offensively by us. It appears very probable, however, that the type might very well be used to release for offensive service ships otherwise unavoidably assigned to guard important geographic points such as an advanced base, itself.

3. If the department concurs, this Bureau suggests the inauguration of an experimental development program of such boats and will endeavor to have included in its appropriations for experimental work, funds for the construction of two such boats each year, preferably one by contract on designs of private naval architects and one from Departmental designs.

4. To permit such designs to be prepared or at least outlined, the Bureau requests to be furnished with the military characteristics which are considered desirable in such a type.

E. S. Land
Chief of Bureau[3]

Eleven days later, Rear Adm. H. G. Bowen, chief of the Bureau of Engineering, signed off on Land's recommendation, noting that the bureau had already "given limited consideration to the design of boats of the type discussed." He further mentioned that his bureau was negotiating a contract for experimental gasoline engines for use in crash boats, also usable for MTBs, and hoped to begin developing a suitable diesel engine for such small craft. Bowen then passed the ball to the CNO.[4]

Standley had meanwhile retired, and had been replaced on 2 January 1937 by Adm. William D. Leahy, who would serve as CNO throughout the administrative phase of MTB development, until 1 August 1939. While Leahy got settled into his new office, Adm. William S. Pye handled many of the ongoing administrative details, including Land's MTB proposal. On January 5, Pye wrote to Secretary of the Navy Claude A. Swanson formally recommending that the matter be taken up by the General Board.

Swanson dutifully concurred, requesting that the board offer its opinion on three naturally relevant issues: (1) "the prospective value of motor torpedo boats to the United States Navy"; (2) "the extent, if any, to which development . . . should be undertaken"; and (3) "the characteristics [of the boats] . . . if active development is considered desirable."[5]

All were fair questions. Meanwhile, by coincidence another ranking American military man, Gen. Douglas MacArthur, had been asking himself the same ones half a world away in the Philippines. The potential therefore existed for the Navy Department and MacArthur to form a kind of joint partnership, adding impetus to the navy's budding MTB initiative. That at least became the hope.

Douglas MacArthur's interest in MTBs arose from Congress's passage of the Tydings-McDuffie Act in March 1934. The act authorized commonwealth status for the Philippines until complete independence in 1946. Both the War Department and MacArthur, then army chief of staff, insisted that the American military maintain a presence in the archipelago during the transition period, largely as a counter to growing Japanese aggression in the Far East. MacArthur, in 1935 coming to the end of his four-year term as chief of staff, agreed to become senior military advisor to the Philippine government. He reached Manila in October of that year, carrying with him a ready-made defense plan for the sprawling island group. The Philippine National Assembly passed this plan, embodied in the National Defense Act, in December 1935.

MacArthur's plan for arming the Philippines, based on the purely defensive Swiss model, called for an expenditure of $8 million a year for ten years. It envisioned a land force of eleven thousand regulars and five and one-half months of training annually for forty thousand citizen soldiers, making for a total of four hundred thousand trained reserves after ten years. It also called for an air force of 250 planes and an "Off-Shore Patrol," "the backbone of which would be a fleet of fifty small, high-speed, torpedo-throwing craft. . . ."[6]

MacArthur knew the Philippines could ill afford a battle fleet, a fact he rationalized by insisting there was no need for the Philippines to preserve its overseas communications anyway.[7] All he wanted, in keeping with the strictly defensive nature of his plan, was vessels for in-shore defense, "to deny the use of Philippine territorial waters to a hostile fleet, and to preserve communications between the islands of the Archipelago."[8] He chose MTBs over submarines, another non-battle-fleet, coastal-defense alternative, mainly for reasons of economy:

> Because of lack of funds, multiplicity of types is to be avoided, and, whenever possible, simple, relatively inexpensive items are to be preferred over the more elaborate and expensive varieties. For example, a fast, small torpedo boat is a more appropriate vessel for the Off-Shore Patrol than is a submarine, in spite of the greater effectiveness of the latter weapon under many conditions. A relatively small fleet of such vessels, manned by crews thoroughly familiar with every detail of the coastline and surrounding waters, and carrying, in the torpedo, a definite threat against large ships, will have distinct effect in compelling any hostile fleet to approach cautiously and by small detachments.[9]

The National Defense Act called for the purchase of the Off-Shore Patrol's first MTB in 1938. That in mind, and being an army man through and through, MacArthur chose a retired U.S. naval lieutenant named Sidney L. Huff to get the administrative ball rolling.

Huff had first met MacArthur in October 1935 while serving on the destroyer tender USS *Black Hawk*, attached to the Asiatic Fleet. The following summer, while playing golf with Dwight D. Eisenhower, then MacArthur's chief of staff, he suffered a heart attack. Before Huff was transported to the San Diego Naval Hospital, MacArthur told him that if he resigned from the navy he could come back to be his naval advisor and to "assist the Philippine Government with its steamboat inspection rules." He agreed. Upon his return in December 1936, around the same time Emory Land drafted his MTB proposal for the American navy, MacArthur summoned Huff to his Manila office at No. 1 Calle Victoria, atop the great stone wall the Spanish had erected around the original city. Huff quickly discovered the general had something other than inspection rules in mind:

> [MacArthur's] thinking that day [as he paced the office] concerned . . . the threatening gestures, the acts of aggression of the Japanese in China and elsewhere in the Far East. The fledgling Philippine Republic was coming to life in a troubled, dangerous world.
> "I want a Filipino navy of motor torpedo boats, Sid," he said abruptly. "If I get you the money, how many can you get built in ten years?"
> The question was about as surprising as a punch in the jaw. All I could answer was: "General, never in my life have I even seen a torpedo boat."
> "That's all right," he snapped, a little as if I were wasting precious time. "You will." He stopped at [his] desk again to line up [some] pencils. "Sid, I don't know anything about torpedo boats. But I want you to start work on plans for a navy. You're a navy man and you know what to do."
> "Yes, sir," I said. "I'll need a little time. The U.S. Navy doesn't have any torpedo boats and I'll have to see what's been done in Europe."
> He sat down at his desk and lit a new cigarette. "Go ahead. Work on it. Let me know how you do."[10]

In early 1937, Huff went to work. First he checked on European developments. Apparently unimpressed, he next contacted the United States Navy.

Around this same time, MacArthur attempted to throw his own weight into Huff's effort. On 25 January 1937, MacArthur left Manila on the *Empress of Canada*, accompanying President of the Philippines Manuel Quezon on visits to Japan, Mexico, and the United States. Arriving in Washington in the middle of February, MacArthur discovered his requests for supplies and equipment, needed to implement his Philippine defense plan, had gone

> unheeded by the War Department. But happily, at the Navy Department, when I asked for fast, torpedo-carrying motorboats, both Admiral Harold Stark and Admiral William Leahy listened sympa-

thetically, and promised the development of such a craft. It was the beginning of the PT boats in the United States which were to later play a decisive role in the Pacific War.[11]

Stark left no record of his meeting, or meetings, with MacArthur. Leahy met MacArthur on March 1, writing in his diary that the general

> called at my office to discuss naval bases in the Islands, and the possibility of obtaining from the Navy Department plans for patrol boats that are needed for coast defense purposes in the Islands.[12]

Given the little documentation available, it cannot be known exactly what was said, or what promises were in fact made, in these meetings. In any event, it is hard to imagine they played much of a role in the genesis of the PT—despite MacArthur's rather grandiose assertion. One would expect Leahy, known to be somewhat conservative, to be less than sympathetic to MTBs at this point. Both admirals were probably playing off the knowledge that an experimental MTB program was already in the pipeline—one the navy conceived, not MacArthur (who was hardly a navy favorite). They may also have discussed Huff's initiative. If so, the two navy men could simply have been expressing approval at the thought of the Philippine government's paying for developmental work of eventual benefit to the United States Navy.

Whatever Stark and Leahy's reaction, it is known that the General Board, chaired by Rear Adm. Thomas C. Hart, took Huff and MacArthur's interest in Philippine MTBs into account when it responded to Swanson's three-part request a month and a half after MacArthur's visit, on 14 April 1937. As we will also see, this response signaled the navy's intention to proceed with MTB development, and it offers the best available insight into how the United States Navy viewed PT boats at the beginning of their developmental career.

The board's letter contains fourteen paragraphs. Paragraphs 1 through 7 summarized the administrative paper trail and offered an overview of foreign MTB development and American experimentation to that point. Discussion of the MTB's anticipated value to the United States, its desired characteristics, and recommendations for development, begins in paragraph 8:

> 8. For torpedo carrying motor boats it is clearly evident that because of our strategic situation the type is of much less initial value to our Navy than to most, if not all, of the others. In the early stages of war it is unlikely that small torpedo carrying craft would be useful to us. However, the developments of a prolonged war could

easily change this situation in that operating areas of our own and of enemy fleets would come closer together and, as mentioned in the basic [Land's] letter, motor torpedo boats could replace larger craft which would otherwise have to be employed in defensive missions. Moreover, future situations can occur under which it would be possible for such small craft to be used on directly offensive missions, —as is no doubt contemplated in certain foreign navies. . . .

9. In the initial stages of a war our greatest necessity in the way of small craft, to reinforce our present provision for local defenses, will not necessarily include the ability to carry and launch torpedoes. The essential equipment will include depth charges, machine guns, and listening gear; moderate speeds combined with fair sea endurance will be satisfactory. The conversion of many of the smaller motor pleasure boats to meet such purposes will be relatively easy and require less than will be the case if the general run of such craft are fitted to also carry and launch torpedoes.

10. As far as concerns small craft to be constructed by or for the Navy during peace, the Board believes that we should not go farther than a sufficient expenditure to develop the types. In this field two types are visualized: the one, a comparatively small type with limiting size such as will permit overseas transportation by auxiliaries or cargo vessels; the second type should be larger with better endurance and designed for off-shore work.

11. The Navy Department is at the present time assisting the Philippine Government in the development of motor torpedo boats for its own program for defense. These plans at the present time call for vessels approximately 80 feet in length and easily capable of off-shore patrols. From this work the U.S. Navy should benefit sufficiently to warrant no development work of its own at the present time in this particular type.

12. For the smaller type the stripped weight cannot exceed 20 tons which is the maximum boom capacity of fleet auxiliaries, or that likely to be available in other ships. The comparatively high speed of about 40 knots should be sought for and in order to obtain proper rough weather performance, the hull should be built on the displacement rather than on the step [planing hull] principle. The design should meet the most difficult requirement in this type—[the] ability to carry and launch torpedoes, the number of which, (one or more), will have to be worked out in developing the design. Depth charges as equipment alternative to torpedo armament should be provided for. In so far as is practicable machine gun armaments and listening gear equipment should be included. Radio equipment is also essential.

13. In view of the prospective value to the United States of the smaller type of motor torpedo boats, the Board believes that there should be available a satisfactory design, and therefore recommends the inauguration of an experimental development program on a moderate scale. It is also recommended that at least a part of the development and building be accomplished under contract. Moreover, small boat designers and builders in this country should be kept in touch with our development in order to utilize the very general desire of owners of such craft to have them of use in the event of a national emergency.

14. Based on the above considerations, the Board recommends the following characteristics:
    Hoisting weight: Not to exceed 20 tons.
    Length: Approximately 60 ft.
    Speed: In excess of 40 knots.
    Armament: Torpedoes, depth charges alternative, machine guns, .50-caliber. Smoke devices.
    Crew: Approximately 2 officers and 8 men (standard accommodations not required.)
    Provisions: Self-sustaining for 5 days.
    Communications: Fitted with radio and listening devices.[13]

Clearly, this document demonstrates a significant shift in the General Board's thinking on MTBs. No longer did it seek to completely deny the small torpedo boat a place within the navy's domineering sea-control philosophy. The board notes, justifiably, that at the outset of war, American MTBs would probably be of limited value compared to those employed by the Europeans, given the nation's "strategic position," i.e., geographic isolation. That, however, does not stop the board from recognizing the MTB's real potential as a ship-killer. In a "prolonged war," once the navy locked horns with an enemy in home or distant waters, the MTB could be of some use. Even initially, as Land pointed out and the board agreed, they could free larger craft from static defensive roles, such as guarding "advanced bases." The board also saw an eventual role for the MTB in "directly offensive missions."

While purely speculative, these musings should not be taken lightly when considering the actual operational history of the PT. When the war began in December 1941, the navy deployed, or was close to deploying, every operational PT boat it had guarding the advanced bases—Manila, Pearl Harbor, and the Panama Canal—Land referred to in his "basic" letter almost exactly five years earlier. (Though he did not mention the above bases by name, they were the only significant "advance" ones the United States had at the time.) Also, with the exception of Squadron Three in the Philippines, American PTs found little to do in the war's initial stage. Once, however, the navy came to grips with the Japanese in the Solomons, and later against the Germans and Italians in Europe, it put PTs to good use—and in "directly offensive missions" at that.

Predictably, with Germany again considered a likely opponent, the board emphasized the antisubmarine capabilities of the prospective class, though noting that private vessels—as in World War I—could be easily converted to this purpose, especially if unencumbered by torpedoes. Although the use of MTB-type small craft for antisubmarine work would prove to be a dead end for the navy, the original emphasis on the class's antisub efficacy was to prove useful in gaining its acceptance in naval and Congressional circles. Small craft had played a significant role in patrolling for submarines in the Great War, and the thought of building small, strictly defensive naval vessels played well with isolationist segments in Congress.

Once having found a use for an American MTB, the General Board had no trouble recommending its development. Significantly, neither the board nor Emory Land called for an actual building program of deployable units. Both merely called for the peacetime expenditure of sufficient funds to develop the MTB "types" that might prove necessary in case of war. Believing that a "successful type cannot be achieved in a single design, [the board] therefore recommend[ed] the inauguration of an experimental development program on a moderate scale." The board "also recommended that at least a part of the development and building be accomplished under [private] contract," and that small-boat builders "should be kept in touch with our development. . . ."

Characteristics? They flowed naturally enough from the General Board's views as to the American MTB's anticipated uses. Some would be torpedo-throwing, others equipped for antisubmarine work. All should be able to carry torpedoes and should be outfitted with machine guns. The call for a displacement hull versus step planing hull should not be construed as indicating a desire to produce slow, ponderous boats. The stepped planing-hull type, as pioneered by the British, was on its way out. Such hulls worked fine in smooth seas, but in rough weather they tended to pound and become unstable. Ever more powerful and efficient gasoline and diesel engines could now be counted on to drive more stable round-bilge, displacement-type hulls at acceptably high speeds. As it turned out, the British were now using the hard-chine V-bottom planing hull in their new MTBs. This design also reduced pounding and provided stability in rough weather. Because of British influence in the American program, as discussed more fully later on, the V-bottom design was adopted for use in the American PT.[14]

British influence in all probability also contributed to the board's choice of 60 feet as the boat's approximate length. In 1936 the Royal Navy began rearming itself with MTBs. Its initial choice fell on a 60-foot V-bottom boat designed and built by racing champion Hubert Scott-Paine and his British Power Boat Company. Six were in service by early 1937, when the board made its report. The 20-ton weight restriction eventually proved unworkable, though one can sympathize with the board's desire to be able to transport the boats as quickly as possible to join the fleet in offensive operations overseas.

With the questions of value, extent of development, and boat characteristics answered to his satisfaction, the secretary of the navy approved the General Board's recommendations on 7 May 1935. A week later the CNO's office "quoted [this fact] for the information and guidance of the Bureaus concerned." With the secretary's endorsement, the naval bureaucracy was now behind a modest experimental MTB program. There remained one modest stumbling block: money.

Obviously the navy expected Huff and MacArthur's Philippine MTB initiative, referred to in paragraph 11, to help provide the funds to jump-start the program. As promised, the navy soon drew up plans for the "approximately 80[-foot boat] . . . easily capable of off-shore patrols," and things seemed to progress smoothly. That summer, Lt. Col. James B. Ord, along with Eisenhower attached to the Philippine military advisor's office, was in Washington overseeing the loan of antiquated American military equipment to the Philippine army. On July 27 he wrote to Eisenhower in Manila:

> The Navy has done a splendid job on the [motor torpedo] boats [we ordered plans for] and I believe we are going to have something that is really superior to anything that the Italians, Germans or British have let us see. The hull construction is totally new and it is pricipally [sic] for this reason that I consider it extremely advisable to have the construction carried out at the Norfolk Navy Yard under direct supervision of the Bureau [of Construction and Repair] here. The cost of the first two types will probably be around $112,000 each, but we will then go into manufacture at Cavite [Navy Yard in Manila Bay] at a considerable saving over this price. It is for this reason that I feel our budget estimates compiled thus far would cover the average cost per ship.[15]

Eisenhower nonetheless disagreed. On August 13 he replied that "the information on the patrol boats staggered me a bit. The cost of the *two* ships will be 500,000 pesos—dangerously close to the *total sum* we have in the item for Off-Shore Patrol [for 1938, the first official year of the program]." He went on to write, "I don't see the real advantage of getting *two* [boats], particularly as they are pilot, which means experimental models. . . . Of course, if the model should turn out perfectly, then we'd be that much ahead, and we'd win on the gamble. But I'm afraid of 'bugs' and consequent necessary revision in design. . . ."[16]

The cost of experimentation therefore became the sticking point of the deal. While the Off-Shore Patrol plan for 1938 called for the purchase of one boat at 245,000 pesos—comparable to the navy's asking price for one boat based on its new experimental design—the navy seemed insistent on selling the Philippines two experimental boats instead, at a total cost, including a 50,000-peso savings, double what Huff and Eisenhower were willing to spend.

The navy's attitude here was perhaps understandable: At precisely the time it was considering an experimental MTB program of its own, along comes a foreign government apparently willing to foot the experimental bill for one of the two desirable boat types under consideration. Why not take advantage? Huff's reaction, as a representative of that foreign government in increasingly desperate need of a navy, is, however, equally understandable. "I dropped [the deal with the United States Navy]," he later wrote, "when I realized our Navy would use the money for experimental purposes rather than for producing well-tested boats for the Philippine Navy."[17]

It is difficult to assess the impact, if any, the cancellation of the Philippine order had on the American MTB program even then gaining steam in the Navy Department. Arguably, experimentation on behalf of the Philippines could have given the navy a major head start on a viable "offshore" type, the kind that eventually became the American PT. This is, of course, speculation. What is known is that later in 1937, as a result of Huff's decision to call off the deal for offshore 80-footers, cooperation between the United States and the Philippines on MTB development took a nose dive.

In 1938, Huff turned back to Europe, coming away convinced that "the British Thornycroft model was the best torpedo boat for our purposes, considering the money available."[18] The two boats Huff ordered—arbitrarily called "Q-boats" by MacArthur—were 55 feet long, of single-step planing-hull design, and capable of up to 41 knots in trials. Armament consisted of two machine guns and a trough at the stern for launching two 18-inch torpedoes.[19] They were constructed in England and underwent trials in the winter of 1939, the first one arriving in the Philippines on March 2.[20] Though Huff ordered more, the outbreak of war in September 1939 prevented any further deliveries. By the time the Pacific war broke out he had only three boats in the water, with twelve others in varying stages of completion at Cavite.

MacArthur, meanwhile, seems to have had his doubts about the Thornycroft deal, perhaps fearing—justifiably—that threatening war in Europe would cut off his flow of boats. On 29 March 1939 he wrote a personal letter to Admiral Leahy asking him to authorize the Bureau of Construction and Repair "to make available to him any information the Navy might have about progress made in motor torpedo boat development." The letter further stated: "It is only natural that if a suitable boat is developed there [in the United States] within our means that we purchase these boats there rather than abroad."[21]

Nothing came of this second, high-level request by the Philippines for American assistance with its nascent MTB program. In the end, the two programs developed along mutually exclusive lines—not surprising, considering the generally low priority the American military assigned to the Philippines in the years before Pearl Harbor.

As for America's nascent MTB program, with Philippine government funding no longer an option by the fall of 1937, it was now up to the secretary of the navy's office to get Congress to authorize experimental funds for the larger offshore-type MTB as well as the smaller one. Fortunately, Assistant Secretary of the Navy Charles Edison eagerly accepted the challenge. Indeed, the MTB program could not have found a better advocate.

Under normal circumstances it fell to the civilian head of the Navy Department, the secretary of the navy, to work with the White House and Congress on overall naval policy and on naval bills and appropriations. The assistant secretary handled more routine administrative matters involving the navy bureaus, negotiated purchase contracts for shipbuilding materials and naval stores, and oversaw shore installations, including labor relations with civilian workers in navy yards. In the spring of 1937, however, circumstances in the Navy Department were far from normal, nor had they been normal for some time.

Claude A. Swanson, Roosevelt's navy secretary since the beginning of his first term in 1933, had been constantly ill, suffering from high blood pressure and a host of other circulatory problems. Unfortunately Swanson, a former senator and chairman of the Senate Naval Affairs Committee, was a tenacious scrapper, determined to stick to his post unto death. Roosevelt, for his part, "hadn't the heart to let him go."[22] To make matters worse, on 22 February 1936, Henry Latrobe Roosevelt, the assistant secretary of the navy—and a distant cousin of FDR's—died. So when fishing about for a replacement, Roosevelt had to have someone who might be expected to fill both the secretary's and the assistant secretary's shoes. "How about Charles Edison—the son of Thomas A.

Edison?" Roosevelt wrote Swanson soon after Henry Latrobe's death. "He is an excellent businessman, has familiarity with government methods, has a sense of humor, and, best of all, is wholeheartedly devoted to our cause."[23] The cause was the New Deal; as its principal architect, FDR had every reason to be impressed with his choice.

Charles Edison was born on 3 August 1890 in his famous father's gabled mansion in Llewellyn Park, "a private haven for wealthy families in West Orange, New Jersey." Though a product of some of the best Eastern prep schools—Dearborn-Morgan, Carteret, Hotchkiss—and the beneficiary of three years at MIT (1909–12), Charles possessed little of his father's interest in science. With his matinee-idol good looks and love of poetry, he felt more at home in the arts. Still, Charles did have a flair for management; early on, his father earmarked him to be executive head of Edison Industries. He took over in 1926, at the age of thirty-six.[24]

After Roosevelt became president in 1933, Charles Edison became involved in the new chief executive's various New Deal attempts to combat the Great Depression. He administered several state and regional emergency and business relief projects, under the aegis of the National Recovery Act (NRA), such as the New Jersey State Recovery Board and the regional labor board. In January 1934 he was named compliance director for the NRA in New Jersey and state director for the New Jersey Division of the National Emergency Council (NEC). Later, in April 1935, Roosevelt appointed him to the National Recovery Board. These were the efforts that prompted FDR to note that Charles Edison was "wholeheartedly devoted to our cause."

Charles Edison's efforts were, however, far from tireless. By 1936 he suffered from exhaustion and was determined, after three years of double duty as an NRA administrator and president of Edison Industries, to leave government service to devote full time to his father's company. (Thomas A. had died in 1931 at age 84.) Throughout the year, the younger Edison turned aside "informal overtures about [his] availability for the navy post." In November, though, while returning to New Jersey after vacationing with his wife, Carolyn, in White Sulphur Springs, Virginia, he stopped off in Washington "to gather firsthand reaction to the Democratic administration's sweeping election victories."[25] For the future PT boat, it was a fateful side trip.

In Washington, Roosevelt formally offered Edison the assistant secretary's post. Edison declined, but FDR insisted he postpone his decision until after he had had a chance to talk to Claude Swanson personally. As Edison relates,

[the] meeting . . . followed in a day or two, and while I heard the secretary's health was not of the best, I was totally unprepared for what I
found. As I entered his office, he looked at me with a vague expression and, as though groping to assemble his thoughts, tried ineffec-
tively to identify me or the reason for my visit. Our meeting was brief,
and during one period of lucidity Mr. Swanson assured me that he did
want me to become the assistant secretary.

I returned immediately to my New Jersey home. Mr. Swanson's de-
bility was most alarming, particularly so because, along with many
Americans, I was convinced that war in Europe was inevitable and,
just as inevitably, that the United States would be drawn into it. The
following day, after a night of soul-searching that left no time for
sleep, I contacted the White House and told the president I would ac-
cept the post.[26]

Roosevelt announced the appointment on November 17; after Senate confirmation in early January, Charles Edison was sworn in as assistant secretary on 18 January 1937. Straightway, he concluded Roosevelt
was "no respector of normal channels of communication," and that his
"duties were to transcend those normally handled by an assistant secretary." One of those duties, ship construction, was normally the province
of the secretary, but because of Swanson's uncertain medical condition,
Roosevelt quickly handed this ball off to the secretary's new assistant.

In a surprise meeting a bare ten days after Edison took office,
Roosevelt spelled out his wishes in regard to ship construction. Specifically, he wanted ships completed more quickly than was currently the
case. FDR also stressed that greater "speed [in construction] was not
necessarily more expensive." Edison concluded that Roosevelt "asked
me to use my best efforts to overcome the difficulties in the way of
speeding construction of vessels and to do everything reasonably necessary to accomplish this end."[27] While FDR was referring to larger
warships and not MTBs, his tone no doubt helped create a sympathetic
administrative climate Edison later put to good use in speeding up the
construction of operational, versus strictly experimental, PTs.

Unfortunately, in the summer of 1937, the prospects for obtaining
funds for even experimental PTs were rather bleak. It was a recession-
ary year—in effect, a recession within a depression—and for an isolationist country at peace, the last thing people wanted was increased defense spending. Despite Great Britain's February announcement of a
significant new naval construction program and Admiral Leahy's subsequent call for parity, Roosevelt ordered a $75 million cut in naval
estimates for FY 1938, and on April 7 even "demanded cuts in current

Secretary of the Navy Charles Edison, "Father of the PT Boat Service." *Naval Historical Center*

expenditures."[28] Clearly, with the navy struggling to maintain its existing ships and building programs, funding for experimental purposes was apt to find tough going. However, on 7 July 1937, that began to change when Japan invaded China.

Many fine works have been written about the slow but inexorable escalation of words and deeds that culminated in the Japanese attack on Pearl Harbor and the Philippines in December 1941. In the end, of course, the PT owes its colorful legacy, indeed its very existence, first to the perceived threat of that war in the late 1930s and secondly to the war itself. Suffice to say, as the Far Eastern war intensified and American ships came increasingly in the crossfire during 1937 (most notably the gunboat *Panay*, sunk on December 12), the navy and the Roosevelt administration sought successfully to greatly expand the fleet in growing anticipation of eventual full-scale hostilities. This is not to say expansion was a foregone conclusion. Far from it. As we will see, Congress still needed a lot of persuading before it approved the naval expansion package of which the experimental MTB program was a part.

Happily, in Edison's efforts to shepherd the experimental MTB program—and other increasingly huge naval appropriations requests for FY 1938—through the 75th Congress, he had a lot of persuasive help, in the person of Franklin Delano Roosevelt. This should come as no surprise to even the most casual student of American naval history. Roosevelt, a former assistant secretary of the navy (1913–20), was ardently pro-navy, his almost "childlike affection" for the sea service tempered only by budgetary limitations and the political realities on any given day.

There is, sadly, a lack of documentary evidence describing the exact nature of Roosevelt's support for Edison's efforts to obtain Congressional funding for the MTB program. Edison's biography completely sums up the president's aid in precisely that wording: "With support from President Roosevelt. . . ."[29] Frank A. Tredinnick and Harrison L. Bennett's "An Administrative History of PT's in World War II" makes no specific mention of FDR's role; nor does Bulkley's *At Close Quarters.* The earliest official source mentioning such support is a paper presented by Lt. Comdr. William C. Specht, USN, one of the first officers involved with the PT on the operational level, to the Naval War College on 17 March 1943. Specht wrote that the "experimental appropriation [was] put through Congress personally by President Roosevelt and Secretary [sic] Edison. . . ."[30]

Roosevelt himself, whose restive temperament allowed relatively little time for writing, left no documents describing his efforts on behalf of the nascent PT.[31] Consequently, it comes as no shock that his numerous biographers, including Kenneth Davis, say nothing of this admittedly minor aspect of his presidency. Still, we know that by January 1938, FDR endorsed the Navy Department's request for experimental MTB funds. Moreover, we find in his background every reason to believe that when Charles Edison (presumably) first broached the MTB program to him sometime in 1937, he was favorably disposed to help out.

Roosevelt loved the sea and ships. In 1913, when he became assistant secretary of the navy, he wanted to pass muster with the uniformed navy men whose ships and shore installations he was supposed to administer. According to Kenneth Davis, Roosevelt

> soon convinced the naval officers he met that he did truly possess nautical knowledge and skill and was one with them in his feeling for

ships and blue water. He loved to sail on fighting ships and did so whenever he could, preferring destroyers because they were so small and fast, so swiftly responsive to the moods of the sea and hence so demanding of those who sailed them.[32]

FDR also took an interest in small craft. After he pushed for the creation of the National Naval Reserve, signed into law in the summer of 1916, Roosevelt oversaw the conversion of a small flotilla of 40-foot, 21-knot patrol boats to be used by the reservists during World War I. And if toying with the real thing was not enough, one of FDR's few enduring passions besides politics in the between-war years was his model boat hobby.

> [This] hobby was especially absorbing during his Hyde Park summers, he striving to answer the question "How fast can a small boat be made to sail?" Having settled on an overall length of 38 inches, as he wrote in a letter published in a hobbies magazine in 1923, he used "balsa wood for the hull, balsa or oiled silk for the deck and aluminum for the spars," simultaneously experimenting with different designs of hull and rigging. He was immensely proud of the speed he achieved.[33]

Based on the above, it is fair to suggest Roosevelt took a more than casual interest in the proposed MTB experimentation program and was more than happy to support the funding request. It is something else again to suggest he "personally" rode the request through Congress, any more or less than he personally supported any naval funding requests during his presidency. FDR, Congress, and the navy itself had bigger fish to fry.

Congress approved the initial naval appropriations bill for FY 1938 in August 1937, calling for a couple of battleships and some cruisers and destroyers. In September, though, the Japanese Ministry of Marine refused to divulge its naval rearmament plans, a sure sign that the grudging spirit of disarmament characterizing the 1920s and 1930s was dead; worsening relations, if not war, were in the offing. Throughout the fall and early winter the navy pushed Roosevelt for more battleships and cruisers, hoping to give teeth to its plans for a naval war against Japan codified in War Plan Orange. This plan, unlike the more defensive antisubmarine war envisioned in the Atlantic against Germany, called for an offensive thrust across the broad expanses of the Pacific, ostensibly to relieve the Philippines. The navy needed even more ships, including all-important auxiliary vessels such as tenders, in hopes of finally achieving the "balanced fleet" the navy had pushed for since the 1920s.

On 28 January 1938, FDR complied, asking Congress for a massive 20% increase in the navy's authorized underage combat tonnage, to cost an estimated $1.1 billion. Included in the wish list were 3 battle-ships, 2 aircraft carriers, 9 light cruisers, 23 destroyers, 9 submarines, 22 auxiliary vessels, and 950 additional naval aircraft. Roosevelt also asked Congress to

> authorize and appropriate a sum not to exceed $15,000,000 for the construction of a number of new types of small vessels, such construc-tion to be regarded as experimental in the light of new developments among navies; and to include the preparation of plans for other types of ships in the event that it may be necessary to construct such ships in the future.[34]

One salient aspect of this funding request is that it includes more than MTBs. The money was intended to cover experiments with other small craft as well, primarily 110-foot wood subchasers and 165-foot steel subchasers. MTB experimentation involved only a relatively small fraction of the total money requested, which is why a March 4 amend-ment to the bill by the House Committee for Naval Affairs should not be viewed with too much alarm. Under the sympathetic chairmanship of Carl Vinson of Georgia, the committee recommended passage of the president's fleet expansion request, amending the experimental-craft provision to read:

> There is hereby authorized to be appropriated . . . the sum of $15,000,000 to be expended at the discretion of the President of the United States for purposes of experimenting with surface craft, lighter-than-air craft, heavier-than-air craft, aerial bombs, aerial mines, torpedoes, and other inventions and material developments for the national defense, of which sum $5,000,000 shall be expended for the construction of experimental vessels, none of which shall exceed three thousand tons standard displacement, and $3,000,000 . . . for the con-struction of a rigid air-ship. . . . *Provided,* That the Secretary of the Navy is hereby authorized to enter into contracts with inventors and manufacturers for experimental work, models, plans, materials, and the development of projects useful to the national defense to the ex-tent of $15,000,000 in addition to the sum authorized by this section to be authorized.[35]

The changes reflect the committee's intent to make the experimen-tal provision of the bill (H.R. 9218) more broad-based, with $7 million of the $15 million going toward much-needed experiments in naval aviation. The committee, "anticipating that the experiments autho-rized to be undertaken by this section will develop projects useful to the national defense," added $15 million more to grease the contractual wheels. Since this additional money would conceivably be of eventual benefit to the experimental MTB program, the $10 million loss of funds for experimental surface ships would probably not have seriously affected the MTB program.

The committee's report made clear why it felt such a program would be desirable, noting that overseas powers were "developing and building small high-speed ships and boats for coastal defense purposes" and that this country should do so as well. Admiral Leahy also emphasized the coastal defense aspect of the small-craft provision in testimony before the Senate Committee on Naval Affairs on April 6. When asked by Chairman David I. Walsh if any other naval craft had been designed for harbor defense besides the submarine, Leahy replied that the experimental small vessels under consideration were being built for "that exact purpose." He added, "They will be used for the defense of harbors and for the patrol of the sea just outside the harbors to keep the submarines away."[36] Though Congress spent a good deal of time debating the rigid airship (dirigible), with Roosevelt suggesting that it be funded with other money instead, the legislators spent virtually no time debating the experimental-small-craft provision.[37]

The Senate Naval Affairs Committee did, however, object to two aspects of the House amendment—the inclusion of naval aviation projects in the total and the addition of the $15 million for contractual purposes. After a compromise agreement was hammered out in conference committee in early May, the bill was sent to Roosevelt, who signed it (Public Law 528) on May 17. The provision in its final, Congressionally approved form now read:

> There is hereby authorized to be appropriated . . . the sum of $15,000,000 to be expended at the discretion of the President of the United States for the construction of experimental vessels, none of which shall exceed three thousand tons standard displacement, and the sum of $3,000,000 . . . for the construction of a rigid airship. . . .[38]

On 7 June 1938, the House Appropriations Committee submitted its report on the actual money to be appropriated for that year (FY 1938). Small-craft experimentation received only around $3 million, which provided for experimental work to begin on the subchasers and "two 70-foot motor torpedo boats, at a cost ranging from $233,000 to $300,000 each; and two 54-foot motor torpedo boats at a cost ranging from $214,000 to $235,000 each—the price depending on whether one or several of each type were built."[39] Start-up funding for the United States Navy's experimental MTB program was in place at last.

Now the question centered on just what to do with it.

CHAPTER FIVE

A Scandalous Birth

Dissatisfied with their place in the world, the Japanese struck Russian positions on Changkufeng Hill near the Tumen River on the Korea–USSR border. They called the attack a "reconnaissance in force," to determine Soviet intentions before launching their Wuhan offensive, a renewed effort to take Hankow, Chiang Kai-shek's capital on the Yangtze. The date was 11 July 1938.

On that same date in Washington, D.C., on the other side of the International Date Line, the United States Navy was also on the move. Taking its first concrete, post-appropriations step toward the development of the experimental small craft authorized by Public Law 528, the navy, at President Roosevelt's behest, publicly announced a design contest. The contest gave private American speedboat designers the opportunity to submit plans for the newly envisioned boats.

The intentions of the Imperial Japanese Army and the United States Navy on that date in July 1938 could not have been more different. Japanese army hotheads hoped to instigate a general war with the Soviet Union.[1] American naval officials hoped, as they had with the Newport torpedo experiments of the 1870s and 1880s, to encourage the creation of truly original American designs for navy subchasers and MTBs. The Japanese clearly saw Changkufeng Hill as an opportunity to provoke the Russians; the navy, of course, had no intention of provoking anyone. But provoke it did.

The MTB design contest raised the American small-boat industry's expectations—expectations squashed sixteen months later when the navy placed an order for twenty-three British MTBs designed by Hubert Scott-Paine. The resulting controversy rocked the Navy Department. Like the German and Japanese provocations that eventually led to war, the Scott-Paine scandal cast a dark, yet ultimately energizing, shadow over the birth of the American PT.

No one foresaw a public relations disaster arising from the experimental design contest. By all appearances, the Roosevelt administration and Navy Department conceived the contest with the best intentions. FDR, being an amateur model-boat designer himself, no doubt enjoyed the prospect of this sort of civilian involvement in naval affairs; he always had, ever since his days as assistant secretary of the navy. Besides, contests were fun—and a politically expedient way of spreading a little additional federal largesse.

For the navy, the contest seemed a perfect way to do what Emory Land and the General Board originally hoped to do: involve private American small-boat designers and manufacturers in national defense. They knew the Royal Navy had involved civilian experts in the design and construction of its military small craft for decades—since the 1870s. They clearly figured it high time the United States Navy started doing the same.

To drumroll such involvement, the navy straightway went public. On 8 June 1938, the day after the House Appropriations Committee defined the sums immediately available for the experimental ship program, Assistant Secretary of the Navy Edison met with President Roosevelt at the White House. As he left, Edison announced to the press his and FDR's desire to "call upon the skill of American speedboat designers to help create a mosquito fleet of superlative speed." Taking pains to assure reporters the contest would be fair, he emphasized the navy would only request "competitive designs from ship builders who [had] never before held navy contracts."[2]

Rear Adm. William Dubose, chief of the Bureau of Construction and Repair, also made clear the navy's intentions with regard to the proposed contest. Testifying before the House Appropriations Committee, he stated: "After we get the designs from the private boat builders we will decide whether we will use those designs or our own or make up a composite design."[3] His matter-of-fact wording gave notice to American small-boat designers that although their input was desired, there was no guarantee their designs would serve, by themselves, as the basis for the new-breed American subchasers and MTBs. The leaders of the American small-boat industry should have heeded his words. Doing so might have saved them, and the Navy Department, a lot of headaches later on.

The experimental design contest, like all contests, came with rules, timetables, and prizes. On 29 June 1938, Capt. A. J. Chantry of the Bureau of Construction and Repair submitted the first draft of the invitation for approval by the Navy Department.[4] On July 11, the navy sent out the formal invitations. The contest was open only to qualified and experienced designers. It called for designs for a 165-foot steel subchaser, a 110-foot wood subchaser, and 70- and 54-foot MTBs. The rules gave the competing civilian architects the "greatest possible latitude" in designing what they wanted without being too inhibited by purely military considerations. The rules, however, also made implicit the navy's desire to have sturdy boats with good seakeeping abilities—beyond those normally expected of private pleasure craft. They also, naturally, wanted boats that could fight.

For the MTBs, our concern here, the navy wanted what the General Board said it wanted in April 1937: a smaller boat capable of being hoisted on board fleet auxiliaries and cargo vessels, and a larger boat capable of independent offshore operations. Specifically, the larger boat was to be between 70 and 80 feet overall; capable of being operated by two officers and eight men; have a trial speed of 40 knots, with a minimum cruising radius of 275 miles at top speed and 550 miles at cruising speed; be of metal or wood, round- or V-hulled; powered by gasoline or diesel; and equipped with at least two .50-caliber machine guns, two 21-inch torpedo tubes, and four depth charges.

The smaller boat was to be no longer than 60 feet and have a hoisting weight of not more than 20 tons and a hull structure "of sufficient strength to permit of hoisting over side by means of slings under moderate weather conditions."[5] Called-for armament was even less specific: two torpedo tubes and depth charges, or an alternative armament of machine guns and smoke generators. The hoisting requirements reflect, as will be recalled, the navy's preoccupation with getting these boats overseas as soon as possible to operate with the fleet. This design class eventually went by the board during sea trials—an illustrative example, perhaps, of what happens when a boat is designed more to fulfill its expectations out of the water than in it.

The navy divided the contest into two phases: preliminary and final. Top prize for the winner in each class was $15,000, while all designers who made it to the final phase would get $1,500. The preliminary design phase, originally scheduled to run for six weeks, to August 24, had to be extended—three times—to September 30 to give the designers more time. There was no lack of interest. The Navy Department received twenty-four designs from twenty-one designers for the small boat; thirteen designs from thirteen designers for the bigger one. All but three were eliminated in the smaller class; all but five in the larger.

The navy set the opening date of the final phase as 7 November 1938, giving the remaining designers 10 weeks to expand on their preliminary inspiration. Their final submission was to "include everything expected in a finished design, [of] sufficient detail . . . to form a proper basis for placing a [construction] contract."[6] One designer, represented in both classes, dropped out of the running for the 70-footer, but the rest complied. On 21 March 1939, the navy announced the winners.

A Professor George Crouch of Tams, Inc., a New York designer of racing motorboats, won in the 70-foot category. Sparkman & Stephens, a New York naval architectural firm known primarily for its sailing craft designs, bagged the top award for the 54-footer. President Roosevelt, ever the mothering type when it came to designing small craft, sent a personal reminder to the Navy Department not to overload the boats; he also let it be known he was anxious for construction on the experimental vessels to begin as soon as possible.[7] So prodded, beginning in May 1939 the department opened bidding for contracts.

At this stage, consistent with the navy's ongoing intention of splitting experimental small-craft design and construction between the Bureau of Construction and Repair and private contractors, the department envisioned the building of eight boats, designated PTs 1 through 8. The navy contracted Fogal Boat Yard of Miami, Florida, to build PTs 1 and 2; PTs 3 and 4 went to the Fisher Boat Works of Detroit, Michigan. All four were based on Crouch's smaller PT design, with 3 and 4's engines modified per Bureau of Construction and Repair instructions. Higgins Industries, Inc., of New Orleans, received PTs 5 and 6. These two boats, the first actually contracted (on 25 May 1939), were based on the larger Sparkman & Stephens design, scaled up to 81 feet. The contract signaled the beginning of Higgins Industries' prominent association, under the dynamic ownership of Andrew Jackson Higgins (1886–1952), with the American MTB program. Meanwhile, not to be outdone, the Bureau of Construction and Repair began work in the Philadelphia Navy Yard on a pair of 81-footers, PTs 7 and 8, the latter being the only aluminum PT ever produced.

Though based, as Admiral Dubose had anticipated, on a varied combination of private and navy-inspired designs, the first eight American PTs all had one thing in common: They proved unsuccessful. This should not have been especially disappointing. Producing high-performance motor torpedo boats, ones sufficiently advanced to compete with modern, seaworthy European designs, was something new to American small-boat builders. The polished European boats then coming off the ways were the result of literally years—even decades—of trial and error. They could be expected to measure up. Which brings us to Hubert Scott-Paine, and PT-9, the inspiration for the most widely used PT of World War II, the 80-foot Elco.

The Elco-Scott-Paine saga began late in 1938, even as the seven unsuspecting winners of the preliminary design contest slaved over their

Henry R. Sutphen, executive vice-president of the Electric Boat Company (Elco). *PT Boats, Inc.*

final entries. Numerously held navy contracts prohibited the Electric Boat Company, specifically its Elco Division in Bayonne, New Jersey, from submitting experimental MTB designs to the contest. That, of course, did not stop Elco from taking note of the proceedings. Company officials, especially Elco president Henry R. Sutphen (1875–1950), saw distinctly enough the United States Navy's interest in MTBs. He resolved to circumvent the contest somehow and hitch Elco's star to the navy's potentially profitable new effort.

Sutphen's interest in producing American MTBs, aside from profit, stemmed from his company's unique suitability for the job. Elco had gained considerable experience building motor launches (MLs) for the British and Italian navies in World War I. As previously mentioned, during Prohibition the company also built a number of "fast, weight-carrying boats which alternately served the rumrunners and the Coast Guard."[8] From these and other boats, Elco became especially adept at solving the number one design issue facing naval small craft since the 1870s: how to combine small size with high speed in a craft capable of keeping the sea in all kinds of weather.[9]

Sutphen's company may have had the technical expertise, but without a workable MTB design of its own, it could not be assured of any significant near-future involvement in the navy's program. While in England late in 1938, Sutphen learned of a British boat that seemed the perfect solution to this problem. If he could buy this proven, pre-existing MTB design, better yet a finished boat, perhaps the navy could be persuaded to purchase it.

The boat Sutphen discovered, somewhat *sub rosa* according to Charles Edison's biographer, was designed and built by a man whose involvement in the American PT program remains the subject of sharp controversy: Hubert Scott-Paine (1891–1954). He began his flamboyant career in 1910 as a designer and builder of land planes. In 1914 he switched to marine types, subsequently patenting many original developments for flying boats. He helped start Imperial Airways in 1924. Scott-Paine's work with flying-boat hulls led to his founding the British Power Boat Company in 1927. Not content with merely designing his boats and overseeing their construction, he personally competed in many international motorboat races, winning several.

In 1934, the Royal Air Force, dissatisfied with the performance of its round-bilge seaplane tenders, contracted British Power Boat to build a number of "rugged, seaworthy, and fairly fast" crash boats and tenders. These boats were of the V-hulled planing type, with a hard chine to minimize roll. In October of that year, Scott-Paine, building on success of his crash-boat design, approached the Admiralty with plans for a 60-foot MTB. The Royal Navy purchased two, then a total of six. They joined the fleet in 1936. These boats, as well as German and Italian MTBs, were what attracted Emory Land's attention, prompting his basic letter of 5 December 1936 that got the American MTB program underway.

Meanwhile, the British put the six Scott-Paine boats through their paces. One was tested in an English Channel gale measuring Force 8—winds in the 34-to-40-knot range, seas running 12 to 18 feet—and was still able to do between 20 and 30 knots. In 1937 all the boats ventured under their own power from Portsmouth to the British-held island of Malta in the central Mediterranean. There they continued to impress their handlers, notably the flotilla leader, Comdr. G. B. Sayer, RN:

> The seaworthiness of M.T.B.'s is remarkable for craft of their size. Their particular form of hull with its high freeboard, great buoyancy and shallow draft (2 feet, 11 inches at rest) allows them to ride over seas rather than through them, and with reasonable handling it is extremely unlikely for green (i.e., solid sheets of) water to be shipped,

Hubert Scott-Paine, after winning the world water speed record in 1933. *Southampton City Heritage Services*

even at fairly high speeds. When stopped the boats lie to in rough seas, beam on to wind and sea, very comfortably, riding over the seas like a cork and keeping comparatively dry. Hove to, they can weather very severe conditions . . . far in excess of those in which torpedoes can be fired with any accuracy.[10]

Though one of the MTBs was subsequently lost in bad weather, forcing the remaining boats to return to England through French canals, Scott-Paine was encouraged by these reports. Determined to go one better, he built an advanced 70-foot version in 1938. The boat, built extensively of plywood, was powered by three Rolls-Royce Merlin aero engines totally some 3,000 horsepower. Armament, as originally designed, consisted of two 21-inch or four 18-inch torpedo tubes, plus two 20mm antiaircraft guns and one 25mm gun in power-operated turrets. She was held to be extremely maneuverable, quick to accelerate, and, like her 60-foot predecessor, able to handle rough seas without difficulty.[11] This was the new boat, still to undergo her sea trials, that attracted Henry Sutphen's attention.

When Sutphen returned to the United States, he contacted Charles Edison with the exciting news of his discovery. How he expected his fellow New Jersey industrialist to respond is not known. To Edison, "the availability of Scott-Paine's boat was like a heaven-sent answer to one of the navy's problems."[12] On 13 January, 1939, hoping to turn his boyish enthusiasm into an officially sanctioned initiative, Edison asked the General Board to "examine the question of acquiring a British-type 70-foot motor torpedo boat similar to those in use by the British Navy and make recommendation as to the desirability of such acquisition."[13]

The board replied three days later. "Inasmuch as said design is known to be the result of several years' development," wrote Admiral Hart, "the General Board considers it highly advisable that such craft be obtained as a check on our own development. It is accordingly recommended that, if possible, a 70-foot motor torpedo boat be obtained on such design." He also recommended that a 54-foot boat be obtained, "if it can be arranged."[14]

With the navy formally behind the idea of obtaining a British boat or two "as a check on our own development," Edison in late January entered into negotiations with Sutphen regarding the business terms of the actual purchase. The agreement: If Sutphen did go to England and did come back with a satisfactory British boat, the United States Navy would buy it. Though Sutphen had wanted a guarantee that the navy would be obliged to purchase five more if the first "demonstrator" proved acceptable, Edison agreed only that "he would ask Congress for funds for [the] purchase of additional boats if the demonstrator justified such action."[15] Fair enough. On 10 February 1939, so assured of his government's intent to buy, Sutphen, accompanied by his chief designer, Irwin Chase, traveled at his own expense back to England to go MTB shopping.

According to Chase, the Royal Navy granted them "unusual opportunities" to inspect not only the Scott-Paine 70-footer but also boats by Thornycroft and Vosper. They liked all of them, but were won over by the same thing that had impressed Commander Sayer in 1937 about the Scott-Paine design: its remarkable affinity for rough weather. After Sutphen and the American naval attaché reported favorably to the

Navy Department on the 70-footer's superb performance, arrangements were made to purchase the boat then and there.[16]

On March 17, Sutphen radioed from England to say he had concluded the deal, with delivery of the boat to take place in three months. Edison got FDR's approval for it on April 3, provided, as the president wrote on the request, the price was "as low as the proposed American 70 footer."[17] In fact, the price was even lower, because of unexpectedly high engine development costs for the American versions. On June 1, Elco and the Navy Department concluded a formal contract calling for the construction and delivery of one MTB on the Scott-Paine design—actually the English designer's prototype, PV-70—with the new formal delivery date set as November 1.

So far so good. On 5 September 1939, four days after the German attack on Poland set off World War II, the Scott-Paine 70-footer arrived in New York as deck cargo on board the SS *President Roosevelt*. The British boat, designated PT-9 and accompanied by Hubert Scott-Paine himself, was lightered to the Electric Boat plant in Groton, Connecticut—ironically located near the mouth of the Thames River, opposite New London. Elco officials then moved PT-9 over to New London, where it underwent ten days of tests and trials for the benefit of the navy and Coast Guard.

The boat lived up to its expectations, though Bureau of Construction and Repair officials "intimately acquainted with this phase of the PT boat program have stated that Scott-Paine—an exceptional boat-handler, especially with his own design—personally did as much to sell the boat to the Navy as the boat did itself."[18] Despite Scott-Paine's performances, the Coast Guard left unimpressed, finding the "potentialities of the craft for a Coast Guard vessel were too limited to warrant investment."[19]

The navy felt differently—*far* differently. At the end of September, Edison, by now thoroughly sold on PT-9's "potentialities," made the single most controversial decision in the entire PT development saga. Instead of merely building one or two boats based on Scott-Paine's design, to test alongside the other eight experimental boats now undergoing construction, he hoped to build one or two *squadrons*. By doing so he sought, with one swift stroke, to take the PT program beyond the experimental to the operational, to the point where a single proven type suitable for operations with the forces afloat would be mass-produced. While this bold step failed in its immediate objective—the program stayed in its experimental stage for a while longer—Edison's initiative was nevertheless to be of tremendous benefit to the PT pro-

Charles Edison, left, as acting assistant secretary of the Navy, with Adm. Harold R. Stark and President Roosevelt, at the White House on 28 August 1939. *Naval Historical Center*

gram as a whole. In the meantime, though, it caused tremendous trouble for the Navy Department.

The ruckus began on 3 October 1939, when Edison wrote President Roosevelt asking his approval on "a project of acquiring additional motor torpedo boats of the Scott-Paine design, using unexpended funds of the Experimental Appropriation made available by the Second Deficiency Appropriation Act of 1938, and negotiating the best possible bargain with Elco—Scott-Paine's licensee in the United States." The president approved his "project," writing, "OK, How many? How much?" on the request. Edison, now secretary of the navy *ad interim* since Claude Swanson's death on 7 July 1939, replied on the same letter: as to number, "18–20"; as to price, "$271,000 or better."[20]

While the Scott-Paine boat passed additional design tests, including rough-water trials on November 1, Edison haggled with Elco over getting its progeny built. With the $5 million Edison offered, all that remained of the $15 million from the Second Deficiency Act, Sutphen felt he could build sixteen boats. Edison, pointing out that the navy hoped to operate the boats in squadrons of twelve, wanted twenty-three boats: twelve motorboat submarine chasers (or PTCs, numbered 1–12), and eleven PTs (numbered 10–20), the twelfth boat to be PT-9. Already gambling on the possibility of future, more lucrative navy orders for the Scott-Paine MTB, Sutphen reluctantly agreed, later stating that his company lost as much as $600,000 on this first deal.[21] In the same hopeful vein, Elco also put up $700,000 to construct a plant in Bayonne to build the new boats.[22] All twenty-three would be identical to PT-9, except Packard engines would be substituted for the original Rolls-Royce engines. On December 7 the navy granted Elco the contract.

Two days later, Edison publicly announced the deal. Included in the official Navy Department announcement was a diplomatically worded attempt to explain the rationale behind it:

> It is hoped a thoroughly satisfactory high-speed military motor boat of American design will be developed from [the eight experimental] ships now building, but to develop a prototype for mass production, if that should become necessary, both American and British boats are to be used in experiments for that purpose, as the military motor boat received considerably more attention abroad during the World War and up to the present time.[23]

The attempt, such as it was, failed miserably. The deal set off a firestorm of protest from the American motorboating industry, which understandably felt its prestige had been dealt a severe blow. Andrew Jackson Higgins, for example, claimed news of the contract resulted in letters from his South American customers "expressing surprise" that the American Navy Department "considers that American designers and builders are not qualified, whereas the English are." He insisted that his dissatisfaction with the Elco deal was "not a question of sour grapes with us," and that his only concern was the damage to the prestige of the American small-craft industry, resulting from the publicity surrounding the purchase of a British boat by America's own navy.[24]

George S. Sutton, Jr., president of the Marine Trades Association and former president of the 220,000-member American Power Boat Association, released a statement on December 30 describing the Elco deal as "American scandal No. 1 of world war No. 2" and "the fishiest smelling deal that has been perpetrated in many a long day in the marine industry." Many in the motor boat fraternity, he stated, were "agog and indignant" over the deal, primarily because a British-designed boat was being mass-produced instead of an American one, and no competitive bidding had taken place.[25]

Angry telegrams and letters poured in to the White House and Navy Department—and to the navy's overseers in Congress. As early as December 11, George W. Rappleyea, the combative chairman of the National Legislative Committee of the American Power Boat Association, wrote to Joachim O. Fernandez of the House Naval Affairs Committee angrily calling for a Congressional investigation into the matter.[26] Nothing came of this heated request—Fernandez did not even query Edison about the charges in Rappleyea's letter until the end of February. Indeed, so far as is known, no serious legal questions were ever raised about the deal. Still, that did not hide the fact that the navy had a potentially serious public relations problem on its hands.

Much of the editorializing, which continued in the national press and boating circles over the winter, could be put down (Higgins notwithstanding) to sour grapes—the fretting of a bunch of intensely competitive businessmen over the loss of a potentially juicy government contract. Judging from the vituperative nature of the writing, the Scott-Paine scandal had more to do with Anglo-American powerboat rivalries than American naval preparedness. Rappleyea, the most persistent critic of the Elco deal, made no secret of his Irish upbringing. He openly professed "little sympathy for the advancement of British supremacy in motor boats or anything else."[27] Scott-Paine's involvement in the deal was like rubbing salt into an open wound, since he had founded British Power Boat in 1927 expressly "to compete with the importation of American motorboats into England."[28] Now here he was, gleefully invading American turf instead; no wonder the industry was up in arms.

Nevertheless, the marine industry telegrams and editorials did raise some legitimate questions about the Elco deal, ones that at the very least required some forthright answers from the Navy Department. Why was the navy building twenty-three identical British-designed boats, rather than just one or two to test against the experimental American designs then building? Why had the navy committed itself to a foreign design before those American boats could even be tested? And why had Elco put up money to build a plant, one "not justified by the present 23-boat order," unless there existed "some secret agreement" to again eliminate competitive bidding for future navy orders?[29]

Other editorialists questioned the fairness of the MTB design contest itself. The January 1940 issue of *Motor Boat and Power Boating* asked

The British Invasion: Hubert Scott-Paine's PT-9 pacing PT-3, the Fisher Boat Works' 58-footer. *Naval Historical Center*

its readers to recall the contest, claiming that "there seemed to be something peculiar about [the contest] at the time, for the original rules did not allow anywhere near enough time for the architects to prepare their preliminary drawings." It went on to chastise the navy for its inexperience in small-craft designing: "Every designer has had experience with the novice boat owner who thinks that a design can be prepared in a couple of days. Within certain limitations the Navy Department took the same unreasonable stand. . . ."

Yachting magazine (February 1940), after criticizing the large number of British boats ("it seems hardly necessary to get 23 to find which are the faster and more satisfactory"), offered what can be taken as the definitive, and certainly heartfelt, marine industry response to news of the Elco deal:

> While it is probably true that the British Admiralty has developed this type of small craft to a greater extent than has our own Navy, we believe that American designers, builders and engine manufacturers are

just as capable of meeting the needs of our Navy if given the opportunity to do so. In time of war we would have to be dependent on our
own designers and builders. They should, therefore, in time of peace
be given every opportunity to fulfill our Government's need.

That, of course, was exactly what the government was trying to do
in building the British-designed boats: fulfill its need. The problem
was, the navy did a poor job of defining that need to the marine industry. The official announcement on December 9 did little to help. It
spoke of developing a prototype for mass production, *if* that should become necessary. What was construction of twenty-three identical boats
if not mass production? And where was the national emergency justify-
ing such necessity? Given what it knew, the marine industry had every
right to see the Elco deal as a slap in the face, an affront to its prestige.

What was this ill-defined government need? What could justify the
navy's cavalier treatment of the very industry it hoped to involve in national defense? Why did Edison do it? *To save time.*

From the beginning of his *de facto* tour as navy secretary, Edison
had been under strict instructions from President Roosevelt to speed
up ship construction and reduce costs in any way he could. He took
those orders seriously. He was a pragmatic business manager, and the
goal of streamlining the ship-procurement process suited him by temperament and training, and he gained personal satisfaction from cutting through bureaucratic red tape. It was he who, in the interest of
greater construction efficiency, brought off the merger of the Bureau
of Construction and Repair and the Bureau of Engineering, thereby
creating the Bureau of Ships in July 1940.

In the case of MTBs, "one of the navy's problems" was how to get
them from the experimental design stage to the operational stage as
quickly as possible. Given the growing threat of war—Hitler flagrantly
swallowed up what remained of Czechoslovakia in March 1939—and
Edison's and Roosevelt's continued special interest in MTBs, it is little
wonder Edison persisted in pulling out the stops.

As for the United States Navy's sending out to the Old World for
help in kick-starting the program, there was nothing new in that. Recall that as far back as 1883, the chief of the Bureau of Ordnance requested the navy to purchase a proven small torpedo boat from overseas (meaning Europe), for use "as a model from which more could be
constructed in this country." Though nothing came of this highly prescient request, seven years later the Navy Department acquired the
Whitehead self-propelled torpedo, and in 1920 it purchased those two
British CMBs for testing purposes. Now with the United States finally

serious about building its own small torpedo boats, it wanted the Scott-Paine boat to use as a yardstick. Nothing could be more natural.

Exactly how Scott-Paine's boat would significantly advance the navy's timetable Comdr. Robert B. Carney, Edison's administrative point man for PTs in the Navy Department, spelled out in a memorandum on 27 April 1939, less than a month after the boat was approved for purchase.

Carney anticipated that once the technical bureaus (Construction and Repair, Engineering, and Ordnance) were satisfied with the experimental boats derived from the contest, they would be turned over "to the forces afloat for service tests with the Fleet." Here he expected some "preliminary [tactical and operational] doctrines" to emerge. Not until 1941, after more technical refinements and the development of plans for a standard, mass-producible type, did he foresee the "building of a certain number of homogeneous units for the continuation of operational tests and development."

This final step in the experimental program, he was then quick to point out, was "not necessarily the last step." Elaborating, he wrote that

> if this type proves to be necessary, it is highly desirable that its tactical potentialities be developed at once. To this end it may be desirable to build a division or squadron at an early date, even though development work is not completed. From present indications it will possibly be about eighteen months (i.e. 1941) before the 1939 boats will be available for operating as a unit with the forces afloat, and it will be considerably longer before a homogeneous unit would be produced under our present program. I therefore consider it advisable . . . that the Department consider the advisability of acquiring a homogeneous unit of some type at an early date for the really important part of the tests—the tactical operations with the forces afloat.[30]

Elco, it seemed, was not the only organization interested in circumventing the design contest. Though Carney failed to mention the Scott-Paine boat specifically, its shadowy presence undoubtedly formed the basis of this soon-to-appear "homogeneous" unit.

In a series of consistently worded responses to the various congressmen and industry leaders who requested clarification about the Elco deal, Edison forthrightly and unapologetically evoked the navy's right, in the name of national defense, to accelerate the PT's developmental timetable—even if it meant using a British rather than American design. Why twenty-three boats?: To create a homogeneous unit of a proven type for the all-important tactical tests with the fleet. Why not wait for the experimental American boats?: war was coming. Why no competitive bidding?: Elco was the sole American licensee of the Scott-

Paine design, the only *proven* design the navy possessed. In essence, although Edison repeatedly professed faith that America's designers would eventually come up with an MTB as good as or better than Scott-Paine's, international tensions did not permit enough time to allow them to do so.

Though generally honest in his answers, Edison was disingenuous on one important issue. He habitually made it sound as if the General Board were initially responsible for the whole idea of acquiring a British boat. For example, on 22 March 1940, in a response to an inquiry into the deal by David I. Walsh of the Senate Naval Affairs Committee, Edison wrote:

> Motor torpedo boats have been used in Europe since early in the world war, but the type has not been developed in this country until recently; in order to profit by the quarter-century of experience abroad, the General Board recommended securing a motor torpedo boat of British design as a yard stick for our own endeavors. I concurred in that very sound recommendation and initiated the necessary measures to get a good boat of foreign design in this country.[31]

Edison, of course, was the one who asked the General Board to consider the idea in the first place, and one wonders why he chose to hide behind the board's official veneer. Was he afraid of the political fallout from appearing to show favoritism toward Sutphen, a fellow New Jersey businessman? Or was he guilty of something far more serious than "winking at legalities" in the Elco deal, as Edison's biographer contends?

Significantly, as for the Elco plant, Edison in his correspondence neither confirmed nor denied that any secret agreement existed to grant Elco exclusive rights to build future PTs of the Scott-Paine variety. Of course, the advantage to the navy, and Elco, in possessing a finished, privately built plant for the mass production of PTs could not be denied. Edison repeatedly stressed during this period that the "construction of the Scott-Paine boat is so radically different that it is a departure from American conventional methods." He no doubt factored in the need for someone in the United States to become adept at mass-producing PT boats using this "radically different" method before war came. Why not Elco? It sought the proven foreign design, took a chance, and constructed a plant to build it. Even if the whole thing smacked a bit of conspiracy, should the navy complain?[32]

Actually, the navy did complain. Edison biographer John Venable notes that "Edison's successful efforts to gain acceptance of PT boats alienated some admirals, who by tradition were wedded to big ships heavily armored."[33] If in fact there were navy admirals who objected to PT boats, the December 1939 Elco deal would have been the ideal time for them to come forward in their opposition. A moderate experimental program was one thing; it was quite another to take experimental money to mass-produce actual combatants for service with the fleet. Sadly, navy records shed virtually no light on the extent of—or even the existence of—such opposition. Nor is one able to find much mention of PT boats, good or otherwise, in the otherwise lengthy memoirs and biographies of the navy's major wartime leaders.

Did the navy "not want" PT boats, as some PT writers have alleged? The answer must be no: The navy wanted PT boats or it would not have experimented with, mass-produced, or manned them. Did some members of the navy brass object to PTs? Probably. They also probably felt that during the heady 1939–41 period, with the navy undergoing massive "big-ship" expansion under threat of war, formally campaigning to get rid of the tiny PT was not worth the bother.

The foregoing also calls into question the popular assertion that President Roosevelt had to "intervene" to keep the brass from thwarting the PT program. There is simply no documentary evidence to support this contention.

Raging motorboat designers; puzzled congressmen; alienated admirals. Was Charles Edison's gamble on the 70-foot Scott-Paine boat worth the hassle? Edison, who was replaced by Frank Knox as secretary of the navy on 24 June 1940, surely thought so, later recalling the entire affair with "special affection."[34] For the navy, the results were more mixed. As things turned out, Edison's enthusiasm for the so-called "Chinese copy" 70-footers was a bit premature. First came the unexpected delays. Elco engineers setting out to duplicate Scott-Paine's politically incorrect brainchild quickly discovered that the blueprints he submitted with the boat were inadequate. They were forced to rely on PT-9 as a working model, delaying delivery of the boat to the fleet until 17 June 1940. Even so, on that date the United States Navy finally had its first motor torpedo boat.

For the navy, though, that was not the final word. By the time the first of the new 70-foot Elcos joined the fleet—along with several of the experimental models—in November 1940, they were in a sense already obsolete. The 70-footers were originally designed to carry four 18-inch torpedo tubes, there then being a surplus of 18-inch torpedoes. Then in June 1940, Lewis Compton, acting secretary until Knox could take over, asked the Bureau of Ordnance and the General Board to determine if the four tubes should be replaced with two 21-inch torpedo tubes instead. He also wondered how future boats should be equipped.[35]

Both the bureau and the board responded in July. They recommended that the existing Elcos should be built as is, with the four 18-inch tubes, but that future PTs should be built with four 21-inch tubes. The reason for the switch was commonsensical: The navy was phasing out the 18-inch torpedo and the 21-inch model was twice as powerful.[36]

If followed, this recommendation would require future boats to be bigger, the 21-inch tube being four feet longer than the 18-inch tube. So the Navy Department asked the General Board to take up this question before making any more contractual decisions.

On August 23 the board came through, presenting the department with a new set of desired characteristics for the next generation of PTs: they would be scaled up to around 80 feet, be of wood construction, be powered by reliable gas engines capable of 40 knots, have a cruising range of at least 500 miles at 20 knots, and possess an armament of four 21-inch torpedo tubes, a smoke screen generator, and four .50-caliber machine guns in two twin turrets. The board also suggested the navy build twenty-four of these new MTBs with funds made available by a $50 million appropriation for small craft for the fiscal year beginning 1 July 1940.[37]

Frank Knox approved these recommendations on September 23, which allowed time to build the last boat of the original twenty-three boat order, PT-20, to the new specifications. Two days later, Elco got the contract, calling for twelve new PTs (numbered 21–32) and twelve PTCs (33–44), all scaled down slightly to 77 feet overall. Eventually, however, the PTCs were all built as PTs, using the same boat numbers, since the navy concluded that larger craft made better antisubmarine vessels.[38] These boats began arriving in the fleet in June and July 1941. With these the navy entered the war in December, while the majority of the 70-footers, including the original PT-9, were sold to the British under Lend-Lease in the spring of 1941.[39]

Meanwhile, Higgins Industries had a success story of its own. It had received the first contract for the Sparkman & Stephens 70-footer, scaled up to 81 feet, but found the submitted design so poor it developed its own, an 81-foot boat eventually delivered to the navy in February 1941. Higgins also built a 76-foot craft, one its naval proponents thought to be superior to the Elco PT. It remained only to compare the two rivals.

The two camps soon got their chance. In the winter of 1940–41, Adm. Harold R. Stark, who had replaced Leahy as chief of naval operations in August 1939, became increasingly anxious about the growing threat of war. He called for PT standardization, in case mass produc-

PT-20, the first Elco-77, in 1941. *Naval Historical Center*

tion soon became necessary, and insisted on the "conduct of comparative service tests without further delay."[40]

The navy complied that summer, staging a series of rough-water tests to compare the reliability, maneuverability, and speeds of the Elco and Higgins boats, and the rest of the experimental designs, off New London, Connecticut. One rough-water test even compared the performance of the boats to that of a destroyer. PT-21, an Elco-77, averaged 27.5 knots, only two knots less than the destroyer (the *Wilkes*), over the six-hour course, with seas running from six to twelve feet. This suitably impressed the board of inspection and survey monitoring the tests. It even opined that

> modern destroyers possess no sensible advantage over the motor [torpedo] boats even under sea conditions highly unfavorable for the latter, and that in areas where limited visibility is not unusual, the motor boats might readily prove much more adaptable than the larger vessels within the limitation of their operating range.[41]

This report, echoed in the board's formal findings, was to bode well for the future willingness of the United States Navy to make use of its new MTBs among the islands of the southwest Pacific and Philippines. Additional recommendations based on the tests included preferring that PTs operate from shore bases, and that patrols, especially in heavy seas, should be kept to a maximum of twenty-four hours, to limit crew fatigue from the incessant pounding. All of these recommendations were to prove highly "visionary."[42]

Dubbed the "Plywood Derbies," the service tests set the stage for the final round of increasingly feverish developmental planning before the onset of war. Both the Elco and Higgins boats (PT-21 and PT-70, respectively), as well as a 72-foot boat manufactured by the Huckins Yacht Company, met the navy's approval. Again, based on the results of the tests, the navy asked the manufacturers for modifications, primarily an increase in size to improve the overall sturdiness and seaworthiness of the craft.

On October 6, Bureau of Ships officials met with representatives of Elco, Higgins, and Huckins to spell out the new specifications, ones that would govern the construction of the American PT throughout World War II. To fulfill performance requirements they must be at least 75 feet long and not more than 82 feet long, "the largest that could be transported easily." Each boat would have three Packard engines, equipped with mufflers to permit silent approaches. Trial speed was set at 40 knots, sustainable for one hour, with a cruising radius of 500 miles. The hull, which showed the permanent influence of the Scott-Paine design, was to be "the hard chine stepless bottom type with lines formed with a view to minimizing stress on the hull and fatigue of crew under all conditions. . . . The sides shall flare outward from chine to gunwale."[43]

Given those specifications, the three companies were invited to submit bids "in lots up to thirty-two, the number allowable with currently available funds." As a result, Higgins was contracted for twenty-four boats, scaled up to 78 feet, Huckins for eight—also increased to 78 feet. Not forgotten, especially given its already demonstrated capacity to mass-produce PTs quickly, Elco received a contract for thirty-six boats, scaled up to 80 feet, soon after Pearl Harbor. The foundation for the PT fleet soon to fight in the greatest of America's wars had been laid.

In sum, the navy bureau system and American ingenuity—that is, trial and error—produced the PT boats the navy employed in World War II, not Charles Edison's importation of a "proven" foreign design. Still, Edison's contributions, which earned him the sobriquet "Father of the PT Boat Service" from John F. Kennedy in 1948, cannot be dismissed.[44] To him goes the honor of finessing the United States' ability to mass-produce PT boats before war made it absolutely necessary. War

PT-84, one of the first Higgins 78-footers. *National Archives*

PT-117, a classic example of an Elco-80, the archetypical PT boat. *National Archives*

intervened before the first generation of PT officers could develop any significant operational or tactical doctrine as Edison had hoped, but that hardly lessens his achievement. He helped make possible, perhaps more than any other single individual, the appearance of the American PT on the firing line in December 1941, when the Japanese were once again on the move.

PART II

A Question of Value
(1941–1945)

CHAPTER SIX

To the Firing Line

We have seen that in the late 1930s, hoping to keep pace with European developments in the field, the United States Navy built, tested, and refined its own unique brand of motor torpedo boat, the PT. PTs emerged from this experimental process technically on par with their European counterparts, but in one important area the Americans lagged far behind: defining the PT's tactical value.

The Europeans, most notably the British and Italians, had employed MTBs on a tactical level before, and when war broke out in September 1939, they promptly put them back to work escorting and interdicting coastal merchant traffic. The United States Navy, having spent the entire interwar period just learning to appreciate and develop the type, had no comparable tactical experience on which to build. This inexperience, combined with uncertainties about how the expected war with the future Axis would shape up, left the navy groping to define what wartime role its new "mosquito boats" might play.

Prewar PT officers, meanwhile, were too busy to give much thought to this broader question of value. They had their hands full providing PT designers with feedback on boat performance and gaining experience in routine boat operations. Upon receiving the new Elco-77s, for example, the crews immediately made a number of suggestions for improvement. Among them were requests for self-sealing gas tanks, "increased pilot house visibility, simplified deck house construction, improvement of midships section to eliminate waste space, and a number of ordnance improvements centered around the mechanical turrets, which were to become a definite nuisance on these boats."[1]

The PT men also worked hard to develop squadron cohesiveness. Admiral Stark decided in April 1940 to make the squadron the operational bedrock of the American MTB. The squadron would be the commissioned adjunct, not the boats themselves. And PT skippers would not, technically speaking, be commanding officers but boat captains. This system was adhered to throughout World War II. It simplified administrative matters tremendously and proved a satisfactory arrangement.[2]

The first actual prewar squadrons came and went, consumed by experimental obsolescence and the dictates of American foreign policy.[3] The navy commissioned Motor Torpedo Boat Squadron One in July 1940. This squadron eventually comprised those experimental boats actually made operational—PTs 3, 4, 5, 7, and 8 and the Higgins-designed PT-6. PTs 1 and 2 had experienced so many delays in having their engines installed that by the time they were delivered in December 1941, the navy downgraded them to small boats. In 1940 the British bought the original Sparkman & Stephens PT-6, along with some 70-foot boats Higgins designed specially for them.

Ordered south for the winter of 1940–41 to undergo a Caribbean shakedown, Squadron One's boats proved so mechanically deficient they had to be confined to Florida. That spring the navy transferred PTs 3, 4, 5, and 7 to the British under Lend-Lease. The navy kept PTs 6 and 8 for training new personnel at the Newport Torpedo Station, PT-6 because it still showed promise from a design standpoint, and PT-8 because the British did not want an aluminum boat. Squadron One then reverted to paper status.

MTB Squadron Two, commissioned in November 1940, consisted of the Elco-70s, including PT-9. Its boats cruised the Caribbean in the winter of 1940–41. Though they proved to be more seaworthy and mechanically sound than their experimental cousins, most—including PT-9, going full circle in less than two years—were similarly handed off to the Royal Navy under Lend-Lease, the remainder being sent to Newport as trainers. This squadron also reverted to paper status, awaiting the arrival of the new Elco-77s.

The dozen PTCs of the original Elco order became Motor Boat Submarine Chaser Squadron One in February 1940. In April, the navy transferred eight of these to the British for use as motor gunboats. The other four were sent to Key West,

> where each was fitted with a separate type of experimental sound gear. None worked. If the boat was underway the noise of its engines drowned out the echoes of the sound equipment. If the boat shut off its engines and lay to in anything but a dead calm, it developed such a short, sharp roll that it could not pick up the echoes. Although admirably armed against submarines (with both stern racks and Y-guns for throwing depth charges), the PTC's had no way of locating them.[4]

The four boats returned to New York in July 1941. Soon afterward, the navy leased them too to the British and promptly decommissioned the squadron.

The swift, unflattering demise of the American PTC is significant when we consider the operational value of the PT program as a whole. By acknowledging that PT-type craft were ill suited for hunting subs, the navy undercut much of its rationale for building them in the first place. Admiral Leahy had touted the proposed PT's antisub efficacy before Congress in April 1938, testimony that helped pave the way for approval of the program's initial funding. Now that role was in question. PTCs, and even PTs, were maybe capable of finding and attacking submarines, but larger naval craft could do the job better. Later wartime experience bore this out.

In the meantime, the extinction of the PTC concept exposed the PT for what it was: a small torpedo boat valuable only against other surface craft. This should not have been a problem, except that throughout their prewar development period the navy generally assumed them to be coastal and harbor defense vessels. At the beginning of a conflict, they would patrol "such bodies of water as Chesapeake Bay, Puget Sound and the mouth of the Mississippi, so as to release destroyers for duty at sea,"[5] a role no more original than that proposed by the Naval Advisory Board in 1885, when it recommended a comprehensive torpedo boat defense of the United States seaboard. The General Board, in its April 1937 endorsement of the experimental MTB program, also mentions using them to release larger patrol craft for use in offensive missions. Unfortunately, all agreed that the enemy vessels most likely to invade inshore areas in the next war would be submarines, not surface craft. If PTs were poorly equipped to hunt subs, what value would they have serving in a modern-day coastal defense capacity?

Admittedly, there is no record this question was raised at the time. In the early summer of 1941 the program entered a bright new phase as the Elco-77s began arriving. PTs 20–30 and PT-42 reconstituted MTB Squadron One. PTs 36–40, 43–44, and 45–48, the latter four also being Elco-77s manufactured beyond the original contract, formed the new Squadron Two. And in early August the navy created Squadron Three (PTs 31–35 and 41) from the remaining 77-footers. Training of crews for the new "coastal defense" squadrons continued.

One would nevertheless think that sooner or later the peacetime navy would have had to concede the general incompatibility of the PT with its assumed coastal defense role. This happened once war came; virtually all PT boats, except those involved in training PT personnel, operated offensively outside the continental waters of the United States. In the months before Pearl Harbor though, the PT had yet to prove its ability to operate anywhere of importance to American interests. What then was in store for the freshly reconstituted squadrons? More Lend-Lease?

As it happened, this potential short-of-war dilemma the PT program never had to face. For the reason, thank the Japanese. Japan had
invaded China proper in July 1937, which helped pave the way for
massive increases in naval spending—including, in May 1938, funds for
the experimental MTB program. Since then the Pacific situation had
grown progressively worse. In May 1940, responding to continued
Japanese aggression on the Chinese mainland, President Roosevelt ordered the United States Fleet—called the Pacific Fleet after 1 February
1941—to base permanently at Pearl Harbor. He hoped the fleet's presence 2,600 miles closer to the Far East would act as a deterrence to
Japan's warlords. He was wrong.

Japan also proved capable of making increasingly provocative decisions. By 1940 it faced stalemate in the vast Chinese hinterland. The
German defeat of France, Belgium, and Holland in May and June 1940
offered the Japanese an opportunity to cut down the flow of Western
arms to the Chinese and obtain new raw materials by extorting military
bases in northern French Indochina from the newly installed Vichy
regime. Roosevelt reacted in July to this move south by barring unli-
censed exports of such things as scrap metal and aviation gas to the
Japanese. He also called for major new increases in defense spending,
and the United States adopted conscription for the first time in its history. Far from being cowed by such steps, Japan formally joined the
Axis in September.

In October, the Japanese decided they wanted the rich resources of
the Netherlands East Indies—part of their self-proclaimed Southern
Resources Area. In January and May 1941 they demanded that Dutch
officials supply them with oil and other necessary resources. The Dutch
responded in July by restricting oil imports instead. That same month
the Japanese completed their occupation of all French Indochina.
Among other provocations, this move brought the British naval base at
Singapore within range of Japanese land-based aircraft.

Faced with this new threat and Japan's continued refusal to leave
China, Roosevelt upped the ante, freezing all Japanese assets in the
United States. This had the effect, among other things, of choking off
Japan's major source of oil. Unless the Japanese could get the crude
flowing again, their war machine and industry would soon grind to a
halt. To extract themselves from this dilemma, they prepared to take
the Southern Resources Area by force, knowing the move would result
in war with the United States and Great Britain.

A detailed account of the frenzied diplomatic and military maneuvering that led up to Pearl Harbor is beyond the scope of this work.
What is pertinent is that these escalating tensions forced the navy to

decide where to employ the new Elco-77s even then joining their squadrons.

It is unknown if Emory Land had the Japanese naval threat specifically in mind when he wrote his basic letter of 5 December 1936, mentioning the use of American MTBs to guard "advance bases." By the end of July 1941, however, Admiral Stark certainly did. As early as 18 February 1941, the new commander in chief of the Pacific Fleet, Adm. Husband E. Kimmel, wrote presciently to Stark that he felt

> a surprise attack (submarine, air, or combined) on Pearl Harbor is a possibility. We are taking immediate practical steps to minimize the damage inflicted and to ensure that the attacking force will pay. We need anti-submarine forces,—DDs [destroyers] and patrol craft.

In this connection, Kimmel also recommended that Stark "send out one squadron of PTs and one squadron of the new PTC subchasers at the earliest possible date."[6] Stark replied on March 22 that he could not send Kimmel any PTs or PTCs because the British had requested— and would eventually receive—twenty-eight of them through Lend-Lease.[7]

Kimmel tried again on July 26, stressing the "urgency for small craft in the Fourteenth Naval District [Hawaii] for patrol purposes, to relieve the load on our limited number of destroyers."[8] This time he had more luck, Stark writing to him on August 2 that he had "just directed sending him [Adm. Claude C. Bloch, commandant of the 14th Naval District] 12 P.T.'s—40 knot craft."[9] Squadron One received these orders to head for Hawaii on August 13.

Meanwhile, Stark ordered Squadron Three to augment the local defenses of the 16th Naval District in Manila. The squadron's six Elco-77s, so selected as they were the most completed, left New York Navy Yard in mid-August piggybacked aboard the fleet oiler *Guadalupe*. They squeezed through the Panama Canal and arrived in Manila Bay on September 28. Stark eventually ordered Squadron Two—the outfitting of its boats having been delayed by a lack of ordnance, most notably a shortage of 21-inch torpedo tubes—south soon after the war began in December to defend the Panama Canal.[10]

Stark later revised these deployments. On October 22, Kimmel wrote to the CNO complaining that

> the urgency for additional patrol craft in this area is as great as ever. Such craft are not worthwhile unless they can operate in trade wind seas which result from winds from 15 to 35 knots blowing almost continuously. The 12 PT's which you sent to us I fear will be of very little

To the firing line: MTB Squadron Three on board the fleet oiler *Guadalupe* en route to the Philippines in 1941. Lt. Bulkeley's famed PT-41 is at lower right. *PT Boats, Inc.*

use in this area. We sent them on an average day to make a trip from Oahu to Molokai. The reports of this trip have gone forward officially. They were practically useless in this sea and could not make more than 10 knots. Several of them had to turn back and a few personnel were quite seriously injured from being thrown about. We need something much more substantial to be of any use out here.[11]

During October, Admiral Hart in Manila also expressed concern about the new PTs, particularly that they lacked spare parts, maintenance personnel, an adequate tender, and supplies of 100-octane gas. Trusting that "the many problems in connection with them can be worked out," Stark replied on November 1 that he "hoped that the PTs will be of real service to you. The British think they are fine." He referred Hart to Kimmel's complaint about the boats being useless in Hawaii and informed Hart he was "considering sending you six (6) more PTs [from Hawaii] and the *Niagara* as a tender."

Of interest is Stark's attempt in the same letter to reassure Hart of the PT boat's durability. Here Stark also acknowledges the failure of the navy's prewar MTB program to produce a wholly satisfactory small combatant in time for war.

> These boats [the Elco-77s] have shown weakness when pounded into heavy seas. I might add that we know the weaknesses of these PTs. We gave them some grueling tests [the "Plywood Derbies"] in fairly heavy weather from New London up around Block Island, down around Fire Island and back. They made a destroyer [the *Wilkes*] hump to stay with them, but all the boats which made the race suffered severe structural damage. We deliberately pounded them to see what they would stand and to develop their weaknesses. Profiting by what we learned, we hope to develop a much sturdier craft. *Meanwhile, we sent out what we had, hoping they would be of some use* [emphasis added].[12]

Thus on the eve of war, not only had the navy dismissed PT boats as antisubmarine vessels, which undermined their assumed potential as harbor and coastal defense craft, but field officers even expressed concern over their suitability as patrol vessels against surface targets, at least in the windy tropical seas off Oahu, and their lack of proper logistical support. Out of desperate need to stiffen his Hawaiian, Philippine, and Panamanian base defenses before the Japanese struck, Stark committed them anyway, "hoping they would be of some use." Maybe they would. At these advance bases there existed more than just a chance of probing attacks by Japanese, or even German, submarines. The PTs might be expected to tangle with Japanese surface ships bent on the bombardment of anchored ships or key facilities, or on outright amphibious invasion. Ready or not, thanks to the Rising Sun the PT program's days as a purely experimental entity born and nurtured in peacetime were fast hurtling to a close.

Coming of age is never easy, but nowhere did the first wartime PT squadrons do so as painfully as in the Philippines, which between December 1941 and May 1942 were the scene of the greatest military disaster in American history. To understand MTB Squadron Three's soon to be famous role in this bloody tragedy, some background is necessary.

The seeds of the Philippines debacle were sown early in the twentieth century. In the years after the United States acquired the Philippines from Spain, President Theodore Roosevelt, anxious to put some muscle behind America's Open Door policy in China, considered making the islands the site of a major naval base. Events soon caused him to question his choice. The principal one was the annihilation of the Russian navy in the 1904–5 Russo-Japanese War, making Japan supreme in Asian waters. Japan's growing power, coupled with its resentment of white racism shown Americans of Japanese ancestry, caused the United States to perceive Japan as a powerful potential enemy—and the Philippines as an undefendable Achilles heel.

From America's point of view, the basic defense problem was distance. The Philippines are 7,000 miles from the West Coast and nearly 5,000 miles from Hawaii. The archipelago was simply too far from the United States' main centers of power. The placement of significant naval and army forces there practically invited their piecemeal annihilation by the locally superior Japanese, who would certainly attack the Philippines in the event of war. Yet American prestige, and a felt obligation to defend the Filipino people, demanded that the United States maintain some sort of defensive entity in the islands. This insistence on keeping up a military presence in the Philippines, though one kept deliberately small so as to neither antagonize the Japanese nor offer them too tempting a target, lies at the root of the American defeat.

Army-navy rivalry further aggravated this defensive dilemma. Early on, the navy wanted a base in Subic Bay, on the west coast of Luzon northwest of Manila. It feared being bottled up in Manila Bay as the Spanish were in 1898. The army, however, did not feel it could defend a naval base in Subic Bay from the landward side. It opted for Manila Bay, and set about placing powerful fortifications and coastal artillery on Corregidor and three other smaller islands at the bay's mouth. Meanwhile, the navy decided in 1909 to set up its main Pacific base at Pearl Harbor.

Army and navy planners took these early force dispositions into account in designing the United States' strategic response to war with Japan. This response, embodied before World War I in War Plan Orange (WPO), called for the defense of Manila Bay for three to four months, ostensibly long enough for it to be reached, and used, by the main American battle fleet thrusting across the Pacific from Pearl Harbor.

The Great War, however, left Japan in control of the former German island possessions in the Central Pacific, the Marianas, Marshalls, and Carolines, all on the route between Pearl Harbor and Manila. Given this new obstacle to a cross-ocean thrust, navy planners were forced to conclude that "the Philippines were doomed. The Japanese could overwhelm the defenders long before the United States fleet could reach the scene."[13]

This conclusion the navy tacitly acknowledged in 1935 when it amended WPO to include the capture of the Marshalls and Carolines before proceeding to the Philippines. That might take years, as indeed it did, meaning the best the Philippine garrison could hope to accomplish was hold out as long as possible.

Meanwhile the army, being responsible for providing that garrison, had its own second thoughts about defending the Philippines. In 1933, Brig. Gen. Stanley D. Embick, harbor defense commander on Corregidor, recommended that all army and naval forces be pulled back from the Philippines to the line Alaska–Hawaii–Panama. The Philippines were too exposed, he wrote, and therefore a military liability.[14] The War Department rejected the idea, later deciding, as noted in Chapter Four, to maintain a limited military presence in the islands until their independence in 1946. How limited is reflected in the army's 1936 decision to scale back its mission, agreeing to defend only the mouth of Manila Bay, thereby denying the bay, but not Manila itself, to the Japanese. To this end the army ground forces were to retreat into the rugged Bataan Peninsula, directly north of the harbor entrance, and make their stand in support of the bay forts. For the next five years, until the summer and fall of 1941, this is roughly where things stood.

In July 1941, with tensions in the Pacific reaching a boiling point, the War Department began to take the defense of the Philippines more seriously. The department recalled MacArthur to the colors and gave him command of United States Army Forces in the Far East (USAFFE). A few small American ground units and American-trained Philippine scouts, about 22,000 men in all, and about 80,000 largely untrained and underequipped Filipino army reservists made up this new command. The army earmarked some additional troops and aircraft, including a small force of modern B-17 bombers, for the islands. Though most of these reinforcements failed to make it to the Philippines before the Japanese attack, the War Department at least tried to do what it could to make sure the strategic retreat to Bataan called for in WPO would succeed in keeping the Japanese at bay—or out of it—for as long as possible.

MacArthur, though, had other ideas. As early as February 1941, he began to feel the revised War Plan Orange (then known as WPO-3) was flawed. Air power, he argued, made merely holding the mouth of Manila Bay impracticable. Only by keeping the Japanese off the islands altogether could he prevent them from seizing or building nearby air bases to support their ground forces. He therefore proposed that the

Lt. Gen. Douglas MacArthur, called once more to the colors in 1941. The flamboyant Army general had a mostly illusory impact on PT boat development. *National Archives*

Philippines be defended on the beaches, expressing confidence that by the spring of 1942—when he expected the Japanese attack—he would have 200,000 men under arms, thus enabling the Philippines to repulse all comers.

In November, encouraged by the arrival of additional aircraft and MacArthur's enthusiastic reports of the progress made by his Filipino recruits, the War Department agreed to revise WPO-3 to allow MacArthur to defend the entire archipelago. Further, the department hoped the air forces deployed there would actively engage in strikes against passing enemy shipping. This would assist the British and Dutch in the defense of the Malay Barrier, the string of islands from the Kra Isthmus in Thailand to Timor.[15]

These revised expectations of USAFFE capabilities turned out to be wholly unrealistic, causing all sorts of difficulties once war actually began. Expectations of naval capabilities in the Philippines tended to be far more realistic but created no less havoc.

Naval leaders gave the United States Pacific Fleet no part to play in the Philippines delaying action. That job fell to the Asiatic Fleet, since July 1939 under the able leadership of Adm. Thomas C. Hart. Hart's responsibilities under WPO were clear: Should war threaten, the Asiatic Fleet's major surface element, two cruisers and a destroyer division, was to avoid destruction by the Japanese Combined Fleet by quickly retiring to the Malay Barrier, there augmenting the British and Dutch defenses. Those forces less vulnerable to superior Japanese surface units and marauding aircraft were to remain, supporting the army in the defense of the Philippines "as long as that defense continues."[16] Hart could, however, shift those units south to a Dutch or British port at his discretion.

Hart's most impressive strike force was composed of twenty-nine Asiatic Fleet submarines. All but six were the new fleet type, superb long-range boats that would eventually devastate Japan's merchant marine and cripple its war production. In the Philippines campaign their goals were more modest: to strike hard at the Japanese invasion fleet and otherwise disrupt Japanese seaborne communications with their units surging south toward the Southern Resources Area. A patrol wing of PBYs, or Catalina flying boats, hoped to provide the subs with up-to-date reconnaissance on Japanese naval and shipping movements.

Also on hand at war's beginning were a few sub and seaplane tenders and a handful of gunboats, useful for protecting Western commercial interests in China but of doubtful value against Japanese dive-bombers and destroyers. And augmenting the 16th Naval District defenses under the command of Rear Adm. Francis W. Rockwell was MTB Squadron Three.

The dire need for district patrol craft had prompted Stark to ship the squadron to Manila in August 1941. Having heard MacArthur's pitch for Philippine MTBs in 1937, he appreciated their utility for work among the myriad shallow, reef-strewn channels and bays of the archipelago. This assumed geographic compatibility with PT operations also explains his intention to send Hart and Rockwell the six "useless" boats from Hawaii. Given the simplistic nature of the army's strategic task, the PTs' mission as district craft was equally clear: to assist the army in the defense of the Bataan Peninsula and the Manila Bay forts by repelling Japanese landings and protecting local shipping. The PTs eventually did both.

However obvious the squadron's strategic role, there still remained the all-important question of exactly how to go about fulfilling it tactically. There was little established doctrine to go by. Luckily for the untried and untested men and boats of MTB Squadron Three, the officer in command was a superb improviser and natural-born leader, not the kind of man to let the absence of a rule book get in his way: Lt. (jg) John D. Bulkeley, USN.

It is difficult to overestimate this pugnacious, irrepressible man's influence. John Bulkeley (1911–96) became to World War II PT boats what William Cushing was to Civil War spar torpedo boats—a dominant presence, an inspiration to his shipmates, and by all accounts an extraordinary American fighting man.

Bulkeley graduated from the Naval Academy in 1933 and was commissioned in 1934. He became fire control officer for the cruiser *Indianapolis*, later serving on board the old gunboat *Sacramento* in China. Bulkeley was a division officer on the aircraft carrier *Saratoga* in February 1941 when the navy assigned him to command PTs. As for why he agreed to a command position with this new, experimental service, Bulkeley biographer William Breuer writes only that he accepted knowing "that to refuse such an 'offer' would squash future promotions." Bulkeley was ill as this work was in progress. He died on 6 April 1996, several weeks after the author attempted contact. For the details requested, his family deferred to Breuer. Thus, unfortunately, we have no sense of how the man who would have so much impact on the PT program really felt about serving in the boats, or how he viewed their wartime potential.[17]

Bulkeley took command of the four PTCs sent to Key West in the spring of 1941 to test their suitability as sub hunters. With the demise of the PTC concept, and squadron, the navy gave Bulkeley newly commissioned Squadron Three that summer. Promising action in "an exciting secret place," he rounded up volunteers from his old boats and set off for Manila, busily conducting sessions on (makeshift) PT tactics en route.[18] After reaching Manila on September 28, the squadron settled into its new home. On Monday, 8 December 1941, the crews were still in residence, anxiously awaiting the Japanese typhoon set to blow in from the north.

That same day, 2,000 miles to the east across the International Date Line, Ens. N. E. Ball, USNR, MTB Squadron One's squadron duty officer, stood on board the barge serving as the PT's tender at the

Lt. Comdr. John D. Bulkeley, USN, in 1942 after he received the Medal of Honor. *Naval Historical Center*

Pearl Harbor Submarine Base. He watched idly for a moment as aircraft appeared and began diving on Battleship Row. When the first bombs began to drop on the squat, unsuspecting mountains of steel resting alongside Ford Island, Ball raced to the on-board mess hall, shouting for the PT crews to man the guns. Within a short time men on board the six PTs of Squadron One, along with the crews of the six boats being loaded on board the fleet oiler *Ramapo* for shipment to Manila, began blasting away at the Japanese aircraft. Between them they claimed two torpedo planes, and possibly they hit several others, before the Japanese sped back to their aircraft carriers, leaving large swatches of Pearl Harbor in shambles.[19]

For those Americans who heard them, they were words not forgotten, not then, not ever: "Yesterday, December 7, 1941, a date which will live in infamy, the United States was suddenly and deliberately attacked by the naval and air forces of the Empire of Japan." President Roosevelt, the man delivering them to a packed joint session of Congress, needed less than six minutes to finish what he had to say. That was enough. Within an hour Congress approved the president's request for a declaration of war against the Japanese.

Japan's surprise attack on Pearl Harbor aroused the American people as nothing had before. They "reeled with a mind-staggering mixture of surprise, awe, mystification, grief, humiliation, and, above all, cataclysmic fury."[20] The physical damage stood at six battleships sunk or sinking and two others damaged, more than 200 aircraft destroyed or out of commission, and 3,600 men dead or wounded. The psychic toll stood even higher. Americans felt utterly betrayed. The Japanese had struck before issuing a formal war declaration. Those Americans who wondered why FDR had lavished so much peacetime cash on more troops, planes, ships, and experimental oddities like PT boats wondered no more. The United States was at war.

CHAPTER SEVEN

Philippine Tragedy

For the men of MTB Squadron Three and the other Americans in the Philippines at the beginning of the United States' involvement in World War II, disaster struck early, decisively. Shortly after 12:30 p.m. on December 8, some nine hours after receipt of the news of the attack on Pearl Harbor, Japanese aircraft decimated General MacArthur's air force on the ground, a gross command failure on MacArthur's part for which he never had to atone.[1] What remained of his bomber force, the long-range B-17s, soon flew to Australia, while the few surviving fighters fought to extinction doing what they could. It was rarely enough.

Suddenly deprived of air cover, Admiral Hart's Asiatic Fleet either died where it stood or fled south sooner than expected to the Malay Barrier. Unopposed, the Japanese bombed Cavite Navy Yard, nine miles south of Manila, on December 10. They smashed the base, destroying valuable fuel stores and torpedoes. The submarine *Sealion* sank alongside her pier and she later had to be blown up. The minesweeper *Bittern* shared a similar fate, while the planes damaged the *Peary*, a World War I–vintage four-stack destroyer. The few remaining destroyers, auxiliaries, and tenders eventually escaped to the south. Two days later, Japanese planes shot up a goodly portion of Patrol Wing 10, forcing Hart to remove it too from the Philippines.

The vaunted fleet submarine force fared no better. With its tenders now vulnerable to air attack and the subs themselves lacking air reconnaissance and deep water to protect against Japanese destroyers, it failed to slow the main Japanese landings at Lingayen Gulf, 100 miles north of Manila, on December 22. Hart ordered them out of the archipelago on New Year's Day, he himself leaving for Java the day after Christmas by submarine. Admiral Rockwell stayed, commanding what ships remained.

Luzon Strait

C. Engaño

Aparri

Scarborough Bank

Lingayen Gulf

LUZON

Cavite Navy Yard
Sangley Pt.
Cañacao

Moron

Corregidor

Manila Bay

Subic Bay

Manila

Batangas

Bataan
Peninsula

Mariveles

Ternate

Mindoro

Verde
Is.

Cape Santiago

MINDORO

Grande
Is.

Legaspi

Cabra Is.

Strait

Apo East Pass

San Bernardino Strait

Apo Is.

MASBATE

SAMAR

Coron Bay

Tagauyan Is.

PANAY

Tañon
Strait

LEYTE

Leyte Gulf
Str.

Iloilo

CEBU

Cebu

Surigao Str.

Palawan Passage

NEGROS

Bohol Str.

BOHOL

PALAWAN

Puerto Princesa

Bais

MINDANAO
SEA

Dumaguete

Zamboanguita

Siquijor Is.

Oroquieta

Cagayan

SULU SEA

Misamis Bay

Iligan

MINDANAO

Lake
Lanao

Davao

Zamboanga

Jolo

Sandakan

Tawitawi

TALAUD
ISLANDS

CELEBES SEA

The Philippines. *Naval Historical Center*

They were a paltry few: three river gunboats, three minesweepers, two district tugs, two civilian tugs, two converted yachts, one submarine tender, the *Canopus*, and Lt. (jg) John D. Bulkeley's six MTBs.[2] All lacked adequate fuel, spare parts, repair facilities, and all possible hope of reinforcement. Periodic air raids whittled down their numbers. Events in the ground war added a further complication: lack of food.

The early date of the Japanese invasion surprised MacArthur, who had believed the Japanese would not attack until the following spring. The Filipino army units he had counted on to repel the invaders at the beaches were still poorly trained and equipped. Many melted away into the hills after their first brushes with the enemy. Other units fought well, but on the whole their performance quickly convinced MacArthur his plan could not succeed. He soon ordered a return to WPO-3, calling for a retreat into Bataan.

By early January 1942, after a series of masterful delaying actions, he pulled off the withdrawal. Tragically, his last-minute revision of WPO-3 resulted in considerable food and ammunition being stashed around Luzon and on the other islands for the benefit of the local beach-defending units. With his strategic shift back to Bataan, many of these supplies were lost. The army command soon ordered daily rations drastically cut for all personnel, including naval; medicine, especially quinine for treating malaria, became scarce. In the end, hunger and disease probably did more to cut short the defense of Bataan and Corregidor than did the Japanese.[3]

For Bulkeley and Squadron Three, the war began the same way it had for Squadron One in Hawaii—from the air. As bombs rained on Cavite on December 10, three of the PTs, alerted in time to get under way, dodged Japanese dive-bombers by maneuvering frantically in Manila Bay. Their skippers waited for the Japanese pilots to release their bombs, then turned the wheel hard over, keeping the boats from being hit. PT gunners claimed three of the planes.

By that time, however, the Japanese had claimed Cavite, forever eliminating any possibility the high-performance PTs would be properly equipped and maintained—as opposed to *barely* equipped and maintained—during the four-month ordeal to come. Spare torpedoes and thousands of drums of the 100-octane aviation gas the PTs needed went up in smoke. Machine shops and food stores were destroyed. Bulkeley had stashed nine spare engines in Manila, but three were lost when the Japanese occupied the city. Of the six others, a bombing raid on Corregidor's North Dock later claimed two, while no opportunity existed to install the remaining four.[4]

Bad gas further contributed to the boats' maintenance woes. With the loss of its gasoline in Cavite, the squadron had to rely on two floating bargefuls in Manila Bay. This gas the men soon found to be laced with paraffin wax, an act of sabotage blamed on two of the Filipinos guarding the barges. The discovery put a serious damper on later operations, since the wax clogged the carburetors and could not be strained out. Though the men spent a great deal of time cleaning the carburetors, this failed to guarantee that the engines, which the crews depended upon for their very lives, would keep running—especially while idling during an attack approach.

The navy aggravated these mechanical difficulties by becoming increasingly reliant on the boats. As the Asiatic Fleet's heavier units went south, the PT emerged as arguably the 16th Naval District command's most valuable and versatile attack and patrol vessel. Demands on them increased accordingly.

From the beginning of the Japanese onslaught the PTs served as dispatch boats, much as the Union spar torpedo boats did during the Civil War, running passengers and messages between Manila and Corregidor, and later between Bataan and Corregidor. After the Cavite bombing they acted as seagoing ambulances, ferrying the wounded to the hospital in Cañacao. Later the squadron moved its base to Sisiman Bay, a small, secluded cove east of Mariveles harbor on the southern tip of Bataan. From there, shortly after midnight on December 17, the boats helped rescue 296 survivors from the SS *Corregidor*, an interisland steamship that struck a mine and sank while fleeing Manila.

Mainly, however, Rockwell called upon the PTs to make routine nightly patrols of the sea approaches to Manila Bay, in hopes of intercepting Japanese warships, shipping, and amphibious landing attempts. The squadron tried running two or three boats together on this so-called Offshore Patrol, for mutual support, but supply and maintenance deficiencies soon made this practice unworkable. Typically Bulkeley could spare only one.[5]

For the first few weeks, converted civilian patrol vessels, Philippine Fisheries craft, or one of the Asiatic Fleet's old flush-deck destroyers often accompanied the boats. The eventual loss of these supporting vessels left the PTs alone in their nightly forays into Japanese-infested waters. Not even the Q-boats brought to the islands by Huff could help out. Only three were in the water when war came (Q-111, Q-112, and Q-113), including the two British prototypes. Huff had twelve other clones building in Cavite, all of which he blew up when the navy abandoned the yard in December.[6] The three working boats helped form the Inshore Patrol, which worked the east, or Manila Bay, side of the Bataan Peninsula. Although the Q-boats did free the PTs from having to patrol that side of the peninsula, they spent little time in tandem with their larger, more seaworthy American cousins.

The Filipino Q-boat crews did not miss much. For the most part the PTs' Offshore Patrol program was fruitless and uneventful. Many of the patrols were wild-goose chases, based on questionable ship sightings by jittery Filipinos or army observers. As such, only a handful of dates throughout the long winter stand out:

December 24: Christmas Eve saw the squadron's first casualty. While on patrol, PT-33 grounded on a coral reef along the Luzon coast south of Manila Bay. Attempts by other PTs to get her off failed. On December 26 she had to be burned to prevent capture.[7]

January 18: District command sent PT-41, under Ens. George E. Cox, Jr., to check out a report that the Japanese were placing heavy guns along the south shore of Manila Bay, near Ternate. Cox found no guns, but two miles east of Ternate he observed several groups of Japanese soldiers on a beach. He took them under fire with his .50-caliber machine guns. According to army intelligence the fire killed eight and wounded at least fourteen of the soldiers.[8]

January 19: On the 18th the army reported "three transports and two war vessels effecting a landing at Binanga Bay [in Subic Bay about four miles north of Moron on the Japanese-held northwest coast of Bataan] and shelling the coast in the vicinity of Bagac [behind American lines]."[9] To investigate, the navy sent two boats, PT-31 and PT-34.

Bulkeley, commanding the joint attack from PT-34, ignored Japanese signal challenges and probing machine gun fire as he idled toward the darkened waters off Port Binanga shortly after midnight. After PT-31, under Lt. (jg) Edward G. DeLong, failed to rendezvous, he crept in alone, firing two torpedoes at what was eventually believed to be a 5,000-ton Japanese transport carrying 5.5-inch guns. One of the torpedoes made a hot run in its tube and failed to clear, but the other was seen to explode about a minute after being fired. As he fled at top speed, Bulkeley observed a fire and two large flashes in the direction of the port.[10]

Though Bulkeley was probably unaware of it, his attack marked the first time since October 1864, when William Cushing steamed up the Roanoke to take on the *Albemarle*, that a small torpedo boat of the United States Navy had gone into action against an enemy vessel. Though the results were less spectacular than the sinking of the Confederate ironclad, the attack proved Bulkeley and crew to be worthy successors of the Cushing legacy.

Meanwhile PT-31, much like picket boat *No. 2*, met an inglorious end. As the PT made its cautious approach to Binanga Bay, DeLong ordered the two wing engines shut down because of "carburetor strainer trouble [resulting in part from the sabotaged fuel]." When the center engine conked out because of problems with its freshwater cooling system, the boat drifted, soon grounding. Attempts to free the PT proved futile. For the second time in less than a month, a boat had to be burned to prevent capture. All but three of the twelve crewmen returned safely through enemy lines to Mariveles the next day.[11]

Aside from the loss of PT-31, the January 19 attack had several important consequences. One, it demonstrated how difficult it was for PT crewmen, attacking at night from a low, pitching deck, to authenticate their handiwork. Was the transport sunk? No one seems to know for sure. Though the army later informed Admiral Rockwell that its observers on Mariveles Mountain, using 20-power glasses, had seen the unidentified transport sink, postwar research of Japanese records fails to confirm this.[12]

Two, the attack, perceived as successful at the time, whatever the truth, made big headlines back home. Bulkeley became a national hero overnight. No doubt for most Americans the sensational press coverage, based on official navy reports from the Philippines but released by PR-savvy admirals in Washington, was the first they had ever heard of PT boats. Thus the PT's ship-hammering reputation was established early on in the war.

Three, the Binanga Bay attack reaffirmed the desirability of making a slow, stealthy approach to a target and graphically demonstrated the need for something to muffle engine noise (preferably better than a wood box and tarpaulin). The loss of PT-31 also made clear the need for engines better able to idle "reliably" at low speeds, what Admiral Rockwell in his official report termed "one of the inherent weaknesses of this particular (PT) model."[13] Thus were some of the PT's design deficiencies also established early on in World War II.

January 21: PT-32 fired two torpedoes at a 6,000-ton tanker off the Bataan coast. Both torpedoes passed ahead.[14]

January 22/23: During the night the Japanese made two roughly battalion-size amphibious landings, well to the rear of the main defense line, at Quinauan Point and Longoskawayan Point on the southwest coast of Bataan. While patrolling, PT-34 and the *Fisheries II* ran into part of this Japanese end run, eventually sinking two 40-foot landing barges with machine gun fire.[15]

Many of these Japanese troops took refuge in caves overlooking the shore. Since the PTs lacked heavy ordnance, the navy had to outfit three 40-foot motor launches, given rude armor plate and armed with a light field piece, to root them out.[16] This episode proved prophetic, as here we have the first suggestion that the PT was too undergunned to counter Japanese tactical methods in the Pacific Theater.

January 24/25: During the night, Bulkeley in PT-41 crept once more into the Subic Bay area. Gunning the engines, he raced in at high speed and fired two torpedoes at what appeared to be a 4,000-to-6,000-ton transport anchored about 800 yards away. The men observed one hit and saw debris falling around the boat—though as before, postwar Japanese sources failed to confirm what damage, if any, the ship might have sustained. On the return, Bulkeley was forced to steer clear of an MTB "obstruction net placed across the entrance of the cove."[17] Obviously, the Japanese had begun taking the PT threat seriously.

February 1: Patrolling off Bataan, PT-32 chased and fired two torpedoes at a ship believed to be a light cruiser. The men observed two hits. Again, Japanese sources confirm little, showing only that a minesweeper, the *Yaeyama*, suffered damage from "shore fire" in Subic Bay during the night.[18]

February 17: PT-35 and PT-41 entered Subic Bay again and fired a torpedo at a small patrol vessel. It passed underneath. They later fired a torpedo at a larger vessel near Olangapo pier. No results were observed. On retiring, Bulkeley noticed a fire near Olangapo. The next day army observers reported a tanker burning at dock. As with the previous reports of torpedo hits, Japanese records fail to confirm the results.[19]

These raids did nothing even to postpone Japanese victory in the Philippines. They did nevertheless give a good inkling of what a properly handled PT could do, thereby helping assure it a future role in the Pacific war. Admiral Rockwell was an early convert. Taking Bulkeley's reports and those of army observers at face value, he wrote to Admiral Hart on January 25, "These boats are proving their worth in operations here, having sunk two ships of three to five thousand tons and three landing boats." He added he felt they would be "invaluable in operations [in the] restricted waters of the Netherlands East Indies."[20]

Unfortunately for Hart, then in Java, defeat came too rapidly for PTs to benefit him or anyone else in that luckless area. Had Rockwell substituted "Solomons," "New Guinea," or "Morotai," he would have been truly prescient. No one in January 1942 foresaw the real significance of those islands in the coming months. Still, should the navy ever need ship- or barge-hunting small craft in those restricted waters to the south, it now knew where to find them.

Sadly, should the navy's call ever come, the PTs of Squadron Three would be unable to answer it: They were literally falling apart. As early as December 25, Rockwell wrote, "Motor Torpedo Boats are rapidly deteriorating due to lack of spare parts and bad gasoline. Because of emergency trips and patrol duties their crews are becoming exhausted and the boats are in poor operating condition."[21]

By the end of January the situation had worsened. Despite heroic efforts by the maintenance crew aboard the beached submarine tender *Canopus* and scheduled visits to Dry Dock *Dewey*, submerged during the day in Mariveles harbor, the boats continued to deteriorate. PT-32, for example, had only one engine in commission. It badly needed hull repairs and replacement parts. All the boats needed bottom cleaning and new paint.[22] And to lend an air of futility to even these stopgap measures, supplies of gas and torpedoes were fast running out. By any measure, Squadron Three's usefulness in the Philippines was coming to an end.

Few options presented themselves to the men as to what they should do next. Like other bluejackets whose ships were beached or sunk, they might burn their MTBs and join the infantry on Bataan, perhaps as part of the Naval Battalion. They might also stick to their guns and die fighting atop the rotting decks of their boats. Either way meant the end of all hope of getting home in one piece.

As it happened, Bulkeley had every intention of getting home in one piece. Never one to back down from a fight, he nevertheless concluded, as early as the end of December, that when the gas and torpedoes were nearly expended, there remained only one sensible thing to do: Load up the boats and escape. At first he intended to try for Hong Kong. Patrol Wing 10 even dropped gas along the proposed escape route. Then on December 25 Hong Kong fell, and the Japanese began overrunning the southern Philippines. That idea squashed, he next opted for China.[23]

Few reliable references to Bulkeley's China escape plan exist, since only a handful of people were aware of the plan while it was under active consideration. One of those people was Associated Press correspondent Clark Lee, a veteran Far East reporter stranded in Manila at the beginning of the war. After the publicity generated by the January 19 Binanga Bay attack, he tagged along on several of the squadron's nightly forays, soon earning Bulkeley's confidence. According to Lee, around the second week in February Bulkeley let him in on the China plan, telling him:

> "We've got only about enough gasoline for one good operation and we have only a few torpedoes left. Then we'll be tied up here. I have suggested that we fill up our boats with the gas that's left and go out and raid Jap shipping along the China coast. After firing all our tor-

pedoes we'll land along the coast, destroy the boats, and hike overland to Chungking."[24]

Lee, also looking for a way out of the Philippines, counted himself in on the trip and put Bulkeley in contact with Lt. Col. Chi-Wang, Chiang Kai-shek's liaison officer to the American forces in the Philippines. The colonel wired Chungking asking permission for the boats to land—somewhere near Swatow, 675 miles north-northwest of Corregidor—and for assistance in getting through Japanese lines. Lee states that Chungking approved the plan, as did Admiral Rockwell. Slated to go were seventy-eight men, presumably the surviving complement of the six PTs, plus Lee and New York *Times* correspondent Nat Floyd.[25]

W. L. White's famous book *They Were Expendable* corroborates the essence of Lee's account. In fact, the book gives great play to the "China trip," even mentioning ruses Bulkeley used to keep knowledge of the proposed escape from his own men.[26] The details of these preparations are not what concerns us here. More interesting is what they imply about the PTs and their crews.

For openers, Rockwell must have considered the PTs capable of getting out of the Philippines—just as the destroyers, submarines, and B-17s had gotten out—or he would not have approved the plan. This confidence in the boats' abilities should come as no surprise: The navy had built them with sufficient range and endurance to enable them to make occasional open-ocean runs if necessary. It had also deliberately built them small and fast enough to escape detection by prowling enemy surface patrols and aircraft. Though engine decay had substantially reduced the boats' top speed by the end of February 1942, the navy still evidently assumed the PTs to have a reasonable chance of getting through—and getting their crews home.

Also, the navy's willingness to let the boats quit the islands leads one to a startling realization: Up to the end of February 1942, when the China plan was irreversibly shelved, the men of MTB Squadron Three were *not* expendable.

This realization is actually old news; according to White, Lt. Robert B. Kelly, Bulkeley's executive officer, knew full well he enjoyed a special lease on life prior to March 1942.[27] Still, knowing that the men of Squadron Three, the most famous of the "expendables" in the Philippines campaign, were actually not expendable throughout most of their time in the archipelago does introduce an element of irony into the historical record. More important, the knowledge colors our perception of what revoked that nonexpendable status: the evacuation of

Gen. Douglas MacArthur and twenty others from the island of Corregidor on the night of March 11.

The story of MacArthur's dramatic escape from Corregidor, and MTB Squadron Three's role in it, begins at the end of January 1942, when Washington reluctantly concluded that trying to reinforce the Philippines was futile. With defeat inevitable, the evacuation of key administrative and military personnel from the archipelago became the top priority. Naturally General MacArthur, the "Hero of the Philippines," headed the list.

Roosevelt and Army Chief of Staff George C. Marshall raised the issue with MacArthur in a series of letters during the first half of February. The general ostensibly resisted the idea, announcing he preferred to stay and share the fate of the Philippine garrison. Finally on February 23 (Manila time), Roosevelt ended the impasse, ordering MacArthur to Australia to take command of the soon to be formed Southwest Pacific Area. He further ordered MacArthur to stop off in Mindanao to check on preparations there for a "prolonged defense" before heading down under.

MacArthur's first reaction was to apparently disobey the order, even to the extent of resigning his commission and taking the field as a simple soldier. His staff nevertheless persuaded him to go, pointing out he would be of more use in Australia. Two days later, MacArthur replied to FDR via Marshall, agreeing to leave but requesting he be allowed to choose the right "psychological time" for his departure. MacArthur's apparent concern centered not so much on his chances of getting through the Japanese blockade but on what impact his leaving might have on the morale of his troops and the Filipino people.

In this same radio communication, dated 24 February 1942 (Manila time), MacArthur first spelled out his plan for getting out of Corregidor.

> I deem it advisable to go to Mindanao by combined use of surface craft and submarine and thence to destination [Australia] by air, further movement by submarine being too time consuming. A flight of three B-24s or B-17s will be able to fight through if intercepted.

He also gave Marshall a revealing hint as to when he would make his move: "To set up the transportation will require a period of time that will probably suffice to make essential psychological and physical adjustments here."[28]

What makes this last comment revealing is not that it sets a specific date for departure, but that it sets conditions for departure seemingly at odds with what he stated earlier in the message. He says he wanted to wait until the right "psychological time" for his departure, yet here he predicts that moment to coincide with the firming up of his travel plans. How convenient. One wonders what the practical difference is between this and simply stating that once his preparations to leave were completed, he would leave.

Whatever MacArthur's sincerity level, Marshall responded on the 26th, stating that the president consented to his choosing the date and method of his departure, "since it is imperative that the Luzon defense be firmly sustained." Marshall agreed that no specific date for departure could yet be set, but informed MacArthur that he would notify the navy "to dispatch, on call from you, a submarine to such point as you may designate." He also said he would have the army command in Australia "dispatch a flight of heavy bombers to Mindanao" when MacArthur desired them.

MacArthur replied the same day that Marshall's proposed arrangements were

> entirely satisfactory. Suggest you request Navy Department order submarine immediately to Corregidor. If navy has doubt as to probability of arrival here, suggest that two be sent to insure arrival. Also suggest directive to Brett [commanding general of U.S. Army forces in Australia] to dispatch planes on call. Anticipate possibility of execution of plan about March fifteenth.[29]

Over the next three days, several messages passed between MacArthur, Marshall, Brett, and Admiral Glassford, commander of the Southwest Pacific naval forces in Australia. On February 28, Brett agreed to have three long-range bombers "held available" and awaiting MacArthur's instructions. Glassford agreed to assign a submarine, initially *Spearfish* but later the *Permit*, to carry ammunition to Corregidor and "patrol off Bataan coast until needed by you [MacArthur]." On March 1, Glassford ordered the *Permit*, then patrolling 1,700 miles to the south off Surabaya in the Java Sea, north to Corregidor; he then notified MacArthur the *Permit* would arrive March 13. The same day MacArthur advised Brett he would need the bombers about March 15.[30]

By all appearances, by March 1 MacArthur had made his dispositions: He would leave Corregidor by submarine on the 13th, sail to Mindanao, and fly from there to Australia on the 15th. He made no further mention of a "combined use of surface craft and submarine" to reach Mindanao. However, while all this high-level, top-secret radio traffic flashed between Washington, Australia, and Corregidor to arrange MacArthur's safe passage out of the Philippines, the general had been busy circumventing the whole process.

John Bulkeley asserts that as early as February 18, Sid Huff, by then a lieutenant colonel serving as MacArthur's aide, approached him in Sisiman Cove. Huff asked him if his "boats could take a party on a sea run of a few hundred miles, say, down to Puerto Princess, on Palawan." Bulkeley said they could, but Huff would not give him any specifics: "I'll be able to tell you more about it later in the month," he said.[31] Ten days later, on February 28, Bulkeley received a further indication that something was afoot when he received word that MacArthur himself wanted to inspect the squadron the next day.

On the morning of March 1, the boats cruised out to Corregidor's North Dock. Soon the general had Bulkeley, whom he warmly referred to as "that bold buckaroo with the cold green eyes," give him, his wife, and several of his officers a brief spin on PT-41 in Manila Bay, air cover courtesy of four decrepit P-40s—all that remained of MacArthur's once vaunted air force. MacArthur wanted to find out if his wife, Jean, to whom he was extremely devoted, could handle the ride. She said she could. According to Huff, Jean MacArthur's nod of approval settled the matter: PT boats, undoubtedly the "surface craft" MacArthur referred to in his February 24 radio to Marshall, were now a viable option.[32]

After the ride, MacArthur formally presented Bulkeley with a Distinguished Service Cross for his gallant actions in the Philippines, and invited him to supper. Once alone with the young lieutenant on Corregidor's Topside, he revealed the real reason for the test spin and presentation: He had been ordered out and wanted Bulkeley and his four boats to take him through the Japanese blockade to Mindanao, 560 miles to the south, where he could be flown out by B-17 to take over his new command in Australia. When MacArthur asked if it could be done, Bulkeley brashly replied, "General, it'll be a piece of cake."[33]

That night, the general broached the idea of going out by PT to several members of his staff. Sid Huff was there:

"I had a talk with Lieutenant Bulkeley," [MacArthur] said. . . . "He tells me we have a chance to get through the blockade in PT boats. It wouldn't be easy. There would be plenty of risks. But four boats are available and, with their machine guns and torpedoes, we could put up a good fight against an enemy warship if necessary. And, of course, the boats have plenty of speed." . . .

"Once we get to Mindanao by boat," he continued, "bombers from Australia could pick us up there and fly us the rest of the way. We'll have at least a fighting chance of getting through." He paused for a moment, a restless, khaki-clad figure in the hot little room. None of us offered any comment. "The other way to go," he resumed, "would be by submarine. Some subs have been getting in and out of Manila

Bay, but it is always a risk. The Japs have control of the seas. It is a long run to Australia, most of it through seas that are not well charted or not charted at all."

As Huff relates, MacArthur's audience was dumbstruck, as were the rest of the men chosen to accompany the general out of Corregidor by PT. Everyone "not only assumed we would go by submarine but definitely wanted to do it that way." Still, MacArthur being MacArthur, no one protested.[34]

Huff goes on to say that MacArthur's chief of staff, Maj. Gen. Richard Sutherland, soon ordered him; Rockwell's chief of staff, Capt. Herbert Ray; and Bulkeley to work out the details of the PT escape. This they did in great secrecy, while during the same period, "for more than a week," Huff and Jean MacArthur scrounged food for the passengers, and "carefully divided it among . . . four duffel bags."[35] By March 10 the three officers had drafted a detailed, eight-page operational order addressed from Rockwell to Bulkeley.[36] The order specified an evening departure the following night, on March 11. The B-17s were now to reach Mindanao two days earlier than originally scheduled, picking up the general's party on the morning of the 13th.

At this point the chronology surrounding MacArthur's departure becomes somewhat muddied. The traditional view holds that MacArthur was reluctant to leave his men and waited until the last possible minute before actually deciding to go. Marshall's and Roosevelt's prodding cables on March 6 and March 9, the continued insistence of his staff that he leave, and ominous new reports of heightened Japanese naval activity on the 9th are generally cited as having forced MacArthur's hand, prompting him to leave as soon as possible by PT and not wait for the *Permit*.

Admiral Rockwell's official report, dated 1 August 1942, contributes to this interpretation, which has found its way into both Samuel Eliot Morison's and Robert Bulkley's brief official renderings of MacArthur's escape from Corregidor.[37] According to Rockwell, MacArthur informed him on March 4 that he had been ordered south and wished to have Rockwell and one or two members of his staff go along.

A submarine had been placed at his disposal for this purpose and the original plan was to use this for the first leg of the trip in coordination with the four remaining boats of Motor Torpedo Boat Squadron Three to assist in escort and disembarkation. . . .

Rockwell writes that "Bulkeley was [then] directed to prepare his squadron for a trip of over 500 miles to an undisclosed destination," presumably in the support role MacArthur mentioned. However, this plan abruptly changed on March 9 when

> there was a very marked increase in the activities of enemy surface craft (including minelayers) off Subic Bay, a surface patrol was reported off Corregidor, and a destroyer division was sighted in the Southern Philippines steaming North at high speed. This was sufficient evidence that orders had been given to prevent General MacArthur's departure, and it was decided not to wait for the PERMIT but to leave by way of M.T.B.s as soon as preparation could be completed. Plans were perfected for General MacArthur's party . . . (a total of 22) to leave at dark of the 11th with M.T.B. Squadron Three. . . .[38]

It is difficult to put much credence in Rockwell's version of events. The available evidence suggests that MacArthur decided to depart as soon as his travel plans were finalized, as he indicated—somewhat disingenuously—in his February 24 radio to Marshall. By March 9, Huff, Ray, and Bulkeley were undoubtedly putting the finishing touches to the March 10 operational order detailing his escape. The arrangements settled, MacArthur notified those concerned that he intended to leave, then left.

There is much to support this contention, despite Rockwell's assertion the trip was last-minute. It is possible to believe that on March 4, MacArthur mentioned to Rockwell his original idea of going "to Mindanao by combined use of surface craft and submarine," the admiral interpreting this to mean that the PTs were "to assist in escort and disembarkation." Making sense of the idea is another matter.

One is hard pressed to imagine how four PT boats could escort a submarine through 500 miles of enemy-infested waters, then be on hand to disembark its passengers afterward. It could not be done, nor would there have been any sense in trying. PTs depended on high speed for their survival; diesel submarines depended on slow, deep submergence for theirs. PTs were ill equipped to signal, detect, or otherwise keep in contact with a submerged submarine. The boats might keep pace if the sub transporting MacArthur ran clandestinely on the surface during the night, but their big, frothy wakes would only have attracted the Japanese, clearly defeating the purpose. It therefore seems incredible that anyone ever seriously considered such a plan. Rockwell, however, would have us believe one was in the works until late in the game. This is not supported by any known documentation, and neither Huff nor Bulkeley mentions being part of such a questionable enterprise.

On the other hand, the eight-page operational order they did help develop shows every indication of at least being workable. It called for a sunset departure on March 11, enabling MacArthur "to take advantage of a very thin moon."[39] Opting for maximum possible darkness made perfect sense, and would have been factored in by the planners. As for the increased Japanese naval activity that Rockwell says accounts for MacArthur's not waiting two extra days for the *Permit*, Annex "D" of the order—Rockwell's own planning document—makes no mention of it.

Annex "D" contains a detailed look at current Japanese air and sea activity. It notes the increase of naval traffic in and out of Subic Bay, but the planners did not know what to make of this. At no time do they mention an *increase* of activity around Corregidor. The blockade was in place, to be sure, but that was a known entity. In other words, everything points to a long-anticipated, well-coordinated escape effort with PT boats serving as the means, not a hasty last-minute act of desperation to beat a tightening blockade.

The plan's execution on March 11 also conveniently allowed time to divert the oncoming *Permit* so it could play an active support role. At 8 p.m. on March 12, the *Permit*, already in the area, received orders to rendezvous with the PT boats at daylight on March 13 at Tagauayan, a small deserted islet halfway to Mindanao in the unoccupied Cuyo Islands, about 250 miles south of Corregidor. The plan strictly saw *Permit* as a backup, to intervene in case the PTs were unable to continue after their first night's journey or were discovered hiding in the islands the next day (the 12th), or in case MacArthur wanted to change his mode of travel.[40]

Rockwell notes these dispositions in his report, though they make for confused reading. He writes that the plans perfected to take MacArthur's party by MTB also called

> for the PERMIT to load [additional select personnel] upon her arrival on the 14th—which *still* [emphasis added] made it possible for her to pick up the first party in case the M.T.B.s were shot up during the first day's hideout (at TAGAUAYAN ISLAND), or to pick them up at MINDANAO in case plane transportation should fail at Del Monte.[41]

His suggestion that the *Permit* could proceed as scheduled to Corregidor by the 14th, pick up more personnel, and still effect a *timely* rescue of the first party if necessary defies logic. At any rate, Rockwell's own operational order calls for the *Permit* to be available at Tagauayan on the morning of the 13th, in other words *before* reaching Corregidor.[42] Was Rockwell's memory faulty? (He even misstated the number of passengers going along—there were 21, not 22.) Or was he having trouble explaining officially when and why MacArthur decided not to wait for the *Permit*, the means of escape overwhelmingly preferred by his traveling companions? Rockwell's difficulty may never be pinpointed, though as we will see, the latter is also a possibility.

Whatever Rockwell's state of mind, preparations for the March 11 trip pressed forward. On March 9, MacArthur, now knowing his departure date with certainty, evidently decided for security purposes to cloud the issue. He told Bulkeley he would be going out by PT on the 15th—"the ides of March"—and cabled Washington giving the same date, but saying that he intended to leave by submarine instead. Finally on March 11 he let the word out: The trip was on for that night—by PT.[43]

To prepare, Bulkeley had the men strap twenty 50-gallon drums of 100-octane aviation fuel to the deck of each of the four boats, a dangerous necessity if they were to reach Mindanao on their own. Because of this extra weight and the weight of the twenty-one expected passengers, many of the squadron's own men, around thirty, had to be left behind. They never rejoined the squadron.

Stories of MacArthur's actual evacuation from Corregidor have been recounted again and again. Since the various eyewitness and secondary accounts of the event are by and large in agreement, there is little point in revisiting the details. For purposes of discussion, only the broad facts need be related.

As described in the operational order dated March 10, Bulkeley in PT-41 picked up MacArthur, his wife, young son, and Cantonese *amah*, and four officers (including Sid Huff) at Corregidor's North Dock just after dark on the 11th, at about 7:30. The other three boats, PT-32, PT-34, and PT-35, embarked the remaining thirteen passengers, all army personnel except for Admiral Rockwell and Captain Ray, at either Sisiman Cove or Mariveles. At 8 p.m., the four boats met at the turning buoy outside the minefield at the entrance to Manila Bay. Once together, they headed southwest in column with PT-41 in the lead, slipping unnoticed around the northern end of the Cabra Islands and the "sinister outlines" of the Japanese blockading squadron.

During the night, heavy seas and persistent engine problems caused the boats, traveling at top speeds in the low 20-knot range in a defensive diamond formation, to become separated. In the half-light of dawn, Lt. (jg) Vince Schumacher in PT-32 thought he saw a Japanese destroyer bearing down on him. As he was running on only two engines, he dumped his barrels of gas overboard to increase speed, but the apparition kept gaining. He turned to fight, only to discover at the last moment his pursuer was PT-41, transporting General MacArthur.

Meanwhile, everyone was behind schedule. Robert Kelly in PT-34 reached Tagauayan first at 7:30 a.m., about two hours late. Bulkeley and Schumacher hid out among the other Cuyo Islands before chancing a daylight run to the rendezvous point that afternoon. Ensign Tony Akers in PT-35 was not heard from until the boat arrived at Cagayan, the port of destination on Mindanao, some time after the others on the 13th.

At Tagauayan, two decisions had to be made. After the rough-weather ride of the previous night, which MacArthur likened to taking a "trip in a concrete mixer," the general was hesitant about going on. Should he brave another potentially gruesome night on board, or wait for the *Permit* to arrive the next morning? After considering the twin possibilities that the sub might never arrive and the seas might quiet down a bit, he decided to continue.

The other decision concerned PT-32. It was down to one working engine, had lost its spare fuel, and was starting to leak. Since it could not make Cagayan, Bulkeley split Schumacher's five passengers among the other two boats and told him to stay and wait for the *Permit* and PT-35. After letting their skippers know that MacArthur had gone on, Schumacher was to use his remaining gas to reach Panay, refuel, and continue to Cagayan.

PT-41 and PT-34 set off just before sunset and immediately ran into what they believed to be a Japanese cruiser. They veered off to starboard and passed unobserved behind the enemy ship, their frothy wakes lost in the quickly gathering dusk. Again that night the seas were storm-tossed. Spray and rain lashed at the men, making navigation without instruments a chancy thing indeed, but "by guess and by God" they managed to make Cagayan on time at 0700 the following morning. MacArthur was appropriately grateful, telling Bulkeley, "It was done in true naval style," and awarding everyone a Silver Star for gallantry.[44]

That same morning the *Permit* arrived at Tagauayan, as scheduled. The *Permit* was one of the navy's first modern fleet boats, large and roomy as submarines went, and well armed. Its skipper, Lt. Wreford G. "Moon" Chapple, had operated out of Manila Bay at the beginning of the war. In the old *S-38* he scored the only significant success against the Japanese invasion fleet at Lingayen Gulf, braving shallow waters and Japanese destroyers to slip in and sink a 5,445-ton transport, the *Hayo Maru*.

Chapple found Schumacher, who reported his boat too unseaworthy to continue on to Panay or anywhere else. He therefore took the crew of fifteen aboard, scuttled the derelict with his deck gun, and continued on to Corregidor. With the loss of PT-32, half of MTB Squadron Three was now gone—destroyed to prevent capture by the omnipresent Japanese.

Before he left the dock area, MacArthur informed Bulkeley he was to conduct offensive operations in the waters north of Mindanao against Japanese shipping. Later the same day, however, the general summoned Bulkeley to the Del Monte plantation, 20 miles south of Cayagan, where he was waiting for a serviceable B-17 to take him to Australia. It turned out that despite all the advance planning, only one barely serviceable B-17 managed to reach Mindanao on March 13. MacArthur had taken one look and angrily ordered it away. Not until March 18 would two navy-owned Flying Fortresses make it to Mindanao to fly the general and his party out.

MacArthur had a special new job for his favorite "pirate." President of the Philippines Manuel Quezon, who had left Corregidor on February 20, was now in hiding on Negros, 100 miles northwest of Mindanao, his loyalty to the cause wavering. Could not Bulkeley snatch him off Negros and deliver him to Mindanao, for transport to Australia? Bulkeley could, and did, that same night, further honing his swashbuckling reputation—one soon splashed across newspapers from coast to coast in the wake of the MacArthur rescue.

In the meantime, Bulkeley's three remaining boats began falling on the kind of hard times no amount of sensational press coverage could assuage. Kelly's PT-34 ran aground shortly after arriving in Mindanao, mangling her propellers and shafts. She was out of action until April 8. And while covering Bulkeley's excursion ashore to pick up Quezon, PT-35 had struck a submerged object, tearing a hole in her bow. She had to be beached and eventually towed to Cebu for repairs. PT-35 never saw action again; she was burned in her slipway on April 12 to prevent capture by the Japanese.

Three days earlier, on April 9, PT-34 also met a fiery end, only this time at the hands of the Japanese. Kelly took his freshly repaired boat and joined Bulkeley, in PT-41, for a night attack on a Japanese light cruiser off the south tip of Cebu. The two men braved heavy gunfire and searchlights to fire off all eight torpedoes at the cruiser. They thought two hit, and reported the cruiser dead in the water, surrounded by a yellowish fog. Both the PT crews and various shore observers felt the cruiser sank. Still, a postwar search of Japanese records showed only that the PTs hit the cruiser, the *Kuma*, once in the bow with a dud. She later sank for real on 11 January 1944, off Penang after being torpedoed by a British submarine.[45]

PT-34 did not have that much time. By zigzagging violently, Kelly escaped from several escorting destroyers. Later, though, as he approached the channel leading to Cebu City, he ran aground. He rocked the boat free by daylight and continued on, hoping to obtain a doctor for a wounded gunner. Once he was in the channel and unable to maneuver, four Japanese floatplanes strafed and bombed him. Two men died and three were wounded by the time Kelly beached his bullet-riddled boat. He tried to salvage her, but later the planes returned. Under a hail of bullets and bombs, PT-34 exploded and burned on the beach, a total loss.

PT-41 survived PT-34 by only a few days. Returning to Mindanao, Bulkeley discovered the Japanese were overrunning Cebu and no more torpedoes were available on Mindanao. PT-41's days as an MTB were therefore at a close. She got a small reprieve on April 13, when the army took her over, removed her torpedo tubes, and put her on a truck for Lake Lanao in Mindanao's interior. The boat was to serve as a motor gunboat, preventing possible Japanese seaplane landings on the lake. PT-41 never made it; en route the Japanese cut the road and the boat had to be blown up to prevent capture. With her demise, coming barely a month after arriving in southern Philippine waters, MTB Squadron Three ceased to exist.

Of Squadron Three's evacuation of General MacArthur from Corregidor, three things are relatively certain. One, the trip was graced by good luck. Had the seas been calmer, the Japanese might well have observed the unavoidably thunderous boats and their foaming white wakes. It is too horrible to imagine the carnage had the boats been taken under fire by the more heavily armed, faster-moving Japanese surface ships of the blockading force. Every PT had a thousand gallons of 100-octane fuel strapped to its decks. One stray machine gun bullet or hot piece of shrapnel and all aboard would have perished in an instant.

Two, the evacuation shelved the China trip for good. The remaining gas needed for the squadron's own escape went to serve the general, as did most of the mileage that could still be coaxed out of the PTs' already overtaxed Packards. A quick glance at the map reveals that Mindanao is some 470 gull-flying miles farther from the Chinese coast than Corregidor. Clearly, once in Mindanao they could not go back. To the south the Japanese controlled everything as far as Australia, some 1,500 miles distant. Clearly they could not go forward. With no hope of escaping the Japanese steamroller, the men of Squadron Three—like the rest of the Americans still fighting in the beleaguered islands—were now truly expendable.[46]

Thus Squadron Three's expendable status did not directly result from decades of ambiguous defensive half-measures taken on behalf of the Philippines; nor did it stem from the capriciousness of some navy brass hat cooling his heels on Corregidor. The United States Navy has, after all, never been an especially suicidal institution. It stemmed rather from the squadron's having to yank MacArthur off "the Rock."

We can even be more specific than that: The single event that ulti-mately made MTB Squadron Three expendable, that doomed it to de-struction in the southern Philippines, was General MacArthur's *decision* to use its boats to pull him off Corregidor.

Which brings us to three: Gen. Douglas MacArthur need not, and should not, have used the PTs of Squadron Three for the first leg of his escape. The reason he did was devoid of sober military considerations. He thereby unnecessarily risked his life and the lives of all the others on the trip, including his family, and needlessly—even recklessly—sac-rificed the squadron, consigning it to inevitable destruction in southern Philippine waters.

The question is, why did MacArthur choose PT boats for his escape from Corregidor in the first place?

Most contemporary biographical accounts of MacArthur's daring escape through enemy lines portray his use of PT boats as an act of defiant nose-thumbing—at the Japanese by roaring out under their noses, and at the United States Navy by proving that the blockade of Luzon, which the navy realistically cited as the reason it could not re-inforce his forces there, could in fact be broken.

Memoirs of actual participants, however, paint a far less heroic pic-ture, one void of such lofty, see-what-you-want-to-see interpretation. Col. Carlos P. Romulo, a Manila newspaper publisher and member of MacArthur's Corregidor staff, wrote that before the escape, MacArthur told him he simply "preferred [mosquito boats] to a submarine." Sid Huff writes that he concluded exactly the same thing the night MacArthur first announced to his staff that he intended to go by PT. "As he talked," Huff reports, "it was obvious the General preferred the PT boats to a submarine." Huff even adds that "much later MacArthur told me that from the beginning he had made up his mind not to go by submarine."[47]

So why did Douglas MacArthur prefer PT boats to submarines? Was it for their greater propaganda value, or to better allow him to demonstrate contempt for his enemies, as his many worshipful con-temporaries asserted? Or was going by PT simply a personal prefer-ence, as his loyal aides suggest? Huff offers what this author believes is probably the most plausible answer to this question. He writes:

> I'm not sure why [MacArthur preferred PTs to submarines], but it was almost as if he suffered a touch of claustrophobia. He had, I remem-bered, shown the same attitude by refusing to sleep in the under-ground tunnel [on Corregidor during bombings], and I felt he in-stinctively disliked the idea of being cooped up.[48]

Is this idle speculation? Did Huff have a solid basis for believing such a thing? Possibly, depending on how one reads MacArthur's own explanation for choosing PT boats. In his autobiography he writes, "I had decided to try and pierce the blockade with PT boats rather than go under with a submarine."[49] That sentence, which constitutes his *entire* discussion of his decision on when and how to leave Corregidor, is frustratingly vague. Do his words "go under" reflect a fear of being trapped underwater in a sub, as Huff speculated, or do they simply mark his preference for going through as opposed to "under" the blockade? It is impossible to tell. One would think, however, that if he had a more noble, heroic motive for piercing the blockade by remaining on the surface rather than piercing it from below the surface, he would have given it great play in his otherwise self-serving memoir.

He does not. This unfortunately proves little, however; speculation that MacArthur chose PT boats because he was claustrophobic must remain just that. But it is not necessary to prove the general was phobic to show what lay behind his decision to go by PT.

This is done by examining the reasons MacArthur gave others—his staff, Bulkeley—for hitching a ride on a PT boat instead of going out by submarine. Throughout, it is important to ask: Do the reasons make sense? Are they sufficient? Are they supported by the facts MacArthur had in his possession at the time? Or are they the musings of a very fallible man desperate to keep the truth of his real motives a secret, lest those dependent on the rationality of those motives think him malicious or irresponsible?

MacArthur gave others two general reasons for wanting to leave Corregidor by PT:

(1) *A submarine would be too risky*. In the meeting at which MacArthur first shocked his staff by saying he wanted to go out by PT, he also mentioned submarines. He squashed that idea, pointing out that going by sub "is always a risk." Compared to what? He also noted, "The Japs have control of the seas. It is a long run to Australia, most of it through seas that are not well charted or not charted at all."

What was MacArthur thinking? By March 1, the day he reportedly made this comment, five different submarines had already made seven successful trips in and out of Corregidor. They had delivered 130 tons of supplies and ammunition, and taken out records and 220 select personnel, including High Commissioner Sayre and President Quezon. Not one of these subs was sunk.

As for its being a long way to Australia through "uncharted" seas, this was true enough. On January 20 the *S-36* went hard aground on a reef in the Makassar Strait between Borneo and Celebes, and it had to be scuttled by her crew the following day. Inadequate charts were blamed.[50] It must be pointed out, however, that numerous Asiatic Fleet and Pacific Fleet submarines were even then operating in and among the Japanese-controlled islands of the West and Southwest Pacific, including the Netherlands East Indies and the Philippines, on a routine basis. Japanese antisubmarine patrols had sunk only one, the *Shark*, prior to March 1942. Therefore his concern over the "risk" of going out by submarine seems overstated at best.

Also, it seems incredibly disingenuous to justify not going by submarine because of the uncharted seas on the way to Australia. Recall MacArthur's February 24 radio to Marshall. He had no intention of going all the way to Australia by submarine, only as far as Mindanao.

Granted, throughout his stay on Corregidor MacArthur remained bitter toward Admiral Hart and the Asiatic Fleet, including the submarine force, for failure to prevent the Japanese landing on Luzon. Both had been ordered out soon afterward, though as part of a long-standing strategic plan to do so. It has been suggested that since Bulkeley and his men stayed behind—as if this were up to them—MacArthur was more favorably disposed toward him and his PT boats than toward the submariners and their undersea boats. However much this might be the case—and it is true the general personally liked Bulkeley—this still makes his preference for PTs an emotional one.

(2) *Going by PT would increase his chances of getting through the Japanese blockade.* On March 1, when MacArthur first asked Bulkeley about the feasibility of using PTs in the escape, the lieutenant asked him if it wouldn't "be safer for [him] to get to Mindanao by submarine or by air." According to Bulkeley, MacArthur

> smiled and said no, that the Nips would expect him to leave like that and would make every effort to intercept him. "They won't be expecting me to make the breakout by PT boat," he added. "Besides, I've got great faith in you and your boys."[51]

This is all well and good. Indeed, the Japanese most certainly did not expect MacArthur to go by PT boat. But so what? It would be one thing if the Japanese expected the general to get out on foot, or by air, only to be fooled by his sudden departure by sea. The truth is that the Japanese *did* expect him to go by sea—by submarine. Their patrols by destroyers and other surface predators, and their air surveillance of the approaches to Corregidor, all steps they took to counter his departure by submarine, were virtually the same as those they would have taken to prevent his escape by PT. Since submarines could escape detection by submerging and PT boats could not, it can even be argued that the steps the Japanese took to snare MacArthur's would-be sub would be even more effective in snaring MacArthur's PT.

Did MacArthur—known to be highly intelligent but largely ignorant of naval matters—truly believe the unexpectedness of his method would give him the edge he needed to pierce the Japanese blockade undetected? Or was it all a line, a lot of macho banter used to disguise less commendable personal motives—perhaps claustrophobia, perhaps something else? Either way, we will never know if he appreciated the essential absurdity of what he was telling Bulkeley.

Whatever the definitive reason MacArthur chose Squadron Three to carry him from Corregidor, the sum of the foregoing evidence strongly suggests he based it more on personal preferences than on sober military considerations. If so, he needlessly, even recklessly, sacrificed the squadron. Had he waited for the *Permit* to arrive on the 15th, as she did, picking up forty men—thirty-six of them codebreakers—and delivering them unharmed to Australia, he could have left with her efficiency unimpaired.[52] Not so the PTs. He used them up, destroyed their crew's only chance of escaping to China and surviving as a unit. Of course, they might not have made it to China either, given the amount of open ocean they had to cross in the face of Japanese patrols. But at least the trip represented a chance to escape intact.

All this is not to say that MacArthur acted maliciously. There is no record he even knew of the China escape plan. Bulkeley could have told the general, hoping the knowledge that he was destroying his unit's only chance of survival might sway him to reconsider a reusable sub instead. However, Bulkeley probably would have considered even bringing up the subject an act of cowardice. As far as he and his men were concerned, getting the great Douglas MacArthur out of harm's way was both a necessary and an honorable thing to do. As Robert Kelly put it: "It was a grim picture for us. But here was our last big job. MacArthur was the brains of the organization—the only general who could take [the Philippines] back. The whole allied defense depended on getting him to Australia."[53]

However hyperbolic this reasoning seems in retrospect, the fact remains that in March 1942, millions regarded MacArthur as a charismatic hero and great military strategist. Even in 1982, Bulkeley affectionately wrote that MacArthur "was the greatest General as well as statesman since George Washington." He added that he felt MacArthur's decision to use his boats was no less than an act of "genius."[54] No wonder both MacArthur's decision to use PT boats for his escape and the reasons he ostensibly put forth to justify it have never before been seriously challenged.

After MacArthur's decision to "transfer" Squadron Three to the southern Philippines led to the loss of the four remaining boats, the general ordered Bulkeley flown out to Australia on April 13. Robert Kelly, Tony Akers, and George Cox followed at the end of the month. Seven others, including Vince Schumacher, reached the same place in *Permit* on April 7.

Of the remaining seventy-two men, most were captured. Some, like Ens. Iliff Richardson, immortalized in Ira Wolfert's *American Guerrilla in the Philippines*, joined the Filipino resistance. In all, three officers and fifteen enlisted men died during the war, including nine in Japanese prisoner of war camps.[55] No one can say they failed to put up a good fight.

While MTB Squadron Three's struggle in defense of the Philippines ended tragically, its enviable record inspired pride in its men, boats, and *apparent* combat effectiveness. Its achievements also inspired confidence. After only four months of war, the American public and navy had come to view the PT boat as a capable antiship weapon, particularly in the hands of swashbuckling types like John Bulkeley.

The Philippine campaign, however, was merely a prelude. The boats had had little opportunity to mesh tactically with the fleet or to prove what well-maintained PTs, given proper logistical and air support, could really accomplish. Proving their worth as small combatants now also depended on another variable: the quality of the growing numbers of volunteers being called upon to roll back the Japanese and stop Hitler. First came Cushing, then Bulkeley. Now it was their turn.

CHAPTER EIGHT

Great Expectations

F or many of the volunteers who served on PT boats during World
War II, John Bulkeley ranked as a truly inspirational figure.
Reading frenzied press accounts of his Philippines exploits in
1942, one would think he had single-handedly sunk half the Japanese
navy. His hyperaggressive personality, his devil-may-care willingness to
press home torpedo attacks against enemy ships no matter what the
risk, made him a hero for the new PT men to emulate. Still, the men
needed more than just a keen desire to follow in Bulkeley's hallowed
footsteps; they needed opportunity. Would they get it?

The next test of arms for the PT, the Battle of Midway, indicated
they might not. While Bulkeley and Squadron Three fought their desperate holding action in the Philippines, Squadron One in Hawaii,
augmented by the six boats Bulkeley did not get, saw no battle action
whatsoever, since the Japanese made no further attacks on Pearl Harbor. Nor did Squadron Two in Panama encounter any German U-boats.
This lull came to an end in May 1942.

On May 20, as part of the effort to forestall the anticipated Japanese invasion of Midway, the Pacific Fleet commander, Adm. Chester W.
Nimitz, ordered Squadron One to the tiny atoll, 1,385 miles northwest
of Pearl Harbor. The twelve 14th Naval District PTs, commanded by
Lt. Clinton McKellar, Jr., left in convoy with the seaplane tender *Ballard* on the 25th, to be used by the Midway commander, Capt. Cyril T.
Simard, "as a striking force at [his] discretion."[1]

As an unexpected boon to the PT crews, Nimitz had also ordered
Comdr. John Ford, USNR, the noted Hollywood film director, to Midway on board the *Ballard* to film the defense of the atoll. During the four-
day trip out, Ford became enamored of PTs and "that wonderful group
of boys," so he filmed them too.[2] His affection for PTs later added to
their glamour; in 1945 Ford produced a film version of W. L. White's
They Were Expendable, starring John Wayne and Robert Montgomery.

Incredibly, the real-life PTs of Squadron One made the long cross-ocean trip to Midway under their own power, refueling three times along the way; only one, PT-23, broke down and had to return to Pearl. Another, PT-25, had engine trouble and had to be towed to Midway by the *Ballard*; despite that, all eleven arrived safely on the 29th.

Simard detached two of the PTs to patrol Kure Island, about 60 miles west of Midway, leaving nine boats on hand in Midway's lagoon on the morning of June 4, when the Japanese launched their only air strike against the small outpost. The PTs provided antiaircraft support, dropping at least one dive-bomber and trying to help the obsolete Marine fighter planes weather the onslaught of Zeroes. In the wake of the attack, PT-boaters rescued downed Marine aircrews and helped fight fires ashore.

That night Simard ordered the boats to search for one of the four Japanese carriers left sinking by U.S. carrier planes during the famous day-long slugfest. The carrier, possibly the *Kaga*, was reported by PBY to be 170 miles to the northwest. McKellar's PTs pressed on toward the enemy in the darkness, their high-speed run plagued by salt spray that contaminated their fuel, causing engines, generators, and in some cases even radios to fail. Though the intermittent rain squalls, low clouds, and smooth sea made conditions for a night torpedo attack ideal, the boats lacked radar and up-to-date intelligence; consequently they found nothing but oil slicks and floating wreckage ("apparently Japanese") before returning to Midway the following morning. Later the PT crews helped bury the flag-draped remains of 11 Midway defenders at sea.[3]

In all then, the PTs of Squadron One played only a minor, though certainly welcome, supporting role in what became a pivotal naval battle in world history. This is hardly a criticism. For three days the cataclysmic event swirled around them. Carrier clashed with carrier; battleships and cruisers tugged at their leashes for a chance to turn the tide; submarines got in their licks. And above it all, the airplane ruled supreme, in both scouting and scoring. But for their machine guns and rescue efforts the 14th Naval District PTs were irrelevant to the outcome of the battle.

And what of the future? At Midway the PTs never once had an opportunity to use their *raison d'être*, their torpedoes, nor, in the absence of any specific Japanese naval threat in their restricted area of operations, did it seem likely they would get the chance anytime soon. Midway, however, altered the whole Pacific equation. Anything was now possible, even for a lowly district patrol craft like the PT.

The enormity of the Japanese defeat lies at the heart of this dramatic reappraisal in the Pacific. On the surface, Japan's Midway invasion had everything going for it. Six months after Pearl Harbor, the Japanese were at the height of their power. Despite a strategic setback a month earlier, when American carriers had turned back an invasion fleet headed for Port Moresby on Papua's southeast coast, they reigned supreme in the West and Southwest Pacific. Their timetable for the conquest of Malaya and the Dutch East Indies was months ahead of schedule; organized American resistance in the Philippines had ceased. After Midway they hoped to invade the South Pacific. If the tenuous supply link between the United States and Australia could be permanently broken, the United States might be forced to sue for peace.

It was not to be. Japan lost four of the six frontline carriers she had used to savage Pearl Harbor, along with all their planes and many of their experienced pilots. The invasion fizzled. Worse yet, the Battle of Midway cast a dark, perpetual shadow over Japan's entire war effort, playing a significant role in ensuring final American victory.

Several specific results of the battle ultimately affected PT operations in the Pacific Theater. Japan's material losses were, of course, all too apparent. In one sudden, dramatic swoop, she lost the majority of her frontline fleet carriers, the principal, indeed indispensable, naval weapon in the Pacific. American losses, mainly the carrier *Yorktown*, were disproportionally far less. The Japanese navy also found it difficult to replace the experienced pilots it had lost. Unlike the Americans, who rotated their naval aviators—and PT crews—between combat and training duties so new recruits could benefit from their experience, the Japanese kept their veteran pilots on the firing line. Seldom again would the Americans face such an experienced foe in the crucial air spaces over the Pacific.

The battle also had a psychological—indeed even spiritual—impact, ultimately far more damaging to Japan's war fortunes than the loss of four carriers. Because of Midway, the Japanese gave up the strategic initiative, though they still had sufficient carrier strength to challenge the small American carrier fleet to another winner-take-all duel. Instead they switched over to the strategic defensive, probably the worst thing they could have done, since it dragged them into a war of attrition. Given the United States' vastly superior industrial base and manpower reserves, the Japanese could not win this kind of war. It is perhaps testimony to the mind-boggling suddenness of the Midway defeat, the sheer magnitude of the disaster, that Adm. Isoroku Yamamoto, who planned the invasion and knew better than most the dangers of such a war, should have sanctioned one after Midway.

The Americans naturally found Midway a different kind of learning experience. Pearl Harbor had, at least in part, been avenged! While no one ever truly doubted the Japanese could, and would, be beaten, here was proof positive. Morale soared. Tactically, the battle pointed out the need for greater coordination between the various components of the air arm—fighters, dive-bombers, and torpedo planes. Strategically, the Americans could now think the unthinkable: going over to the offensive.

As early as March 1942, CNO and Joint Chiefs of Staff member Adm. Ernest J. King had recommended an offensive move into the Solomons, a chain of jungle-clad islands 1,000 miles northeast of Australia. He saw this as a necessary prelude to an offensive against the great Japanese naval and air base at Rabaul, on New Britain immediately northwest of the Solomons, which threatened the line of communications with Australia. After Midway the Japanese heightened that threat by themselves moving into the southern Solomons. They established a seaplane base at Tulagi and began building an airfield on nearby Guadalcanal. When the Americans learned of these actions, they decided to make their move. The first American offensive, code-named Operation Watchtower, would be the seizure of those two bases.

On 7 August 1942, units of the 1st Marine Division waded ashore and captured the nearly completed airfield on Guadalcanal, renaming it Henderson Field. After a short, sharp fight, Tulagi and two smaller Japanese outposts also fell. Japanese reaction was swift and deadly. For the next six months they poured ships and troops into a desperate, though ineptly piecemeal, attempt to retake the airfield.

With opposing aircraft from Henderson Field and Rabaul dominant by day, the opposing navies came by night. The Japanese hoped to reinforce their Guadalcanal garrison and bombard Henderson into impotence; the Americans tried to stop them, while simultaneously keeping their own troops resupplied and reinforced. A series of bloody night surface actions resulted, mostly involving cruisers and destroyers, which cost both navies dear. The Japanese ran reinforcement and bombardment groups down from Rabaul so regularly the Americans began calling them the Tokyo Express. Sometimes the American fleet had the means to contest the Express, sometimes not. Enter the PT.

At the end of July 1942, as planning for the Guadalcanal operation progressed, Admiral King ordered that eight boats from Squadron Two in Panama, since enlarged to fourteen, be transferred to form a new Squadron Three. He then directed the new squadron to prepare for immediate shipment to a combat zone. Bulkley describes this somewhat complicated transshipment process, repeated here as typical of what the short-range PTs had to go through to get from Panama to their operational areas in the Pacific throughout the war:

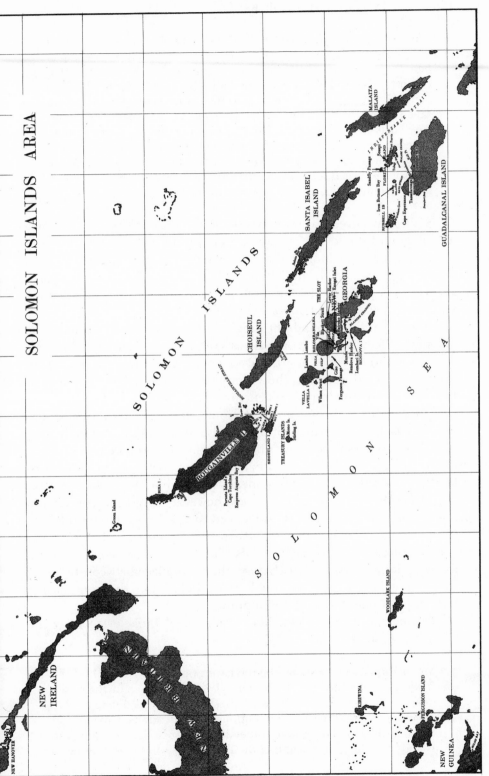

The Solomon Islands. *Naval Historical Center*

The first division of Squadron 3, PTs 38, 46, 48, and 60, departed Balboa [in Panama] on August 29 aboard the Navy oilers *Lackawanna* and *Tappahannock*, two PTs to a ship. They arrived September 19 at Noumea, New Caledonia, were unloaded, and were towed to Espiritu Santo by the cargo ship *Bellatrix* and the tender *Jamestown*, which had sailed from New York early in August to join the PTs in the Solomons. The boats were towed from Espiritu Santo by the high speed minesweepers *Hovey* and *Southard*, converted flush-deck, four-stack destroyers, to a point 300 miles from Tulagi [their new base]. There the boats were turned loose to proceed under their own power, arriving at Government Wharf, Tulagi, at daybreak on October 12.[4]

Squadron Three's second division of four boats arrived via Noumea at Tulagi on October 25. At the end of November the twelve boats of Squadron Two, including six of the first Elco-80s (PTs 109–114), reached the area. With the addition of MTB Squadron Six's first division in early January 1943, a total of twenty-four PTs eventually took part in the Guadalcanal operation.

It is not difficult to fathom King's decision to send PT boats to the Solomons. Because that group consists of two staggered rows of islands running 20 to 60 miles apart, the waters were relatively protected. In similar restricted waters in the Philippines, Bulkeley had showed that PT boats could apparently sink enemy ships. Further, the boats had accomplished this while in support of a long-running land campaign, and despite a lack of air cover—conditions also likely to be found in the new operation. Assuming the navy's basic inability to permanently maintain a force of cruisers and destroyers in "the Slot" between the rows of islands, PTs seemed the next best means of derailing the Tokyo Express.

These reasons suffice. There has, however, long been speculation that General MacArthur both influenced King's decision to send PTs to the South, and later Southwest, Pacific areas and contributed to the navy's desire to build more PT boats. The source of this conjecture is a meeting, long celebrated in PT lore, that took place between Bulkeley and MacArthur in Australia on 14 May 1942, after the general had Bulkeley evacuated from the Philippines.

During the conversation, MacArthur asked Bulkeley to relay the following message to Admiral King:

Motor torpedo boats should be the basis of a separate branch of the service for specialists, and who must have confidence in their own weapons. These boats can be used effectively for coastal defense 200 or 300 miles offshore, in the Philippine Islands, straits, narrows and potential blocks. There is no other location such as the Philippine Islands and the islands south of the Philippines where they can be so effectively used. With enough of this type of craft, hostile Japanese shipping could be kept from invading and island or continent, and kept 200 to 300 miles offshore. I want 100 or more MTBs here of your type (Elco) together with the improvements which have been developed since the outbreak of the war. Two hundred boats if possible with the tenders, spare parts, and equipment necessary for them within eight months.[5]

It is doubtful MacArthur's message had much impact, for several reasons. One, the general's relationship with the navy still left much to be desired. Two, the message demonstrated MacArthur's continued ignorance of naval affairs. PT boats were effective coastal defense vessels not "200 to 300 miles offshore," but close inshore, where they could appear suddenly in the middle of the night, strike, and flee back to base or some secluded cove before sunrise. Further, to suggest that with enough of them he could keep a Japanese invading fleet "200 to 300 miles offshore" from an island or continent, like Australia, is ludicrous.

Obviously star-struck by MacArthur, Bulkeley himself contributed heavily to the general's "juvenile fantasy." On 4 August 1942, he received a Medal of Honor for his Philippine exploits at the White House, where later that night he lectured President Roosevelt on the need for 200 PTs to be rushed to the Pacific. With them, he promised, America could win the war against Japan.

Bulkeley later went around the country on a recruitment drive for the PT service. He reportedly was a magnificent orator, at one point getting 1,024 young ensigns to volunteer for 50 PT officer vacancies. During his speeches he repeated MacArthur's delusion, namely that "500 PT boats could give the United States mastery over all the Pacific, and that a sufficient force could stop any kind of land invasion."

Alvin Cluster, John F. Kennedy's PT squadron commander in the Solomons, later had this to say about Bulkeley's tour as a war hero:

He and I served on the *Saratoga* before we went to PT boats—he was about a month ahead of me. I liked John. It was only in later years that I realized that his zeal in promoting himself was outsize to the man himself.

The big thing was MacArthur. If MacArthur had traveled out of the Philippines by any other method, you probably never would have heard of John Bulkeley. And that would have been a blessing.

America desperately needed heroes after Pearl Harbor, and they would seize on any exploit or any battle to show how great we were. The only reason PT boats got the attention they did was that we had nothing else! They really didn't do a lot of damage. But Roosevelt had to point to somebody, and that's why Bulkeley and PT boats got

John Bulkeley (far right), with his wife, Alice, at the launching of the PT-103, 16 May 1942, at Elco's Bayonne, New Jersey, plant. The two officers between the Bulkeleys are Tony Akers (at left) and Robert Kelly. The man in civilian clothes is none other than Charles Edison, who became governor of New Jersey in 1940. *National Archives*

> all the attention. William White, who wrote *They Were Expendable*, seized on the exploits of Bulkeley's poor boats out there and expanded on them quite a bit. . . . John Bulkeley was really a joke to a lot of officers.[6]

Other than assuring a plenitude of PT volunteers, MacArthur and Bulkeley's grandstanding therefore accomplished little, other than to make them both look silly. As for the determining factor in the PT buildup, Admiral King himself summed it up succinctly and without fanfare: "They were produced at intervals in accordance with military requirements."[7]

One of those military requirements, tangling with the Tokyo Express off Guadalcanal, came soon after the arrival of Squadron Three at Tulagi. On the night of October 13/14, a Japanese force built around the battleships *Kongo* and *Haruna* bombarded Henderson for some ninety devastating minutes. They killed scores of marines and army troops, badly cratered the airfield, and knocked out forty-eight aircraft. The attack coming only two days after the costly Battle of Cape Esperance, was uncontested by heavy American surface units. That left the four PTs of Squadron Three's first division.

The PT crews, awakened by the gunfire, quickly manned their boats and swept in among the escorting cruisers and destroyers. The PTs fired six torpedoes, then successfully evaded the pursuing destroyers by machine-gunning their searchlights, making smoke, zigzagging, even dropping depth charges in their path. Except for one boat running aground, they suffered no casualties.

The results of this first PT surface action since Cebu in April are uncertain. The PT crews thought three torpedoes hit; they claimed one cruiser probably sunk, another damaged. Radio Tokyo acknowledged the loss of a cruiser that night, and a coastwatcher reported that natives had seen a large vessel sink the next day off New Georgia. Again, however, there is no conclusive evidence that the PTs sank anything that night.[8]

One thing is certain about this engagement. The Japanese, commanded by Adm. Takeo Kurita—who later ran for home prematurely off Samar in the Battle of Leyte Gulf—broke off the bombardment soon after the PTs arrived on the scene. It has never been conclusively established that the PT boats prompted this and were therefore responsible for sparing Henderson additional carnage. Still, as Bern Keating points out, the

> Japanese navy had an inordinate horror of torpedo boats—possibly because the Japanese themselves were so diabolically good at surface torpedo attack. The knowledge that American torpedo boats were back on the scene must have been a jolt to their sensitivities.[9]

This may be true. If so, the Japanese soon got over it. Over the next four months, until the Japanese evacuated their last emaciated troops from Guadalcanal on the night of 7 February 1943, PTs from Tulagi battled the Tokyo Express a total of fourteen times. It seemed the Japanese navy was always willing to come back for more.

There is a certain sameness to the accounts of these spirited matches, mostly between the PTs and Japanese destroyers. The PTs would lie to off Savo Island, located roughly between Tulagi and Guadalcanal. Often they would know of the approach of the Express from air reconnaissance or coastwatcher reports; other times the ominous dark swells created by the silent passing of a large ship somewhere in the night would be their only warning. Upon sighting the enemy they would try to creep in as close as possible, thereby avoiding telltale engine noise and wake, before launching torpedoes. Once alerted, the Japanese ships would sweep the area with their searchlights and let loose with their heavy guns. The PTs would evade, laying smoke and weaving to and fro. Generally, once they lost tactical surprise, speed, smoke, and superior maneuverability became the PT's best friends, in both attack and retreat.

From William Cushing onward, navies looked upon small, unarmored torpedo boats strictly as weapons of opportunity. Complete surprise, naturally enough, maximized that opportunity. As Cushing, Bulkeley, and the PT-boaters who fought at Guadalcanal discovered, such surprise rarely came about. At Guadalcanal it happened only twice.

The first time came early in the morning of November 14, in the midst of the Naval Battle of Guadalcanal—the last large-scale attempt by the Japanese to reinforce their beleaguered garrison. Two boats, attacking independently, closed completely undetected on a cruiser-destroyer formation bombarding Henderson. Each picked out a destroyer, both well lit by their own flares and gun flashes. They launched a total of five torpedoes, claiming one hit on one of the destroyers, two on another. The boats retired under smoke; Japanese counterfire was negligible and way off the mark. Though records never confirmed any sinkings, the Japanese, undoubtedly unnerved by such an unexpected attack by forces unknown, retreated immediately up the Slot. Henderson had been spared a further roughing-up.[10]

The second occurred on December 9, when two PTs sighted barges unloading supplies from a surfaced Japanese submarine. They shot at the barges while PT-59, commanded by Lt. (jg) Robert Searles, USNR, quickly fired off two torpedoes at the surprised sub. One hit amidships. Postwar records confirm that Searles destroyed the *I-3*, 1,955 tons.[11] It was the first verifiable sinking of an enemy warship by a small American torpedo boat since October 1864.

The PTs scored again two nights later, sinking the destroyer *Terutsuki*. This time the cost came high. PT-44, hit squarely by gunfire from a destroyer, sank in a sea of flames; two officers and seven enlisted men perished. Five more boats joined her on the bottom before the campaign's end in early February 1943. Destroyers sank four, while a bomb from a night-flying floatplane claimed the fifth.

Throughout the successful six-month-long effort to expel the Japanese from the southern Solomons, the American blue-water fleet and aircraft from Henderson were the decisive players. As for what the

Tulagi PTs contributed, besides blood and sweat, that will never be accurately known.

According to Bulkley, in 14 separate engagements the PTs fired 111 torpedoes, 29 (26%) of which the crews perceived as hits. The men believed they sank or damaged 1 heavy cruiser, 2 light cruisers, 19 destroyers, and 1 submarine. Records, though, confirmed little of this destruction: only 3 torpedo hits for 1 submarine and 1 destroyer sunk, 1 destroyer damaged. Given the confusion that reigns in night surface actions and the questionable accuracy of armchair surveys, the actual damage was probably higher than Japanese records suggest—but not by much. The PT crews later discovered their torpedo, the vintage Mk 8, was too slow, had too small a warhead, and ran too erratically to do much damage. The "hits" they observed were often no more than destroyer gun flashes or torpedoes hitting a wake.

However ambiguous these results, at the time they seemed real enough. Though the PTs' torpedo potency left much to be desired, they often succeeded, by the threat of their shadowy presence and the aggressiveness of their attacks, in "rendering the transport of supplies exceptionally difficult" and giving the Japanese ships "many a bitter pill to swallow." The Tokyo Express had been derailed, and the PT had unquestionably done its fair share.[12] For the exhausted crews the reward was real enough, too: a four-month lull in operations, time to prepare for a move into the central Solomons on the road to Rabaul.

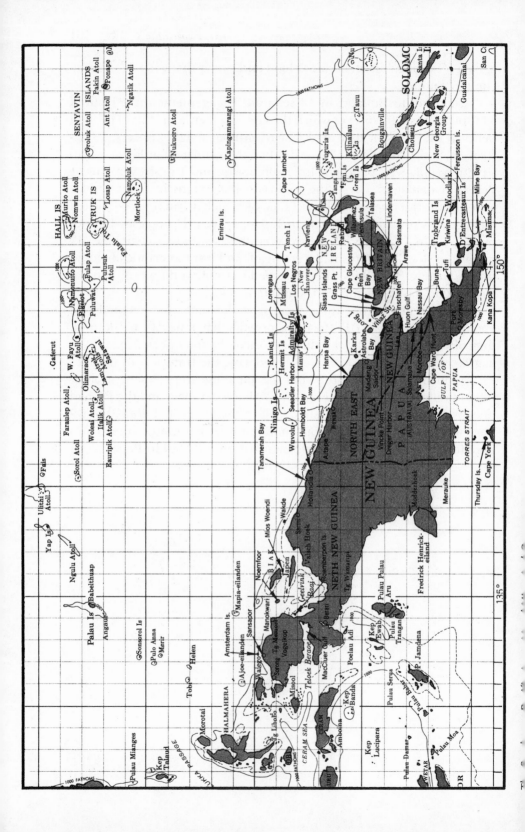

CHAPTER NINE

Transformation

While the Tulagi PTs played their high-stakes game of torpedo tag with the Tokyo Express off Guadalcanal, the navy decided to expand the PTs' area of operations, to the Australian territories of Papua and New Guinea, immediately west of the Solomons in General MacArthur's Southwest Pacific Area. As we will see, this decision had some rather unexpected results, ones that would radically alter the scope of American MTB operations in World War II.

In May 1942, the Battle of the Coral Sea thwarted a Japanese amphibious invasion of Port Moresby, on Papua's southeast coast. Still hoping to isolate Australia despite this setback, the Japanese tried again that summer. On July 21 they landed troops at Buna, on Papua's northeast coast, forestalling a similar Allied move. From there the Japanese marched over the jagged, nearly impassable Owen Stanley Mountains in order to take Port Moresby from the land. By mid-September they had nearly succeeded. Australian troops and American combat engineers subsequently beat back a second invasion prong, a landing at Milne Bay on Papua's eastern tip. At the same time the Japanese high command turned its full attention to retaking Guadalcanal. These events reduced the Port Moresby attack to a holding action, then a retreat. In the Southwest Pacific, as at Midway, the Japanese lost the initiative.

The Allies promptly seized it, beginning a campaign to take the northeastern coast of New Guinea. The Joint Chiefs of Staff considered this move the second phase of the assault on Rabaul, in conjunction with the advance up the Solomons. By 7 November 1942, Australian troops had pushed the Japanese back over the Owen Stanleys and reached Papua's northeast coast near Buna and Gona. On November 19, American troops—lacking heavy naval support because of the shallow waters—landed near Buna and bogged down in the dense, roadless jungle outside of town. The need for shallow-draft vessels to operate offshore in support of the ground forces now became obvious. Shortly after the Buna landing the call went out to send in the PTs.

Squadron Two at Guadalcanal detached two boats for this expanded area of operations. Newly arriving Squadron Six provided four more. Together they created Division 17, becoming the first PT boats in General MacArthur's Southwest Pacific command, which on 15 March 1943 became the U.S. Seventh Fleet. Division 17, initially serviced by the tender *Hilo*, began arriving in Papua–New Guinea waters, via Australia, on 11 December 1942.

Milne Bay was a fine place for the *Hilo*, but too far from the fighting around Buna, 200 miles west, to be used as an operational base by the short-range, nocturnal PTs. Too much travel time to and from the operational area meant too little time on station and too much wear and tear on the engines. This being the case, on December 19 the crews set up a new base at Tufi, on the east side of Cape Nelson about 70 miles east of Buna. Regular patrols began. PT boats were in Papua–New Guinea to stay.

For the next two and one-half months, until the end of February 1943, Division 17's six boats were the only PTs in the area. As in the Philippines campaign a year earlier, a lack of boats and inadequate repair facilities often meant they had to work alone on patrol, rather than in pairs. Nevertheless, they soon made their presence known.

On their very first nightly patrol, on December 18, two boats fired two torpedoes at a surfaced supply submarine. Both appeared to hit but failed to explode. Five nights later one of the same boats, PT-122, fired four torpedoes at another surfaced sub on a supply run. The crew observed two sure hits, but postwar investigation failed to confirm a sinking.

That same night, December 23/24, saw the Papua–New Guinea PTs' first contact with Japanese troop barges. PT-114 and PT-121 crept up on two of the troop-laden vessels in Douglas Harbor and sprayed them with machine gun and 20mm fire. The Japanese soldiers replied with small arms. The resulting melee sank both barges. The PTs suffered no casualties, though this luck soon changed. On the night of January 17/18, when PT-120 intercepted three well-armed barges loaded with escaping Japanese officers, the lethal slugging match killed one crewman. In exchange the PT sank two of the barges and set the third afire, killing most of the officers.[1]

As the PT crews soon discovered, this deadly nocturnal dance with Japanese barges came to be a regular occurrence, even to the extent of threatening to dwarf the PT's torpedo role. No one could have foreseen this; certainly not the Japanese. As early as 1942, with the Allies entrenched in the Solomons and their airpower gaining ascendancy, Japan found it increasingly difficult to reinforce and supply the many far-flung garrisons of its new, rapidly acquired island empire. The barge became the Japanese solution to this growing dilemma; intercepting them by day with aircraft and by night with PTs became the Allied response.

The barges themselves came from native builders in occupied China, Malaya, and the Philippines. They constructed hundreds of the mostly wooden diesel-powered amphibious vessels during the war, the Japanese arming them with machine guns and 20mm, even 40mm, guns. Doctrine called for the barges to load up with troops and supplies, at major bases like Rabaul, and hole up during the day in some wooded creek or cove to escape marauding Allied aircraft. At night they ventured out, hugging the reef-strewn shore to escape deep-draft enemy surface ships. As attacks by planes and PTs intensified, the Japanese even posted artillery along the barge routes to give the sluggish vessels added protection.

Sometimes these tactics worked, sometimes they did not. While at Tufi the PTs sank 18, possibly 20, barges. The boats, along with Maj. Gen. George C. Kenney's low-flying, ship-busting Fifth Air Force, made it costly for the Japanese to keep their troops supplied in the Buna–Gona–Sanananda area, where weariness and hunger contributed greatly to the success of the final Allied offensive. The Allies had seized all three towns by 22 January 1943, ending the Papua campaign and setting the stage for that of New Guinea.[2]

Japan's dependency on barges increased dramatically in this new phase of operations, largely because of the disastrous big-ship losses the Japanese sustained during the Battle of the Bismarck Sea, in early March 1943. With the loss of Papua, the Japanese determined to slam the gate shut on the Allied Rabaul advance by hanging onto the Huon Peninsula, across the Vitiaz Strait from New Britain. To do this they risked a convoy of large troop transports, eight in all, escorted by an equal number of destroyers and protected by upward of 100 planes. None of these precautions did much good.

Detected by air reconnaissance on March 1, the convoy came under two days of increasingly accurate strafing and bombing attacks by B-17s, and by B-25s specially adapted to make low-level antiship runs. On the night of March 3, eight PTs from Tufi and Milne Bay reached the scene, but found only a burning derelict transport. They finished her off with torpedoes. All but four of the destroyers had been sunk; some 3,000 men of the Japanese 51st Division perished, many under the guns of the PTs, which roamed the area for several days afterward, shooting up lifeboats and survivors in the water, who, typically, refused to surrender. On March 5, two PTs did manage to fire a couple of torpedoes at a submarine picking up survivors, but both missed.[3] As at Midway, the PTs played only a minor role; the airplane once again proved decisive.

During the winter and spring of 1943, after taking Sanananda, the Allies consolidated their positions in preparation for knocking at Japan's Huon gate. MTB Squadrons Eight and Seven, the latter commanded by returning Philippines hero John Bulkeley, arrived on the scene. Forward operations moved west to a new base on the Marobe River on April 20. Meanwhile, the JCS laid the strategic groundwork that would carry the PT boat up the Solomons ladder, westward along the New Guinea coast, and ultimately back to the Philippines themselves.

Despite the intense efforts of its sailors and airmen to expel the Japanese from the southern Solomons and Papua, the United States Navy wanted the principal Allied blow against the Japanese to fall elsewhere: in an all-navy drive westward from Pearl Harbor through the scattered island groups of the Central Pacific. General MacArthur, never one to take a backseat, instead envisioned an army-dominated thrust to the northwest along the New Guinea–Mindanao axis. Which drive should the JCS authorize? Who should command it? For months the debate raged. The JCS, beset by interservice rivalries of its own, felt obliged to keep both the army and navy happy. So in the spring of 1943 the JCS authorized both drives, soon known to history as the Dual Advance.

Despite the politicized nature of the JCS decision, both the navy and army put forth compelling arguments for their favored drive. After all, everyone agreed Japan must be decisively defeated, invaded if necessary. To do that, Japan's island defense perimeter had to be pierced, and siege laid to its home islands. Very few acceptable attack routes across the trackless Pacific were open to the Allies. The fewer those options, the better each could be made to look.

For the navy, the Central Pacific drive was an old dream come true. Recall that War Plan Orange had called for such an operation to relieve or retake the Philippines. The JCS merely revived this notion, only now aircraft carriers instead of battleships would spearhead this "main line of advance" against Japan. The JCS reasoned that the existing Allied offensive up the Solomon chain and New Guinea had essentially outlived its original purpose of defending the U.S.–Australia supply line. It seemed pointless to plod along down south when a new offensive could be opened farther north, closer to Japan. Cutting Japanese communications would leave the southern forces to wither on the vine.

The Central Pacific offensive, set to begin in the late fall of 1943, had other advantages as well. The navy would be attacking isolated island groups incapable of supporting one another. The offensive would take maximum advantage of all the new battleships and carriers reaching the Pacific and help speed up victory. By attacking the inner ring of Japanese defenses, the navy might force the Japanese navy into a decisive battle of annihilation, thereby opening Japan itself to invasion.

This all made perfect strategic sense, yet the JCS authorized a second drive through New Guinea to the Philippines, needlessly dividing forces between two simultaneous offensives and inviting defeat in detail by the still-formidable Japanese. The reason for this potentially hazardous state of affairs has repeatedly managed to find his way into these pages: Gen. Douglas MacArthur.

MacArthur, as a former army chief of staff and "Hero of the Philippines," enjoyed considerable political and popular clout among ruling circles in Washington. His name came up more than once to become supreme commander in the Pacific, but the navy adamantly rejected the idea. Still, the JCS could not very well subordinate the godlike MacArthur to Admiral Nimitz. Unable to decide which of the men should command, the Joint Chiefs left the question open, figuring it more politically and militarily expedient to simply give them their own way in their own backyards.[4]

MacArthur's drive nevertheless had merit. Landmasses suitable for airfields were generally available on his route to the Philippines, so MacArthur could dispense with huge, vulnerable carrier fleets and massive fleet trains to supply them. He also argued that America's prestige was on the line. He had promised the Filipinos that he, meaning the United States, would return. America would lose face if it bypassed the Philippines, leaving the loyal Filipinos in the hands of the brutal Japanese.

In the end, fortunately, the Dual Advance worked. It kept the Japanese off balance, never knowing where the next blow would fall. Though coordination of the two drives created *potentially* serious problems, as at Bougainville and later at Biak, by and large the dual offensives just kept hammering relentlessly at the Japanese until they caved in.

For the PT, destined to do its fair share of that hammering by war's end, the JCS decision to continue the New Guinea–Mindanao offensive had enormous implications. Foremost, it gave them a steady job at the cutting edge of the Allied offensive. PTs needed shallow, coastal waters and plenty of enemy surface targets such as barges to be of value. In New Guinea and the Philippines they had both; in the Central Pacific they would have had neither. One could speculate on PT fortunes had

New Guinea been relegated to a backwater and the Philippines by-passed. This did not happen. From 1943 to 1945, MacArthur kept the PT boat very busy, not out of gratitude to John Bulkeley or any special desire to give the PT a role, but simply as a by-product of his status and stubborn persistence in carrying on an active offensive in his shallow-water command area.

One immediate offshoot of the JCS decision, Operation Cartwheel, saw MacArthur move against the Huon Peninsula in late June 1943, prefatory to landing on Cape Gloucester on the opposite end of New Britain from Rabaul. At the same time, Adm. William F. Halsey, commanding in the South Pacific, landed on New Georgia in the central Solomons and began his advance north to Bougainville. Cartwheel postponed the attack on Rabaul itself, because of lack of forces.

PTs in both New Guinea and the Solomons participated in Cartwheel. From Morobe, boats spent the spring hunting supply submarines, without result. On July 6 they had better luck landing troops at Nassau Bay, to establish a supply base for advancing Australian troops. Transporting troops, landing secret reconnaissance patrols, and performing other close-support duties for the land forces were to become common PT functions throughout the remainder of the war, in both the Mediterranean and the Pacific. During the summer the Morobe boats also got back into barge-busting in the Huon Gulf, sinking 44 and possibly as many as 51 of the nocturnal Japanese craft.[5]

On June 30 the Tulagi boats arrived with the initial central Solomons invasion wave and established a base at Rendova Harbor, south of New Georgia and opposite the main American objective on that island, the Japanese airfield at Munda. From there they began patrols, having the inglorious bad fortune to torpedo and sink the damaged attack transport *McCawley* the first night out.[6]

The *McCawley* incident prompted a transfer of PT operational control from local naval base commanders to the local amphibious force commander. This improved communications between PT commanders and the rest of the operating naval, air, and land forces. Nevertheless, incidents where aircraft or friendly ships fired on and even sank PTs, and vice versa, did occur all too frequently. This tragic "friendly fire" phenomenon existed primarily because of the command and control complexities of fighting a combined land, sea, and air campaign over thousands of square miles of ocean dotted with tropical islands. The phenomenon has little to do with the fact the PTs had no opportunity to operate with the fleet before the war.

For the Rendova PTs, the New Georgia campaign saw a brief return to fighting Tokyo Express destroyers. During July and early August they tangled with the Express twice. On July 3, three PTs fired six torpedoes at four Japanese destroyers apparently on their way to bombard Rendova. After a brisk melee, in which the crews thought they hit one destroyer, the enemy retired at high speed, unable to complete its mission.

The second, last, and certainly most celebrated run-in with the Express occurred on the night of August 1/2, as four Japanese destroyers headed down the west coast of neighboring Kolombangara Island, through the Blackett Strait, to discharge 900 troops and 70 tons of supplies at Vila on Kolombangara.

Fifteen PTs, in four groups each built around a boat with radar, fought a confused, shamefully uncoordinated night action with these ships as they ran along the shore, dropped off their cargoes, and retired. The PTs fired a total of thirty torpedoes at the destroyers, and thought five hit. No damage was ever confirmed, nor did anyone even believe the skippers' claims at the time.[7] As the Japanese ships swept north up the western side of Kolombangara on their return, one of them, the *Amagiri*, had a close, lethal encounter with the single most famous PT skipper and boat in PT history: Lt. John F. Kennedy, USNR, and PT-109.

It is safe to say that more pages have been written about JFK and the 109 than about all the other five-hundred-plus PT boats that participated in World War II combined. Most adults know what a PT boat is, almost certainly largely because of the 109. More to the point, of course, people know about PT-109 because they know about John F. Kennedy, the 35th president of the United States and arguably one of the most charismatic men of the twentieth century.

Although the PT-109 saga played a significant role in the making of the Kennedy legend, and hence his presidency, the story deserves no hallowed place in our discussion here. After the MacArthur rescue, the plight of PT-109 is easily the most shameful chapter in the history of the American PT. In some ways it is even worse, since this time the damage was self-inflicted, a result of incompetence on several levels within the PT command structure.

The PT-109 saga, in essence, is as follows. The night of August 1/2 was black, moonless, with heavy cloud cover, making for bad visibility in the Blackett Strait. Despite this, the Rendova PT commander, Lt. Comdr. Thomas G. Warfield, disdainfully referred to by his officers as "the biggest shit in the Pacific," ordered the four groups of boats to maintain complete radio silence except in emergencies. The PTs in each section were thus somehow expected to stay in visual contact with

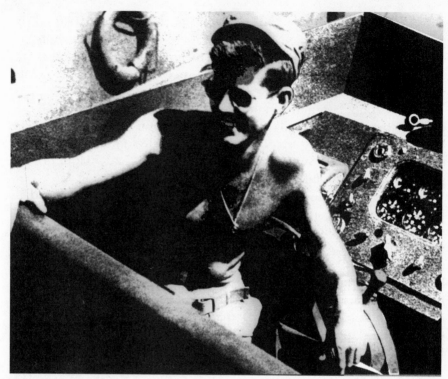

Lt. John F. Kennedy, USNR, in the cockpit of the PT-109, 1943. *PT Boats, Inc.*

the radar-equipped leader, reacting to that boat's moves without the benefit of either radio or visual communications. The PT skippers, most of whom were inexperienced newcomers, also had standing orders to head for home independently once they had expended their torpedoes.

These questionable orders, designed to maintain secrecy and minimize confusion, combined with the bad visibility to produce catastrophe. One by one the four radar-equipped "leaders" made contact with the four Japanese destroyers. They raced ahead without being seen by nearly all their section mates, fired their torpedoes at too great a distance to be effective, and headed for home with nary a word to the boats left blind and deaf in the darkness behind. Warfield, meanwhile, completely lost control, exhorting the remaining blind boats by radio to press home the attack without apparently having the slightest idea why they were having such trouble doing so.

This critical interpretation of events comes largely from statements by the various PT skippers, and other PT commanders involved, taken from Kennedy biographer Nigel Hamilton's detailed reconstruction of the battle.[8] Based on these statements, Hamilton makes Warfield out as the chief villain in the whole shameful episode. However, when one reads Warfield's official report of this action, dated August 5, he accuses "several" of the PT skippers of "failing to put out immediate intelligible report[s] of contact with the enemy, with the result that the others had no chance to get into position for an attack." Warfield also spelled out that while the boats were to refrain from using the radio, this did *not* mean to refrain from making contact reports. He also recommended that

> PTs should stay together in "V" formation and follow their division leader. All boats should fire their torpedoes when their section leader fires, with deployment. They should spread torpedoes about the base torpedo course of the leader.... [Further], boats should fire at shorter range. Some boats retired without firing and had to be directed to return to station.[9]

The verity of Warfield's report raises the possibility that the inexperienced PT skippers misunderstood his orders about keeping radio silence. Or perhaps Warfield was just trying, after the fact, to divert blame. Perhaps the truth lies somewhere in between. A poor working relationship between Warfield and his officers appears to be the root cause of the Blackett Strait debacle.

In the meantime, to his lasting credit, Lieutenant Kennedy reacted to this sorry mess by forming up with the one remaining boat in his section, and one other, to create a rough skirmish line near his patrol station in the Blackett Strait, between Gizo Island to the west and Kolombangara to the east. He idled along muffled, at 6 knots, on his center engine alone, the wing engines in neutral. This too the skippers considered a sensible tactic, at least at the time, as the propeller on the center engine was set deeper and put out the smallest wake—an important consideration, given the numerous Japanese floatplanes harassing the PTs that night. Their tactic was to follow the phosphorescent wake of a PT and drop their bombs when they thought they had come to the vortex of the V.

At approximately 2:30 a.m., as the 109 slowly crept south, the *Amagiri* raced north at high speed, trying to regain contact with the three destroyers she guarded. Simultaneously, lookouts on both vessels made visual contact, though versions differ somewhat on the exact timing of this and other aspects of the incident. As their courses were roughly parallel and offset by mere yards, Comdr. Kohei Hanami of the *Amagiri* deliberately attempted ramming the PT with a quick swerve to starboard.

Kennedy, for his part, had only about 10 seconds to respond to the sighting call "Ship at two o'clock!"—first made by his gunner in the starboard .50-caliber turret when the destroyer, first thought to be another PT, was only 200 to 300 yards away. He signaled the engine room for more speed and attempted to turn to starboard to get into a firing position. It proved too late for that. The *Amagiri* "rammed [the 109], striking it forward of the forward starboard tube and shearing off the starboard side of the boat aft, including the starboard engine."[10]

The *Amagiri*, contrary to myth, did not actually cut PT-109 in two; it only sheared off a big chunk, which had the same disastrous effect. The gas tanks exploded, though the destroyer's wash carried the flames away, and the stern section soon sank, carried down by the weight of the remaining engines. Two men died, leaving eleven others, including several suffering from serious burns, to an uncertain fate on the 109's canting foredeck.

The rest of the saga is even better known than the collision itself. Kennedy emerged a hero by the time it ended, and rightfully so. When no one returned to pick them up, Kennedy towed a severely burned member of the crew and swam with the rest of his men to a nearby island the next day. After a series of events worthy of the best South Seas adventure book, a PT picked up all eleven men seven days later, on August 8. Two war correspondents accompanied the rescue party. Needless to say, they had a major story on their hands, one Kennedy eventually played up for all it was worth right into the White House.

The impact of Kennedy's rise to the presidency on PT history is worth noting here. The inevitable media attention that accompanied his successful 1960 bid catapulted PT-109, and PT boats in general, into the public spotlight with him, much as Bulkeley's Philippines exploits had done during the war. Several books followed: Robert J. Donovan's *PT 109: John F. Kennedy in World War II* (1961); Richard Tregaskis's *John F. Kennedy: War Hero* (1962); and Chandler Whipple's *Lt. John F. Kennedy—Expendable!* (1962). Donovan was a longtime friend of Kennedy's, which accounts for his favorable portrayal of Kennedy in all aspects of the PT-109 episode. The titles of the other two also give a good idea of how Kennedy fared.[11]

Robert Bulkley's *At Close Quarters* itself owes its existence to JFK. As mentioned previously, the official history of PTs originated as an unpublished manuscript written by Bulkley, at the behest of the Naval History Division, right after World War II. The Naval History Division dusted off, updated, and published it in book form as a result of all the attention generated by the former PT skipper's presidency.[12]

The sinking also attracted attention at the time. There were immediate newspaper stories, and John Hersey wrote a "moving and sensitive" account of the episode, titled "Survival," that appeared in *The New Yorker* of 17 June 1944. It must be noted that Kennedy was already something of a celebrity, at least in upper-crust Eastern circles. His father had been ambassador to Great Britain, while JFK himself had published a book on British unpreparedness in the 1930s, *Why England Slept*. Of course, no matter who had been at the wheel of PT-109 that night, the sinking and subsequent rescue made for a tremendously dramatic wartime story.

The controversies surrounding the loss of the 109 make the story even more worth our attention. There are two: whether Kennedy was negligent in "allowing" his boat to be rammed by a destroyer; and why no one at Rendova bothered to make a concerted effort to rescue possible survivors.

As for the issue of Kennedy's negligence, two distinct camps have formed over the years, those feeling he could not have prevented the ramming and those feeling he should have. First the latter:

Lieutenant Commander Warfield, who judged that Kennedy "wasn't a particularly good boat commander," believed there was simply no excuse for him not to have seen the destroyer, or at least its phosphorescent wake. Lt. Comdr. Jack E. Gibson, who succeeded Warfield and served as an advisor to the 1963 film *PT 109* starring Cliff Robertson, chastises Kennedy for getting separated from his section leader and just cruising around muffled, "out in the middle [of the Blackett Strait]" afterward. He felt Kennedy should have just returned to base instead. Another PT skipper, Patrick Monroe, whom Kennedy corresponded with occasionally during his time in the Pacific, wrote in 1992 that "Kennedy had the most maneuverable vessel in the world. All that power and yet this knight in white armor managed to have his PT boat rammed by a destroyer. Everybody in the fleet laughed about that."

Naval writer Michael Isenberg also takes a critical view of Kennedy's actions, believing him to have been "callow, reckless, and careless in command, although his heroism was never in question." He specifically faults JFK for allowing two of his men to be asleep and two others to lie on deck while on patrol, despite the fact they were "*expecting* Jap destroyers that night." He also points out that one of the other boats in the threesome, PT-169, commanded by Lt. (jg) Philip A. Potter, Jr., saw the *Amagiri's*, phosphorescent wake speeding toward the 109 and gave warning over the radio, but neither Kennedy nor the other boat—PT-162, commanded by Lt. (jg) John R. Lowrey—responded.[13]

Were Kennedy and crew "not on the ball," as suggested by these critics? Did he run a lax boat? Was he not paying proper attention to his job, thereby allowing the 109 to be rammed and sunk, two men to be killed, and others to be badly burned? Was Kennedy, who in 1960 became commander in chief of the armed forces of the United States, negligent in the loss of PT-109?

The available evidence indicates no. The above criticisms appear damning, until one looks closely at the reasons Kennedy did what he did before the collision. For openers, it is difficult to see how he can be faulted for not turning tail and heading for base after his section leader left him and one other boat behind. The PTs were under orders to stay on their station and maintain radio silence, unless they had fired their torpedoes. As for running slow, he did this to avoid Japanese float-planes, as previously explained. To assume that PTs constantly flitted around at 40 knots, utilizing all that "power" and "maneuverability" every minute on patrol, is unrealistic.

It is true Kennedy expected Japanese destroyers, particularly since he had received a radio report a couple of hours previously that told of other PTs being chased by enemy surface ships. This, however, is meaningless; every night they were out on patrol they *expected* enemy destroyers. The reason the two men were sleeping is that they got so little of it as a rule. Watches were two hours on, two off. Anyone who has ever tried to peer intently into pitch darkness from the deck of a PT (or any boat) for any length of time knows the fatigue such eye-bending activity brings on.

As for PT-169's radio warning, neither the official report nor any of the other statements made later by PT-109's crew mentions hearing such a warning. One reason they may not have even received it is offered by Dick Keresey, the skipper of PT-105, another boat also involved in the ill-fated Blackett Strait action. He notes that the pounding the boats took often had the effect of knocking the radios off their assigned frequencies. This may or may not have happened, yet even if the 109 had heard the warning, it is doubtful it would have helped.

The reason is timing. Lieutenant Potter estimates he only observed the destroyer for "ten or fifteen seconds" (the same as the 109 crew's estimate) before it collided with the 109. It seems unlikely Potter could have made the sighting, determined its significance, and directed his radioman standing next to him in the cockpit to send out the warning in time to have done any good.[14]

In sum, faulty command and control probably did more than any other preventable factor to cause the ramming of PT-109. Nevertheless, the major proximate cause of the ramming must be put down to simple bad luck. As Dick Keresey puts it:

If luck had not chosen to put the 109 directly in the path of the on-rushing Japanese destroyer, if the 109 had been a few hundred yards

The *Amagiri* ramming the PT-109, from the official Navy painting by Capt. Gerard Richardson, USNR. Note how even the "official" painting tends to perpetuate controversy surrounding the sinking. Should the 109 have been planing along as fast as Richardson suggests here, it is extremely doubtful she ever would have been hit. *National Archives*

to either side, then that Japanese destroyer might have been the victim of the 109, instead of the other way around.[15]

The other controversy can be more easily dispatched. After seeing the 109 explode, the other two PTs apparently fired torpedoes at the departing destroyer. They observed no hits. They fled, expecting other destroyers to come charging into the area. Potter claimed that about an hour later he returned to the area and conducted a search for survivors for about 30 to 45 minutes. Finding none, he left. He also sent a radio message to Warfield advising him of the collision, but Warfield never issued an area-wide alert to that effect. For its part, PT-162 never returned to the scene. All the boats in the patrol area had left to return to Rendova by 4 a.m.

Later that morning, after Potter and Lowrey reported that they felt there was no hope anyone could have survived the explosion, Warfield decided against any boats going out to the area for a daylight search.

Daylight searches by PTs were too dangerous, given the threat of air attack—from U.S. as well as Japanese planes. More inexplicable is his refusal to send boats to the same area for their nightly patrols during the following few nights. Had he done so, one of them might have found Kennedy with his battle lantern treading water in Ferguson Passage, waiting and hoping.

Some air searches over the general Japanese-occupied area were made, but the planes arrived too late to detect the crew in the water. The 109 crew, out of fear of giving themselves away to enemy aircraft, hesitated to flag down the patrols. Since the night PT patrols avoided the area, those few air searches composed the entire effort to locate the survivors. But for sympathetic natives, ones working for an Australian coastwatcher, Sub-Lt. Arthur R. Evans, the crew might have starved to death or been captured. In all, the PT command failed shamefully in its efforts to locate Kennedy and his men. As Keresey succinctly puts it: "We should have gone back."[16]

Kennedy is known to have expressed bitterness at his mates for not coming back to find them. Rightly so, though he seemed far more interested in getting back at the Japanese. In the fall of 1943 he took command of PT-59, the first of three old Elco-77s to be converted to gunboats. This assignment, however, the navy cut short in December 1943 when it sent him home, citing his chronic back and stomach problems—which would have kept him out of the navy altogether had it not been for his father's connections. Before his premature departure, JFK therefore had the opportunity to witness two pivotal moments in PT history: the last PT run-in with the Tokyo Express, and the beginning of the PT's transformation from torpedo boat to torpedo-gunboat.[17]

The Americans in the Pacific were also caught off guard by the Japanese need to use small, shallow-draft barges to keep their garrisons supplied. Prewar designers had in mind torpedo attacks against ships when they built the PT, intending their machine guns and 20mm gun for use primarily against aircraft. So when, after a series of costly destroyer battles during July and August 1943 in the Slot north of New Georgia, the Japanese turned to barges in the Solomons as well, the PTs had a rude introduction to the low-slung Japanese vessels.

Rendova PTs made their first contact with Japanese barges on July 21; two nights later they sank their first one, driving two others back to their base and preventing three enemy destroyers from off-loading supplies into them. On July 26/27, PTs operating from a new base on the north coast of New Georgia, at Lever Harbor, intercepted six barges evacuating troops from the besieged Japanese base at Bairoko Harbor. They attacked again, only to discover the barges were "so well armored that gunfire . . . ricocheted harmlessly off their sides." Thus protected, the barges did not hesitate to fire back, even closing the range when the PTs had to stop firing to reload.[18]

These barges were unlike those so far encountered by the New Guinea PTs. They were

> Type A *Daihatsu(s)* [an abbreviation meaning "large-type landing barge"], metal-hulled, diesel-powered craft, 41 to 49 feet long, weighing 8 tons, capable of making 8 knots and carrying 100 to 120 men or 10 to 15 tons of cargo. At least two machine guns were standard equipment for each *Daihatsu*, but in battle waters the Japanese added anything up to 37-mm field pieces, while troop passengers contributed automatic weapons.[19]

After engaging upward of seventeen of these barges leaving Bairoko in mid-August, Lt. Comdr. Robert Kelly, of Philippines fame, reported that

> on each occasion the return fire from the barges and shore batteries has been so heavy that the PTs have been unable to close to effective range. Only two barges were seen to be damaged and none are believed to have been sunk or seriously disabled. Without illumination it is impossible for the PTs to see the barges which closely hug the shore. However, the PTs themselves are clearly visible against the horizon in the moonlight. Heavily armored large barges with 40mm. and machineguns escort the medium barges which carry only machineguns and/or 20mm. In order to sink a barge, the range must be closed well within 100 yards and more than 1,000 rounds of .50 caliber and 500 rounds of 20mm are required. . . . This requires laying to at point blank range of shore batteries and barges for approximately 10 minutes which is tantamount to sacrificing the PT boat.[20]

Casualties from barge hunting tended to be remarkably light throughout the war, even at this early stage, so while Kelly overstated the danger to the PTs, he accurately recognized the undesirability of relying on machine guns and 20mm guns for use against the barges. And there were lots of barges. From July to the end of August the Rendova PTs encountered a total of 56 barges and 5 small auxiliary ships, claiming 8 barges and 1 auxiliary sunk, plus others probably sunk or damaged. Lever Harbor boats engaged 43 or 44 barges in August, claiming only 2 and beaching 1. Clearly, with all that traffic the PTs had a major, ongoing job to perform; just as clearly, they were unequal to the task.

For the Solomons PT men, encountering armored *Daihatsus*, shore batteries, and floatplanes in combination in the summer of 1943 produced something of a cumulative shock effect. Kelly even recommended in late August that "the only practical solution for combating this barge traffic would be to employ similarly armored barges of our own or to install appropriate shore batteries capable of interdicting the barge route."

Admiral Halsey, however, disagreed with much of Kelly's report, thereby planting the administrative seed of the PT's wartime transformation. He wrote:

> The use of PT boats as barge destroyers leaves much to be desired. Such employment in daylight or bright moonlight is distinctly hazardous and frequently expensive to an unacceptable degree but Commander South Pacific does not agree that PT boats in anti-barge operations are ineffective and costly under all conditions. However, steps have been taken locally to improve their effectiveness, when so employed, by equipping them with a 37mm. or 40mm. single AA gun. Work is now underway on the conversion of three 77-foot MTB's (original Elco-77s) into motor gunboats by removal of torpedo tubes and depth charges to provide space and weight compensation for an additional 40mm. single AA gun and armor.[21]

Although New Guinea PTs were already experimenting with 37mm and 40mm guns—four boats arrived in late August with a 40mm mounted even before leaving the United States—the heightened use of barges in the Solomons and the decision to convert the three Elco-77s to gunboats make August 1943 a watershed month for the American PT. No longer would the navy think of the PT as a torpedo boat good only against ships; nor could it afford to. Because of losses suffered at the hands of Allied airmen, blue-water seamen, and submariners, the Japanese were risking fewer ships in the shallow-water areas frequented by PT boats, while increasing tougher-to-spot shallow-draft, coastal-hugging barge traffic. With a few modifications the PT could be made to combat this new, desperate Japanese tactic, thereby continuing to justify the navy's investment in the boats.

This does not mean the navy's transformation of the PT from torpedo boat to gunboat was immediate, total, or even universal. As Robert Bulkley describes, the navy adapted the boats only so far as local tactical conditions required:

> After experimentation with the single-shot Army 37mm. cannon, which was not entirely satisfactory because of its slow rate of fire, the automatic Army Air Force 37mm. was made standard installation on

A fleet in transition: PT-61, at right, one of the three Elco-77s converted to gunboats in the fall of 1943. PT-168 is at left. *PT Boats, Inc.*

PTs in the Solomons. Except for [the converted Elco-77s], the 40mm. was not used by the South Pacific PTs until later squadrons came out from the States with them already installed. . . . [In] the Southwest Pacific the 40mm., a far more powerful weapon than the 37mm., became standard armament for PTs. This divergence in armament in the two areas resulted partly from differences in background, partly from differences in operating conditions.

In the Southwest Pacific [and later in the Philippines] PTs were used from the start and almost exclusively as barge destroyers. The 40mm. was the most potent and most accurate antibarge gun. Ergo, it was adopted. In the South Pacific, on the other hand, PTs had a background of action against destroyers and cruisers: the torpedo was regarded as the primary weapon. The 40mm. was a heavy gun, and it was feared that the extra weight would slow down the boats if they continued to carry four torpedoes. This fear was justified. Unless PTs are maintained in top condition, frequently a difficult thing to do under combat conditions in forward areas, extra weight does tend to slow them down. In many sections of the Southwest Pacific, PTs armed with the 40mm. were authorized to carry two, instead of the customary four, torpedoes. Although South Pacific PTs did not meet destroyers after August 1, 1943, the possibility that they would meet them still existed. The Japanese still had destroyers at Rabaul and could have run the Tokyo Express again had they been willing to risk their ships.

So much for differences in background. The difference in operating conditions was a matter of distance. South Pacific patrol areas were usually close to the PT operating bases. So it was possible to act on Kelly's suggestion and convert some LCMs [Landing Craft, Mechanized, 50 feet long] to gunboats to accompany the PTs on their missions. Each LCM gunboat carried a 3-inch gun, and their low speed [12 knots] was acceptable where distances were short. Later, larger landing craft, LCIs [Landing Craft, Infantry, 157 feet long], were converted to gunboats to operate with the PTs. Similarly converted were some wooden-hulled 110-foot submarine chasers, which came to be known as PGMs. These were somewhat faster than the landing craft, and so could operate further from their base. Thus, in the South Pacific, the PT was preserved primarily as a torpedo boat, strengthened against barges by the 37mm. cannon, but largely dependent on slower gunboats for heavy firepower. In the Southwest Pacific, where patrol areas usually were 100 to 150 miles from base, LCM and LCI gunboats and PGMs lacked the speed necessary to proceed to station and return during the hours of darkness. Consequently PTs had to carry their own heavy guns.[22]

That same August, as the Southwest and South Pacific PTs began beefing up their anti-barge firepower, the Joint Chiefs, with their British counterparts at the Quadrant Conference in Quebec, made some important decisions affecting what the PTs would be called upon to do with it.

The JCS decided first to bypass Rabaul, the objective of both the Solomon thrust and MacArthur's New Guinea campaign. Instead of taking the huge Japanese base, where after the war some 100,000 well-entrenched Japanese soldiers were found waiting to die for the emperor, the Allies would neutralize it, thereby freeing forces badly needed for the Central Pacific drive opening that fall. The JCS next let MacArthur continue to charge westward along the long northern back of New Guinea to the Vogelkop Peninsula, in preparation for the leap to the Philippines. These two decisions ultimately had the effect of reducing the Solomons PTs to backwater caretakers, while placing the New Guinea squadrons at the forefront of an ambitious offensive to the west.

A detailed operational account of the PT as barge-hunting gunboat is beyond the scope of this study. For the sake of continuity, though, I will present an overview of this facet of PT operations, one that unquestionably dominates their non-torpedo-boat record in the Pacific War.

In the Solomons, Admiral Halsey pressed northward in his quest to isolate Rabaul. After taking Munda airfield on New Georgia, he bypassed Kolombangara with its 12,000 Japanese troops and landed unopposed on neighboring Vella Lavella on 15 August 1943. Bypassing Choiseul, he landed in the Treasury Islands on October 27, in preparation for the Bougainville landing at Empress Augusta Bay on November 1. On Bougainville, despite intensive Japanese air, sea, and land attempts to drive off the invaders, the Americans established an airfield, which was soon in use by fighters supporting Munda- and New Guinea–based bombers in raids on Rabaul.

Meanwhile, a series of massive air battles, including two bold raids by Halsey's carriers in November 1943, whittled down Rabaul's air strength and made its harbor increasingly untenable for ships. In December, Halsey unleashed a systematic air offensive to finish the job. By mid-February 1944 the Japanese had been forced to withdraw all their remaining aircraft and ships; by May, on schedule, the airfields and airdromes had been wrecked, finishing Rabaul as a base. Active naval operations then shifted to the north and west.

The Solomons PTs followed close on the heels of these moves. They established a base on the northeast coast of Vella Lavella on 25 September 1943, and another in the Treasury Islands on October 25. Two days after the main Bougainville landing on November 1, PTs began patrolling from Cape Torokina. Later, in February and March 1944, the navy established advanced PT bases to assist in the permanent isolation of Rabaul at Green Island, between Bougainville and New Britain, and at Emirau, north of New Britain itself. Sailing from Green, on March 1, PT-319 had the distinction of becoming the first Allied warship to enter Rabaul Harbor since its occupation by Japan. As the visibility was only a hundred yards, the crew found nothing, there being little left for them to find.[23]

From the above South Pacific bases the PTs primarily hunted Japanese supply and evacuation barges. Nocturnal combat conditions and understandably poor Japanese record-keeping make it impossible to do more than estimate the number of barges the PTs eventually shot up: PT action reports for the Solomons put the totals at 146 sunk or probably sunk and 86 damaged, between 21 July 1943 and the end of October 1944. Still, these totals fail to tell the whole story.

As the official history points out, these figures—and those tallied by the New Guinea boats—are probably conservative. Advancing ground forces often found beached barges not originally listed as destroyed. Not only that, the figures are unrevealing. Frequently the PTs thwarted resupply operations without necessarily causing much damage, and since "strangulation of the [Japanese] supply line was the paramount objective . . . the boats accomplished this objective to a far greater degree than any mere 'box score' of barge sinkings could possibly indicate."[24]

During the height of the Solomons advance, the boats also landed and picked up reconnaissance parties and otherwise provided fire support for small landings. Even these familiar PT functions died down, though, along with barge sinkings, after Rabaul's neutralization. After the end of March 1944, the South Pacific PTs "were to devote themselves to 'containing' the Japanese in their sealed-off areas of occupation; disrupting any remaining barge traffic, and strafing coastal installations."[25] This they did to the extent necessary until mid-February 1945. At that time the navy pulled the last of the squadrons out and sent them to other areas of the Pacific.

PT operations in the New Guinea campaign followed a pattern similar to those in the Solomons, though at a more feverish pace. As the Allies advanced, sometimes for hundreds of miles at a jump, the PTs would be right up at the front. They had to be at the front to be of any use. The base crews would establish advanced operating bases for as long as the local barge traffic continued, then close up shop and leap to the next target area. This process repeated itself until no serious Japanese resistance remained on New Guinea and MacArthur moved on to the Philippines in October 1944.

Like Halsey in the Solomons, MacArthur's first objective was to seal off Rabaul. This he accomplished from his end by March 1944, securing the Huon Peninsula, the western and southern sections of New Britain itself, and the Admiralty Islands. PTs from Dreger Harbor and Morobe, and later from Saidor, Arawe on New Britain, and Seeadler Harbor in the Admiralties, all patrolled in support of this aggressive amphibious effort, spearheaded by Rear Adm. Daniel E. Barbey's VII Amphibious Force.

Beginning in April 1944, MacArthur's Southwest Pacific forces then began a series of equally bold leapfrogs 1,200 miles to the west along New Guinea's northern coastline. PTs moved to Aitape at the end of April in support. Here they saw the heaviest fighting yet as the trapped Japanese 18th Army tried to receive supplies by barge from its main supply base at Wewak, 100 miles east of Aitape.

Over a five-month period the Aitape boats sank some 115 barges and destroyed 12 Japanese army trucks along coastal roads. Despite the determined enemy use of shore batteries in support of their barges, PT losses were extremely modest: three men dead, seven wounded, one boat lost. The fact that PTs were so hard to hit accounts for this low casualty rate, so characteristic of torpedo boat operations since the American Civil War despite doomsday rhetoric to the contrary. Whereas the barges trudged along, the PTs sped into range, made as many passes as necessary to punch the barges full of holes and silence return fire, then sped off. Except when PTs grounded on a reef, the single greatest cause of PT losses in the war, they avoided giving the enemy a stationary target at all costs.

This period also saw the introduction of comparatively exotic new weaponry, such as racks of 4.5-inch barrage rockets used to plaster hard-to-reach shore installations and batteries. Mortars were installed on some boats; one boat even experimented with mounting a 75mm gun. The crew eventually removed the big weapon, since its rate of fire was too slow.

The introduction of an improved version of the Mk 13 aerial torpedo ranks as another major advance in PT weaponry. The Mk 13 outdid the World War I–vintage Mk 8 in every category, being faster by a good 5 knots (33.5 vs. 28), packing twice the warhead (600 pounds vs. 300), and being shorter, more reliable, and side-dropping, allowing the boats to rid themselves of the big bulky torpedo tubes. For PTs everywhere, the weight savings alone made the Mk 13 worth its weight in extra armament.

Being so superbly equipped, and protected by Allied air cover, the boats even began venturing out in the daylight, sometimes in tandem with destroyers. By the time MacArthur moved on Biak in June 1944 and Cape Sansapor on the Vogelkop Peninsula in late July, the Allies enjoyed nearly absolute air and naval superiority in New Guinea waters. The PTs, now totaling fourteen squadrons of roughly twelve boats each, naturally moved forward in support of these final amphibious adventures, though they encountered fewer and fewer barges as the Allied steamroller moved west.

When October arrived the navy transferred forty-five boats north to the Philippines from the giant PT base at Mios Woendi, south of Biak. It sent many more in the coming days. The remaining PTs spent most of their final weeks of the campaign locating and evacuating former Japanese prisoners of war.

Throughout twenty-three months of nearly continuous patrolling in New Guinea waters, PTs sank or destroyed an estimated 486 barges, possibly sank 10 others, and damaged 40. In addition they sank 2 small cargo ships, 6 luggers, 1 picket boat, 1 submersible barge, and 31 canoes. Again, these totals do not truly begin to tell the story of the carnage the PTs wrought, in conjunction with Allied airmen and soldiers. Along the coast they left behind "the wreckage of hundreds of blasted barges," and inland the "bodies of thousands of [Japanese] soldiers who died for lack of supplies."[26]

Torpedo actions were predictably few and far between. According to Bulkley, the New Guinea PTs fired a total of only thirty torpedoes the entire time, the same number fired by the boats in Blackett Strait the night PT-109 sank. They claimed four submarines sunk or damaged, though none were confirmed. A derelict merchant ship, the

In the Pacific to stay. PTs tied to finger piers at Camp Taylor, Mios Woendi, the largest PT base in New Guinea, September 1944. *National Archives*

Oigawa Maru, and one 200-foot minelayer were the PTs' only torpedo victims.[27]

In New Guinea's shallow, reef-infested waters, PT boats came into their own, emerging as an unambiguously effective first-tier response to changing Japanese tactics. This fortuitous transition required faith in the boats' basic design—and a whole lot more gunpower. The resulting disparity between the PT's gunboat and torpedo functions did not, however, signal the end of the PT as a torpedo boat. The transformation to gunboat was not universal, but geared to local operating conditions. It is now time to examine a far different set of such operating conditions, half a world away in the Mediterranean.

CHAPTER TEN

From Lend-Lease to Leyte Gulf

*I*n retrospect, it is obvious why the United States Navy committed roughly 80% of the PT boats it commissioned during World War II to the Pacific Theater: The navy fought its main show against Japan. In purely tactical terms, the Pacific also proved extremely conducive to PT operations—at least for the PT as gunboat. Further, Japanese aggression had helped shape the PT program's destiny from the beginning. It spurred funding for the experimental PT program in 1938, encouraged Charles Edison to accelerate the pace of experimentation in 1939–40, and determined the initial deployment of the first operational boats in 1941.

Ironically, the navy's purpose in the prewar years had been to create a torpedo boat, not a hybrid gunboat. In this respect, and viewed strictly from hindsight, the navy's effort to thwart the Japanese by building PT boats was misguided. In the case of the Germans and Italians, however, the navy's experimental MTB initiative proved to be more on the mark.

From the spring of 1941, when the navy transferred the first batch of experimental Elco-70s to the British under Lend-Lease, American industry had supplied increasing numbers of MTBs to British Coastal Forces. In the spring of 1943, the United States Navy took a more direct interest in assisting its British cousins, assigning Squadron Fifteen, eighteen boats (PTs 201–218) under Lt. Comdr. Stanley M. Barnes, USN, to work with Coastal Forces in the Mediterranean.

This deployment proved advantageous for several reasons. Firstly, Squadron Fifteen had originally been slated for service at Midway Island, by the winter of 1943 a relative backwater. It would have been of little value there. Secondly, the PTs would be doing what they did best: support active coastal land operations. Thirdly, at least during the spring of 1943, the squadron composed almost the only strictly offen-

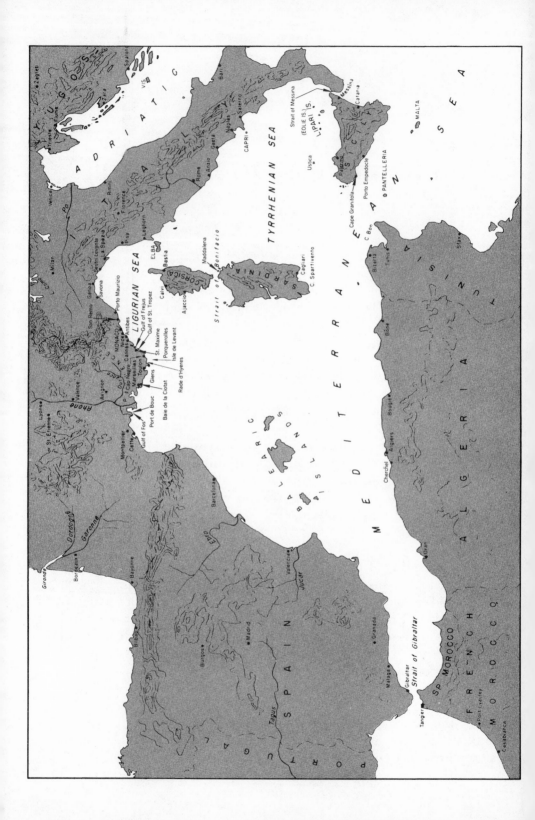

sive force the United States Navy had in the Mediterranean. Its presence demonstrated solidarity with the Royal Navy at a time when the U.S. Navy's main commitments were elsewhere. Lastly, the Americans benefited from British experience—and the British benefited from American radar.

Radar proved the key to the PTs' usefulness in the Mediterranean, a notion the navy seems to have appreciated from the start. Ten of Squadron Fifteen's boats were equipped with a set even before leaving the United States; the first eight arrived without radar, but all had it installed within three months after beginning operations, by July 1943. Compare the preponderance of radar in Squadron Fifteen to the South and Southwest Pacific squadrons during that same summer. The latter were lucky to have four boats out of fifteen with radar on the night of August 1/2 in the Blackett Strait battle. Even so, the emphasis on the value of the Mediterranean PTs' radar should not imply that the navy regarded the PTs themselves as otherwise irrelevant. Stanley Barnes, one of the "most dashing of PT men," in either the Pacific or European Theaters, was not about to let that happen.[1]

Barnes's first four boats arrived in Gibraltar aboard a fleet oiler on April 13. They proceeded on their own power first to Oran, then to Bone in eastern Algeria, at the time the most advanced naval base possessed by the Torch invasion forces in North Africa. They were to attack, in conjunction with British MTBs and MGBs, ships supplying the beleaguered German and Italian armies in Tunisia. Some 275,000 Axis troops eventually surrendered in mid-May, the Italian navy making no attempt to evacuate them.

The PTs meanwhile began joint patrols on April 28, though they did not make their first contact with the enemy until May 8/9. Barnes rode PT-206 quietly into the blackness of Ras Idda Bay, on the east side of Cape Bon, and torpedoed and blew up what later turned out to be a German tanker. So far so good. The promise of scoring in the Mediterranean was very real. So too were the hazards. Within minutes Barnes had to dodge two torpedoes fired at him by the MTB leader. That same night, PT-203 had to pull the crew off a grounded MTB while under fire from a German fort. And two nights later, three PTs were fired on and chased for over an hour by two British destroyers involved in a confused melee with two German E-boats. In the process the PTs strafed one of the German craft, leaving it burning. The British, who were operating out of their assigned patrol area, later apologized.

Such friendly-fire problems arising from the joint PT–MTB operations were inevitably the result of that "old bugbear of varying communication procedure and equipment as well as disparities in doctrine."[2]

Lt. Comdr. Stanley M. Barnes, USN. *PT Boats, Inc.*

In any event, after a few weeks the problems subsided as the two allies worked congenially to iron out the bugs. The German E-boats, however, were around to stay. They became the PTs' chief foe in both the Mediterranean and the English Channel.

The E-boat, or *Schnellboot* (German for "fast boat"), was the enviable product of ongoing German MTB experimentation between the wars. Though characteristics varied, the basic E-boat was about 115 feet long and was driven by three diesel engines at speeds of up to 42 knots. Its wood hull, backed by a light metal frame, was of a round-bilge displacement type, making the E-boat extremely seaworthy. Armament consisted of four torpedoes for two bow tubes, a 40mm gun, and one or more 20mm guns.

The E-boat blended gunboat-torpedo functions very well, so that no less astute an observer of fast attack craft than John Bulkeley came to express "great admiration" for its design.[3] Their crews were every bit as deserving of that admiration as well; they were as bold and tenacious as any of the British and American MTB men, and were equally determined to win.

Fortunately, the E-boats did not win. After the Allies rolled up the Axis armies in North Africa, they attacked Sicily (10 July 1943); invaded Italy at Salerno (9 September 1943) and Anzio (22 January 1944); overran Elba (17 June 1944); and landed in southern France (15 August 1944). The PTs took an active part in all these landings as part of the U.S. Eighth Fleet, or, in the case of Elba, as part of a special Coastal Forces task group. Between times they patrolled as an operational, but not administrative, element of British Coastal Forces.

Sicily set the tone for PT invasion operations. After the Allies secured North Africa, the remainder of Squadron Fifteen's boats arrived from the United States. They patrolled the western coast of Sicily in tandem with British MTBs and MGBs, landed agents of the OSS (Office of Strategic Services, the forerunner of the CIA), and performed long-range reconnaissance missions. On 11 June 1943 Allied forces took the island of Pantelleria, 60 miles southwest of Sicily. PTs helped patrol in case the Italian garrison attempted evacuation. The garrison did not make such an attempt, but that did not stop the Axis from dive-bombing the boats. The planes dropped thirty to forty bombs, killing one man with shrapnel—the first PT casualty in the Mediterranean.

During the Sicily invasion itself, PTs acted as E-boat screens and helped stage a noisy mock invasion of Cape Granitola, which temporarily had the desired effect of keeping some Axis forces away from the invasion beachhead. These activities—special operations, E-boat screening, reconnaissance, staging mock invasions, and even running generals around—became part and parcel of the PT experience in the Italian and southern France invasions as well. The PTs performed admirably in these functions, but few truly required the attention of fast, radar-equipped torpedo boats. Only between invasions did they really get the chance to show the enemy what they could do.

That opportunity began knocking after Gen. George S. Patton's advancing troops took Palermo. From that northern Sicilian port the boats patrolled the Strait of Messina, to prevent the evacuation of Axis troops to the Italian mainland. On July 24, off Palmi, three PTs torpedoed an 8,800-ton Italian merchant ship and strafed the tug towing it, which later sank. Three nights later the PTs had their first disquieting

With the invasion fleet off Salerno, Italy, 12 September 1943. The two boats are Higgins-78s. *National Archives*

encounter with F-lighters, coastal cargo vessels slated to become their chief prey in the Mediterranean.

In a sense, F-lighters became to Mediterranean PTs what Japanese barges were to Pacific PTs. Beyond that, however, all similarity between the two craft ends. F-lighters were much larger, seagoing vessels "170 feet long, with a cargo carrying capacity of about 120 tons, and their [steel] hulls were so well compartmented that it was impossible for PTs to sink them with anything less than a torpedo hit." On the night of their first encounter, and in subsequent engagements with these craft, the PTs found "that it was foolish to try to fight them with guns; the F-lighters [bristling with 76mm and 20mm guns and machine guns] were far more heavily armed than the PTs and far less vulnerable to gunfire."[4]

During the slow, painful Allied drive north up the mountainous Italian peninsula, from September 1943 to the end of the war, growing Allied airpower forced the German army to rely increasingly on these F-lighters, and a host of other small coastal vessels, to convoy supplies at night from ports in the Gulf of Genoa down the peninsula's west coast. Unlike New Guinea, the Italian coast had few reefs to keep out enemy destroyers, so the Germans planted scores of minefields along the convoy routes. They also set up shore batteries, only these guns were of the 6-to-8-inch variety, not the light infantry guns the Japanese generally used. E-boats, small coastal destroyers, and other armed vessels, including converted, heavily armed F-lighters called Flak-lighters, provided close support.

F-lighter design and the strategic and tactical conditions under which the Axis powers were forced to operate them dictated Allied countermeasures to these formidable convoys. Allied aircraft blasted them by day. The job of hunting and sinking them while en route at night fell to British Coastal Forces, since the minefields effectively kept destroyers and other blue-water combatants at bay. To reach the convoy routes, Coastal Forces set up a base at Bastia, on the northeast coast of Corsica, in mid-October 1943. Squadron Fifteen soon joined them there, and the hunt was on.

Though the PTs scored some success on their own, managing to torpedo and sink an F-lighter in late July, a corvette in October, and a subchaser in early November, tactically they were in a bit of a bind. As we have seen, the Mk 8 torpedoes carried by the PTs were slow, weak, and generally unreliable. They often proved to be duds, or tended to behave erratically, especially when set to run as close to the surface as possible to take on shallow-draft F-lighters. The PTs themselves (Higgins-78s) were undergunned, no match for the lighters or their escorts in a straight fight. They did, however, have radar.

The wood-hulled PTs and MTBs could not afford to expose themselves to all the direct, heavy-caliber fire from Axis convoys and shore batteries. Doctrine therefore called for sneak attacks, using radar if possible to track targets and set up an approach angle. The boats would idle in, fire torpedoes before the enemy became aware of their presence, then hightail it, maneuvering at high speed and making smoke if necessary.

Since the PTs had radar but lacked decent torpedoes and heavy deck armament, Lieutenant Barnes formulated a joint tactical plan with the British in November 1943. Each type of Allied small combatant would do what it did best, relying on the other types to make up for what it lacked. The PTs provided the radar for convoy tracking, the MTBs the reliable torpedoes for making the actual torpedo attack, and the MGBs the heavier gunpower to deal with enemy counterfire.

Barnes's plan worked well, though even in combination with the PTs, Coastal Forces possessed insufficient strength to do more than harass and dent the traffic, far less to cripple the convoy system itself. From November to the end of April 1944, despite lots of stormy win-

ter weather, the joint British–PT patrols engaged enemy convoys fourteen times. They sank 15 F-lighters, 2 E-boats, 1 tug, and 1 oil barge.
Enemy vessels damaged included 3 F-lighters, 1 destroyer, 1 trawler,
and 1 E-boat. Alone during the same period PTs met the enemy ten
times. They claimed 1 F-lighter sunk, 1 E-boat damaged, and a possible hit on a small coaster.

Not all the actions were offensive—or successful. On two occasions,
small Italian coastal "torpedo boat" destroyers, manned by Germans,
raided Bastia. The second time (December 18/19) the PTs drove them
off, firing seventeen torpedoes in the process. None hit. The same dismal score resulted when three PTs attacked two of the small, fast destroyers in February. The boats launched five torpedoes; again none
hit. The problem here even Robert Whitehead would have recognized:
a slow torpedo (the Mk 8) trying to catch too fast a target. Happily,
early May saw Squadron Fifteen's conversion to the faster, more lethal
Mk 13, and the addition of 40mm guns on the stern of each boat.

May also saw the addition of two new PT squadrons to the Mediterranean, Twenty-two (Higgins) and Twenty-nine (Elco), both of which
already had the Mk 13. Barnes assumed overall command, splitting the
three squadrons between Bastia and Calvi, on Corsica's west coast. This
extended the area of operations farther west. In May and June the
boats claimed three corvettes sunk and another permanently crippled.

The invasion of southern France kept the PTs busy in the summer
of 1944. The boats, eventually operating from bases on French soil,
created the usual diversions, landed troops to capture coastal batteries,
and even maintained a daily blood bank shuttle. Two PTs were lost
when mines blew their sterns off. At the end of August they drove off
or sank numerous explosive boats and human torpedoes. None ever
got through to the invasion fleet. It was all in a night's work.

Throughout the summer, patrols out of Bastia continued. The
boats harassed more coastal convoys and sank or damaged more barges
and F-lighters, though again not enough to make the cost of running
the convoys prohibitive to the Axis. The traffic only ceased in the winter of 1944–45 during the general Axis collapse.

By September 1944, PT operations had begun to wind down.
Squadron Fifteen's boats were turned over to the British under Lend-
Lease in October, and the squadron was decommissioned. Squadron
Twenty-nine was withdrawn from operations on October 28; eight of
the boats were Lend-Leased to Russia, four went to the PT training cen-
ter in Melville. Squadron Twenty-two operated over the winter from
Leghorn on the Italian mainland. Patrolling was hazardous, with rough
seas tearing mines loose; PT-311 hit one and sank, and 10 men died.
On 28 April 1945, the PTs made their last patrol, though with all the

ports in friendly hands by that time there seemed little point. The navy shipped the squadron home shortly afterward, ending the PT's war in the Mediterranean.[5]

Since the PT remained first and foremost a torpedo boat in the Mediterranean, the "box score" cited in Bulkley's *At Close Quarters* is a valid way of summing up their activities:

> The three squadrons had operated in the Mediterranean for 2 years. Their losses were four boats destroyed by mines; 5 officers and 19 men killed in action; 7 officers and 28 men wounded in action. They fired 354 torpedoes and claimed on their own to have sunk 38 vessels totaling 23,700 tons and to have damaged 49, totaling 22,600 tons; and in joint patrols with British boats to have sunk 15 vessels totaling 13,000 tons and to have damaged 17, totaling 5,650 tons.[6]

Of special note is a conclusion Lieutenant Barnes reached at the end of his tour of duty as PT commander in the Mediterranean. He originally felt joint PT–MTB patrols would not work, because of the "radical differences which exist between British and U.S. boats with regard to communications equipment and procedure, military characteristics of boats, and tactical doctrine." That, though, was before the PTs acquired radar and joint patrols began out of Bastia. There the crews of the PTs and British boats developed a workable joint tactical doctrine, proving small craft of different types could work together—provided teamwork existed. This prompted Barnes to conclude that "successful [joint] operations require only tactical unity and not homogeneous types."[7]

This conclusion is interesting in a broad historical sense. Recall Charles Edison's reasoning behind his controversial request for funding the original twenty-three Elco-70s in 1939. At the time he and his naval advisors believed operational testing with the fleet required a "homogeneous unit" of PTs to be successful. While homogeneity certainly would have simplified testing, Barnes's experience in the Mediterranean indicates such standardization need not have been a prerequisite.

Before turning to the last major PT campaign of World War II, the Philippines, brief mention should be made of the PTs that took part in the Normandy invasion and of subsequent operations in the English Channel.

As the official history points out, the English Channel was British Coastal Forces' own backyard. From the invasion of France in the spring of 1940, Coastal Forces had been in action almost continuously, both preying on German coastal convoys and protecting Allied shipping from E-boats. According to Lt. Comdr. Peter Scott's *The Battle of the Narrow Seas*, the British rough equivalent of Bulkley's *At Close Quarters*, British MTBs, MGBs, and MLs claimed 269 enemy vessels sunk or probably sunk, against the loss of 76 of their own. Only with the increased demand for naval escort and patrol vessels of all kinds for the 1944 Normandy invasion did the Allies see a need for PTs.[8]

A total of thirty-three boats participated. The OSS made use of three boats, commanded by the irrepressible John Bulkeley. They began operations in May, mostly landing and picking up intelligence agents in France in preparation for D-day. The others arrived either right before or after the start of the invasion on June 6. They formed anti-E-boat screens, helped rescue survivors from stricken ships, and ran more than their fair share of important generals and admirals onto the invasion beaches. Probably their most important contribution, since there were no E-boat attacks in their patrol area, was to douse strings of float flares the Germans planted two nights in a row, to guide night bombers to the fleet standing off the beaches. Unable to see, the planes dropped their bombs wide of the mark.

By the end of June other PTs patrolled to the west off Cherbourg. Little happened, except on the evening of the 27th. As American troops battled their way into the city, the navy ordered two boats, commanded by Bulkeley, to make a close approach to the Cherbourg breakwater to see if the harbor fort guns were still in action. They were; the boats beat a hasty retreat after one was nearly hit by a shell from a "large-caliber battery." It conked out the PT's engines for a long five minutes before the engineers could get them going again. No one was hurt. In retrospect, the boats were lucky. It is odd the navy chose to risk them in such a fashion. Bulkeley's derring-do reputation may have played a role, though the decision probably stemmed from the boats' well-deserved reputation of being hard to hit from shore.

By early August the navy had withdrawn PTs from the invasion area, sending eighteen to patrol the Channel Islands, Jersey, Guernsey, and Alderney, to disrupt enemy shipping between them and the French mainland. Their first action came on the night of August 8/9. Off Jersey in a thick fog, a destroyer vectored five boats in two sections into attack positions against six German minesweepers. They fired nine torpedoes; all missed. While moving in to attack, PT-509 hung her bow up on one of the minesweepers. Germans raked the deck with small arms while desperately trying to free themselves from the burning PT. The boat sank; all but one man perished.

In two subsequent actions with minesweepers, the boats fired eight more torpedoes. None hit. By mid-August, Allied forces had taken the coast and traffic dried up. Thereafter, over the winter and into the spring of 1945, some boats were retained in Cherbourg to escort convoys and to patrol to prevent German personnel from the Channel Islands from escaping to the mainland. They saw virtually no surface action.

Farther east, in early August other PTs augmented a successful attempt by Coastal Forces to prevent the German reinforcement and eventual evacuation of Le Havre. Most of the battles against German E-boats, trawlers, minesweepers, and other small craft were gun battles. On four occasions in August, however, the PTs fired an estimated total of twenty torpedoes. Only one probably hit anything—a tank landing craft. Le Havre fell the first week in September and the battle subsided. Most of the boats were soon Lend-Leased to Russia.[9]

So ended the American MTB experience in the European Theater. In two years the boats, composing only 20% of the entire United States PT fleet, fired more torpedoes at the enemy than did the other 80% serving in the Pacific over a period nearly twice as long. The implication is obvious: In European waters the PTs' intended torpedo function remained dominant, whereas in the Pacific it did not. This result could be expected. Americans originally conceived the PT boat to keep pace with European torpedo boat development. British notions of what MTBs were supposed to accomplish in European waters heavily influenced its very design. Ironically, during the war British Coastal Forces did well enough on its own, rendering the PT by and large unnecessary in Europe. Thus where PTs were most at home as torpedo boats, they were also most redundant.

Back in the Pacific Theater, PTs were anything but redundant. The Allies needed all they could find, and with good reason: The time had come to make good on General MacArthur's pledge to return to the Philippines—the very place the PT had first established its fast, hard-hitting reputation in the dark early days of 1942.

On 20 October 1944, a massive Allied invasion force, of a size and complexity dwarfing anything thought possible two years earlier, landed troops on the east coast of Leyte, three months ahead of the original JCS schedule. Meanwhile, five squadrons of PTs, forty-five boats in all, had sailed from Mios Woendi on October 13. Accompanied by three tenders, the boats refueled at Palau in the Marianas and reached Leyte on the morning of October 21, the day after the landings.

The uses to which the PT was eventually assigned in the Philippines will by now sound quite familiar: barge-hunting, strafing shore installations, rescue work, landing troops and famous returning generals and reconnaissance parties, providing escort and extra antiaircraft fire-

MacArthur returning to the Philippines on board PT-525, October 1944. At right is Lt. Gen. Walter C. Krueger, commander of the U.S. Sixth Army. *National Archives*

power for landing craft, even stalking occasional destroyers and possible submarines. Before they could settle into any of these missions, however, the Japanese struck back.

The Japanese could not ignore the Allied landing at Leyte. It came as an unacceptable breach of their inner island defense perimeter. The Imperial Japanese Navy therefore responded by committing the cream of its still-formidable surface fleet to crush it. A Northern Force, built around Japan's remaining carriers and a handful of planes, was to serve as a decoy to lure Admiral Halsey's supporting carrier fleet to the north, away from the invasion beachhead at Leyte Gulf. Then a Center Force and Southern Force, both consisting of battleships, cruisers, and destroyers, would launch a simultaneous pincers movement against the invasion shipping itself, and annihilate it.

The Japanese plan resulted in a four-day clash with the American and Australian navies known collectively as the Battle of Leyte Gulf, from 23–26 October 1944. It ranks as the greatest naval battle of all time in terms of the sheer numbers of men and ships involved. Fittingly, the battle also involved more PT boats in a single engagement than any other campaign of the war.

To counter the Center Force approach eastward through the San Bernardino Strait, north of Samar, the navy employed Admiral Halsey's powerful Third Fleet, consisting of the big carriers and fast battleships. Though things did not quite turn out that way, the subject of much controversy over the years, this huge aspect of the battle is not our concern here.[10]

Our interest is in the Southern Force, detected by air reconnaissance on the morning of October 24 heading east through the Sulu Sea toward Surigao Strait, south of Leyte itself. It consisted of two uncoordinated groups. The first, commanded by Vice Adm. Shoji Nishimura, comprised two battleships, one heavy cruiser, and four destroyers; the second group, lagging about forty miles behind the first, was made up of two heavy cruisers, one light cruiser, and four destroyers, under the command of Vice Adm. Kiyohide Shima.

To stop this prong, Rear Adm. Jesse B. Oldendorf, with six old but modernized battleships and a host of cruisers and destroyers, was ordered to take up positions at the northern end of the Surigao Strait on the night of the 24th. There they would wait to slug it out with the far smaller Japanese force. Prior to that gritty prospect, the Japanese would also have to run a gauntlet, one made up of PTs.

Thirty-nine boats out of the original forty-five were in shape to put to sea that night. They were organized into thirteen sections of three boats each and told to lie to at various advantageous choke points along the supposed Japanese route into Surigao Strait, and inside the strait itself. As the fleet temporarily lacked night-flying patrol planes, the PTs' first mission was to report all radar or visual contacts, then attack independently.

Conditions for torpedo attack were excellent—a smooth, glassy sea, partly overcast skies, occasional rain squalls, no moon after midnight. The first PTs made radar contact with Nishimura's group shortly before 11 p.m. The boats were soon illuminated by star shells and straddled by destroyer gunfire, forcing them to beat a hasty retreat by zigzagging violently and making smoke. By the time they were able to send off a contact report, it was after midnight. Admiral Oldendorf received it at 12:26 a.m., October 25. That one report, "the first definite information received by him of the enemy since around 1000 the previous morning," was all he needed. "It confirmed the wisdom of his dispositions, and required no change in his battle plan."[11]

As it turned out, that contact report and others like it constituted the lion's share of the PTs' contribution to the subsequent route of Nishimura's and Shima's two battle forces that night. Samuel Eliot Morison notes:

It was the same story right up the Strait. Each succeeding motor torpedo boat section along the enemy's course observed gun flashes of the previous fight; made contact itself; attempted to get off its report (and sometimes did); went in for attack; fired torpedoes which missed; became brightly illuminated by enemy searchlights; came under brisk but inaccurate gunfire, and retired under a smoke screen.[12]

There are two notable exceptions to the above description. PT-493 was hit by three 4.7-inch shells from an all too accurate destroyer. Two men were killed, five wounded. The crew managed to beach it, but later the tide lifted the boat off and it sank in deep water—the only U.S. warship to be sunk in the Surigao Strait battle. As for the torpedo record, 15 boats fired 35 torpedoes, of which only one is known to have *not* missed—and even that was an accident. PT-137 tried to torpedo a destroyer but missed, hitting Shima's light cruiser, the *Abukuma*, in the bow. The cruiser slowed to 10 knots and dropped out of formation. Army bombers sank her the next day off Mindanao.[13]

Shima's force never did catch up with Nishimura's. It retired without hardly even getting into the battle, while the latter admiral's entire force, with the exception of one destroyer, was blasted by Oldendorf's destroyers, cruisers, and battleships later that morning. For the United States Navy, it was a magnificently one-sided sweep.

For the PTs, however, the battle must rank as a magnificent disappointment. Conditions were excellent. They had first crack at both Japanese task groups, yet out of thirty-five torpedoes fired, only one— or possibly two—hits were confirmed. What caused such a dismal score is, oddly enough, the same reason the English Channel boats did so poorly: inexperience.

Morison writes:

[Attacking Japanese ships in the Surigao Strait] was just what the PT sailors had been longing to do. Their boats, designed for fast, hit-and-run torpedo attacks on enemy ships, had had little or no torpedo experience since the struggle for Guadalcanal and the action in Blackett Strait on 2 August 1943. In the Southwest Pacific, as in the South Pacific, they had been usefully employed as patrol craft and fast gunboats, but torpedo training had been neglected. The only "fish" that most of them had fired since 1943 was in a practice before departing Mios Woendi.[14]

Yet as in so many instances in the past, the PTs managed to make a worthwhile contribution despite their poor torpedo record. Admiral Nimitz summed up their value in the fight as follows:

The skill, determination, and courage displayed by the personnel of these small boats is worthy of the highest praise. Their contact reports, as well as the firing and illumination they drew from the enemy, gave ample warning to our own main body; and while the issue of the later main engagement was never in doubt, the PTs' action very probably threw the Japanese command off balance and contributed to the completeness of their subsequent defeat.[15]

Despite their questionable torpedo performance, in other words, the crews earned their pay that night.

In the remaining months of the war, in the Philippines and off Morotai and Okinawa, PT crews earned their pay over and over again. No attempt will be made here, though, to describe these final operations. The reason is partly to save space, but mainly to drive home a point: By the fall of 1944, PT boats were a permanent fixture of the colossal Allied war machine that had marched across the South and Southwest Pacific to Imperial Japan's very doorstep. The many important, diverse missions they performed in the final months were essentially the same ones they performed to such a high professional degree in New Guinea and the Solomons.

We have come then to the end of the story of the American PT. When World War II came to a violent end amid the radioactive ruins of Hiroshima and Nagasaki, the wood PTs, unlike steel-hulled craft that could be stored away, were either scrapped or sold off. In the Philippines, 118 especially broken and battle-worn boats were stripped of equipment and burned right on the beach on Samar. A few were kept for experimental purposes, but soon even these went the way of the MAS boats and CMBs of old. By 1962, none could even be found to film the movie *PT 109*. The studio had to outbid Fidel Castro for three air-sea rescue craft, which were later converted to PTs. The American PT, born in 1940, had lived usefully all of five years.[16]

What five years! If the accolades PTs received from the navy brass are any clue, they were well worth every dime spent on their short, eventful careers. Though many regular navy men considered PTs part of the "hooligan navy," no less a regular navy man than Admiral King himself defended their worth on several occasions.

King first praised their performance in the southern Solomons. Their repeated attacks on Japanese surface craft, he wrote, made the Japanese realize they could never "sufficiently improve" their position by continued night landings of supplies and reinforcements alone. The

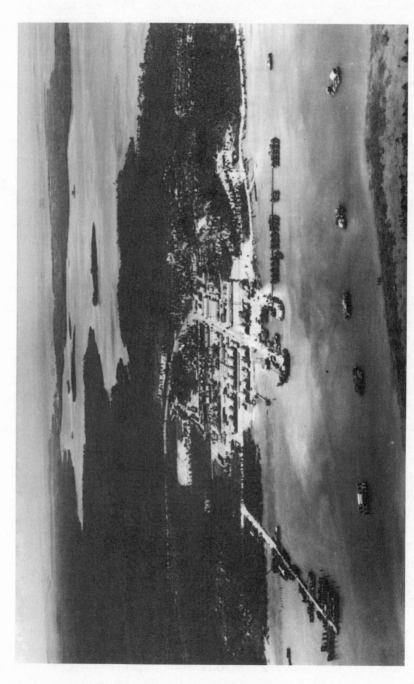

PT Base 17 on Bobon Point, Samar, Philippines, in mid-1945. Said to be the largest, most complete motor torpedo boat base in the world, Base 17 gives testimony to the transformation of the PT from a specialized weapon of opportunity into an integrated component of the Allied juggernaut. *Naval Historical Center*

result: the decisive Naval Battle of Guadalcanal. Later King lauded the PTs' "admirable service" in New Guinea, where they roamed "east and west along the coast, harassing enemy barge traffic and preventing reinforcements from being put ashore."

Admiral Nimitz, in addition to praising the Surigao Strait PTs, felt the boats and their crews "turned in a highly creditable performance" during the war. Admiral Leahy, who served on the JCS with King, was more specific in his praise. He thought the boats he helped win funding for in 1938 "became excellent substitutes for destroyers."[17] His description is fitting; it helps us define the PT's overall naval role during World War II. Still, we can go one better.

Judging from the varied uses to which PT boats were put, the navy came to look upon them as miniature versions of virtually every ship in the United States naval arsenal. Whenever the real thing was unavailable, too deep-draft, or too big a target for enemy planes, the PTs were there, providing gunfire support for amphibious landings, torpedoing and gunning for enemy ships and small craft, landing troops, and even dropping off secret agents in rubber boats.

Perhaps the most eloquent summation of this versatility comes from a former PT officer seldom at a loss for eloquent summations, John F. Kennedy. "PT boats," he wrote from the White House, "filled an important need in World War II in shallow waters, complementing the achievements of greater ships in greater seas."[18]

This is the PT's wartime legacy, indeed the legacy of all the small Allied torpedo boats and gunboats that served in World War II. The Allies would probably have beaten the Axis without their many gallant contributions, but would have had to pay an even higher price.

EPILOGUE

The PT as Torpedo Boat: An Assessment of Value

*T*he PT boat is something of an anomaly in American naval history. In the beginning, the young republic wanted fast ships that packed plenty of firepower and could keep the sea for long periods on distant station. Later, as the colonial outlook gave way to pretensions of national greatness, big ships and big guns became the rage. Small torpedo boats were considered an irrelevancy.

That attitude appeared to change in the mid-1930s, as the United States geared up for likely involvement in another general European war. The navy's bureau system generated the idea of building motor torpedo boats to keep pace with similar European developments. Experimentation began, its pace accelerated by Assistant Secretary of the Navy Charles Edison's rush to build an operational "homogeneous unit" of the PTs for service tests with the fleet.

Because of Edison's administrative zeal, twenty-nine PTs were on the firing line when the Japanese attacked Pearl Harbor. Dozens more were on order. Their anticipated mission: to conduct stealthy, hit-and-run torpedo attacks on enemy ships. The PTs did so on numerous occasions, their apparent successes catching the eye of the wartime public. Woe to the Axis Goliaths having the misfortune of crossing wakes with the Yankee Davids! After the war, however, the PT's legendary reputation as a big-ship killer suffered in the history books.

In 1953, Samuel Eliot Morison, author of the monumental fifteen-volume series *History of United States Naval Operations in World War II*, viewed postwar damage assessment surveys, noted the PTs' dismally low "box score" of ships actually confirmed sunk or damaged, and labeled the PT "useless" as a torpedo boat. He called their attacks "futile" and "suicidal."[1] While Morison had nothing but praise for the PT as gunboat, he clearly believed it would have been best if the American navy had continued to ignore the PT's potential as a small torpedo boat.

Morison's contention that PT torpedo attacks were suicidal is not supported by PT casualty figures. We have seen that while losses naturally did occur, over the decades small torpedo boat crews rarely suffered the heavy casualties naval observers feared they would. They were simply too small, maneuverable, and hard to see in the dark to be hit consistently. On the other hand, Morison's belief that PTs were useless as torpedo boats, their attacks futile, is definitely a notion worthy of further analysis. It turns out the word "useless" is a poor choice: PTs were *unsuccessful* as torpedo boats, but hardly useless.

For the PT to be successful as torpedo boat, it had to have three things going for it: exploitable attack opportunities; reliable equipment, especially its torpedo; and competent, experienced crews. Rarely did all three occur together; rarely, therefore, was the PT successful in a torpedo role.

As we have seen, except in the Philippines, at Guadalcanal, and in isolated battles like Surigao Strait, PTs in the Pacific had few torpedo targets. Obviously, this vastly diminished their value as torpedo boats, though it does not account for the PT's poor showing per se.

There are two primary reasons PTs were unsuccessful as torpedo boats. The first is the Mk 8 torpedo. It is unknown how many of these World War I–vintage "fish" hit home but failed to explode, ran erratically, or exploded but were too undercharged to do any real damage. Postwar studies reported that more than half of the Mk 8s were duds.[2] This bad torpedo heavily undercut much of the success the early PTs might have enjoyed as torpedo boats.

Another limiting success factor, one that even tended to offset the improved performance of the later Mk 13 torpedo, is crew inexperience.

The PT was a specialized weapon. It required a great deal of specialized training and practice to master the art of lining up a boat, often under fire, to shoot torpedoes effectively at a darkened, fast-moving enemy ship. Few of the officers were hard-core navy men like Bulkeley and Barnes—or William Cushing. They were reservists like Kennedy, called up by the thousands because of the wartime emergency. This suggests nothing derogatory about their intelligence or willingness to fight; most inexperienced reservists simply lacked the training to deliver a PT torpedo attack successfully. Couple this to the fact that most of them seldom ever *made* an actual torpedo attack, because of the boats' primary employment as gunboats, and the poor showing of the boats on the whole is readily explained.

Other factors contributed. PTs were small, often tossed about by the sea, making precise coastal navigation and torpedo sighting difficult. The radar sets installed on the later boats were small, too, less effective than those placed on larger warships like destroyers. The jarring of the boats often upset their radios, knocking them off their assigned frequencies and leaving the boats deaf.

To all this add a lack of adequate logistics and maintenance facilities for the boats, especially during the first Philippine and Guadalcanal campaigns. The high-performance standards of the PTs, their constant usage, and the greater demands placed on naval maintenance commands by the blue-water fleet often left them in poor shape to fight—or even to put to sea at all.

None of the above is meant to imply that the PTs themselves were poorly designed, or so technically deficient as to render them useless, or unsuccessful, as torpedo boats from the start. If a PT boat had a decent opportunity to attack, possessed an experienced, determined crew, and had reliable torpedoes, it could be—and at times was!—a formidable torpedo-delivery vehicle. If any of these three things were not present, and they frequently were not, the attack generally failed.

From this a fascinating contradiction emerges. PTs were technically sound, for the times, but unsuccessful as torpedo boats, whereas William Cushing's picket boat *No. 1* was technically deficient but ultimately successful as a torpedo boat. The reason for this strange twist is understandable in view of the PT's later experiences: *No. 1* had a readily exploitable opportunity to attack the *Albemarle*, which for several months rotted in its lair practically asking to be sunk. It also had Cushing, an extremely competent, experienced, and determined officer. Lastly, while *No. 1*'s spar torpedo was too unwieldy to be of much practical use, when it was supposed to work, it did. Many a PT crewman in 1943 or 1944, whether staring into the darkness or into the harsh glare of a destroyer's searchlight, would have given many a prayer for a torpedo as ultimately reliable as the one dangling on the end of William Cushing's spar eighty years earlier.

During World War II, over five-hundred PTs were built in American yards. With the exception of thirty-six boats Lend-Leased to the USSR and Great Britain before commissioning, all served for varying lengths of time under American colors. According to the official history, all those PT boats fired only about 700 torpedoes during the entire war, as follows:

Campaign	Number Expended	Average number per boat
Philippines I	18	3
Guadalcanal	111	5
Central Solomons	53	less than 1
New Guinea	30	less than 1
Mediterranean	354	8
English Channel	37	1
Philippines II	94	less than 1
Total:	697	1.6

Approximately 350 PTs served in the Pacific, while only 33 served in the Channel and 42 in the Mediterranean. Two squadrons saw service in the Aleutian Islands between September 1942 and May 1944. They were wasted there, accomplishing nothing but staying afloat in the icy, storm-tossed waters. Considering the tremendous disparity between the two global theaters, the overwhelming majority of PT boats in World War II fired less than two torpedoes, and probably less than one, during their entire operational existence. Obviously, the average PT had little opportunity to actually launch its fish.[3] Nor from 1943 onward did it spend much time bothering to do so.

The above statistics give one pause. The navy conceived and built the PT as a torpedo boat, yet it spent relatively little time being one once it found full expression overseas. It is fair, therefore, to ask if the navy made a mistake in investing in PTs.

The question is answerable only in the context of the times, and that answer must be no. The United States Navy was more than justified in experimenting with PT boats in the late 1930s. Given the growing threat of war and the strong likelihood that similar European MTBs might have to be either counteracted or reinforced, it would have been negligent of the navy to continue ignoring their potential.

The prewar navy was also justified in building the particular PT boat it did. During the war, after the PT's torpedo function waned, the PT's hull and engines gave the Allies a readily available, mass-producible, seaworthy, fast, maneuverable, shallow-draft gun platform for dealing with Japanese coast-hugging logistical traffic—that is, a gunboat.

PT-601, one of the last Elco-80s, built in 1945. While the PT's weaponry and role changed dramatically during the war, its mass-produced design stayed essentially the same. *National Archives*

There is no record anyone anticipated this role-saving wartime use for the PT, nor should anyone have been expected to. Considerable credit is nonetheless due to navy men like Admirals Land and Stark, politicians such as Edison and Roosevelt, and private boat designers and builders like Scott-Paine, Chase, Sutphen, and Higgins. Because of them the United States Navy built not just a torpedo boat or a gunboat, but one superbly versatile man-of-war.

Notes

Abbreviations Used

B and L:
    Battles and Leaders of the Civil War: Being for the Most Part Contributions by Union and Confederate Officers. Based upon "The Century War Series," ed. Robert Underwood Johnson and Clarence Clough Buel of the editorial staff of *The Century Magazine.* 4 vols. Reprint. Secaucus, N.J.: Castle, 1983.

ORN:
    Official Records of the Union and Confederate Navies in the War of the Rebellion. 31 vols. Washington, D.C.: Government Printing Office, 1894–1922.

Introduction

    1. Douglas MacArthur, *Reminiscences*, 155.

    2. According to the Naval Vessel Register, PT boats are considered as follows. Type: Patrol Vessel; Class: Motor Torpedo Boat; Symbol: PT. "PT" is therefore a letter designator like "BB" for battleship or "CV" for aircraft carrier; the letters do not necessarily correspond to the actual first letters of the words describing the vessel class. "Patrol Torpedo" is a popular, not official, designation.

    3. Bern Keating, *The Mosquito Fleet*, 4.

    4. PT Boats, Inc., of Memphis, Tenn., a nationwide nonprofit PT veterans' organization, refers to Bulkley's *At Close Quarters* as the "bible" of PT boat history. They say they consult it daily.

Chapter One: The First Yankee Torpedo Boats

    1. "Small torpedo boat" is an unofficial designation for the purposes of this work only. The navy called them picket boats, picket launches, or tugs, though it did describe their conversion by noting they were "Fitted as torpedo boat[s]." Lee to Welles, giving stations of ships in North Atlantic Blockading Squadron, 16 September 1864, *ORN*, Series 1, vol. 10, 463. Later on they

were given names—*Alpha, Beta, Gamma, Delta, Epsilon*, and *Zeta*. *ORN*, Series 1, vol. 11, 881.

2. Ralph J. Roske and Charles Van Doren, *Lincoln's Commando: The Biography of Commander William B. Cushing, U.S.N.*, 195.

3. Ibid.

4. Ibid., 200.

5. Ibid., 207.

6. Ibid., 208.

7. Ibid., 89.

8. Ibid., 163.

9. Cushing to Lee, 9 May 1864, *ORN*, Series 1, vol. 10, 39–40.

10. Ibid., 40.

11. Cushing to Welles, 21 May 1864, *ORN*, Series 1, vol. 10, 77.

12. Roske and Van Doren, 28.

13. Lee to Welles, 9 July 1864, *ORN*, Series 1, vol. 10, 247–248.

14. Ibid.

15. Cushing to Lee (forwarded to Welles), 9 July 1864, *ORN*, Series 1, vol. 10, 248.

16. *B and L*, 634.

17. Bryan Cooper, *PT Boats*, 66–67.

18. Telegram from Welles to Admiral Gregory, 7 August 1864, *ORN*, Series 1, vol. 10, 340.

19. *New York Times*, 21 November 1864, 8.

20. For Cushing's postwar journal entry on the length of picket boat *No. 1*, see *B and L*, 634. See also *ORN*, Series 2, vol. 1, Statistical Data of U.S. Ships, 177. Chief Engineer Wood's comments appear in *New York Times*, 21 November 1864, 8. Dana Wegner feels the 30-foot size is just too small given all the equipment on board, which included the steam engine, boiler, coal spaces, 12-pounder gun, and storage space for the 100-pound spar torpedo. The fifteen-man crew during the attack and the fact that *No. 1* sailed under its own power with a seven-man crew from New York to North Carolina are additional factors favoring the larger size. Also, he says the schematic drawing of the picket boat in *ORN*, Series 1, vol. 10, 622 (insert), "worked" when he used it to construct the scale model—to scale based on the 45-foot length—on display at the Smithsonian Institution in Washington. From conversation with the author, 1 March 1996.

21. Cushing asserts here that the boom (spar) itself was "some fourteen feet in length." This figure is almost certainly too low. Most accounts agree that Cushing placed the launch no less than ten feet from the side of the *Albemarle*, which drew about eight feet of water. For Cushing to have been able to manipulate the spar, dangling as it was in the air near the bow, and extend it below the ram's bottom, it would have to have been far longer than fourteen feet. Faulty memory or his known tendency to embellish—placing himself closer to danger than he actually was—may account for this apparent discrepancy in his postwar journal account. *B and L*, 634–35.

22. Roske and Van Doren, 210.

23. Welles to Gregory, 8 September 1864, *ORN*, Series 1, vol. 10, 441.

24. Stockholm to Welles, 26 October 1864, *ORN*, Series 1, vol. 10, 539–40. *No. 2* was later repaired and returned to service.

25. See *B and L*, 641, for Lieutenant Warley's postwar narrative, which combines portions of his official report.

26. Roske and Van Doren, 220–21.

27. Ibid., 222–23.

28. *B and L*, 635.

29. Roske and Van Doren, 226.

30. *Richmond Dispatch*, 4 November 1864 (reprinted in *New York Times*, 8 November 1864, 8).

31. *B and L*, 636.

32. Ibid.

33. Ibid., 637. It was the after gun that stared them in the face, but they were too close for it to depress sufficiently to hit them. See Warley's official report, 28 October 1864, *ORN*, Series 1, vol. 10, 624.

34. *B and L*, 637.

35. Ibid., 640.

36. See R. O. Crowley, "The Confederate Torpedo Service," *Century Magazine*, June 1898, reprinted in Philip Van Doren Stern, *Secret Missions of the Civil War*, Chicago: Rand McNally, 1959, 207–18. For a more extensive look at this fascinating subject, see Milton F. Perry, *Infernal Machines: The Story of Confederate Submarine and Mine Warfare*.

37. *B and L*, 642.

38. Details regarding picket boat *No. 1*'s days at the Naval Academy are courtesy of James Cheevers, curator of the U.S. Naval Academy Museum, Annapolis, Md. Conversation with the author, 26 February 1996.

39. Roske and Van Doren, 248.

40. Ibid., 303.

41. General Orders No. 34, read to officers and men of the North Atlantic Squadron by Admiral Porter, 5 November 1864, *ORN*, Series 1, vol. 10, 618.

42. There are no further references to this request (Lamson to Porter, *ORN*, Series 1, vol. 11, 97), so presumably it was denied. Of note is Lamson's suggestion that the torpedo boats "could be brought down on a steamer's deck and hoisted out here [near Wilmington]." This presages a tactic used by the Russians against the Turks in the Black Sea thirteen years later.

43. Porter to Commander W. A. Parker, 2 December 1864, *ORN*, Series 1, vol. 11, 120.

44. *No. 5* seized the steamers *Skirwan*, *Cotton Plant*, *Fisher*, and *Egypt Mills* on 22 May 1865. *Civil War Naval Chronology, 1861–1865* (Washington, D.C.: Naval History Division, 1971) 5:100.

45. *New York Times*, 21 November 1864, 8.

46. Warley to Mallory, Confederate secretary of the navy, 28 October 1864, *ORN*, Series 1, vol. 10, 624.

47. *B and L*, 637.

Chapter Two: The Ship Killer

1. *Annual Report of the Secretary of the Navy, 1869*, 41st Cong., 2d sess., H.exdoc. 1, 34 (serial set vol. no. 1411).

2. Harold and Margaret Sprout, *The Rise of American Naval Power, 1776–1918*, 205–6.

3. For a closer look at the life of this early military industrialist and his revolutionary invention, see Edwyn Gray, *The Devil's Device: Robert Whitehead and the History of the Torpedo*.

4. R. B. Bradford, *Notes on Movable Torpedoes*, 20.

5. Gray, 57.

6. Ibid., 23.

7. Ibid., 11. Gray is quoting from Admiralty Letter 3/5688/6101, *Report of the Committee on the Whitehead Torpedo*, 28 October 1870.

8. Bradford, 20.

9. According to Bradford (ibid., 22), Turkey came to own the Whitehead rather circuitously. "It was brought about by the capture of two Russian torpedoes of [the 14-inch] pattern [after a Russian attack] at Batoum, December 29, 1877. The captured samples were taken to Constantinople, and Mr. Whitehead, fearing that his secret would become public, immediately commenced negotiations for their purchase. The Turks sold them to him on condition that they should be permitted to purchase torpedoes at any time without paying for the secret or the right to manufacture."

10. Gray, 85.

11. Bradford, 21.

12. Compiled from *Annual Reports of the Secretary of the Navy, 1869–1882*, "Bureau of Ordnance Report," H.exdoc. (serial set vol. nos. 1411, 1448, 1507, 1562, 1600, 1638, 1679, 1748, 1799, 1849, 1909, 1958, and 2016).

13. For an example of Torpedo Corps appropriations see *Statutes at Large*, Vol. 20, 45th Cong., 2d sess., 1877–79, 52. For the fiscal year ending 30 June 1879, approved 4 May 1878, Congress appropriated $45,000, broken down as follows: labor, $15,000; freight and express charges, $500; material, $10,000; general repair of the seawall, $5,000; instruction and general torpedo experiments, $14,500. While these figures do not show the exact amount used in movable torpedo research, they give a good general idea of the level of funding and its relation to Whitehead's asking price at the time.

14. Lance C. Buhl, "Maintaining 'An American Navy,' 1865–1889," in *In Peace and War, Interpretations of American Naval History, 1775–1984*, 148.

15. Norman Friedman, *U.S. Naval Weapons: Every Gun, Missile, Mine and Torpedo Used by the U.S. Navy from 1883 to the Present*, 115.

16. Bradford, 3.

17. Benjamin H. Harris (R-Mass.), House Committee on Naval Affairs, House Report No. 943, 45th Cong., 2d sess., printed to accompany bill H.R. 5183, and committed to the Committee of the Whole House on 11 June 1878, 2 (serial set vol. no. 1826).

18. See *Annual Report of the Secretary of the Navy*, "Bureau of Ordnance Report," for the years 1876 to 1880 (serial set vol. nos. 1748, 1799, 1849, 1909,

and 1958), for evidence of the bureau's dissatisfaction with the level of Congressional support.

19. Friedman, 115.

20. Jaques, "Paper on Naval Torpedo Warfare," prepared for the use of the select committee of the United States Senate on Ordnance and War Ships, 5 January 1886, 49th Cong., 1st sess., Senate Reports 1–90, 149 (serial set vol. no. 2355). Jaques included this particular excerpt from the "Bureau of Ordnance Report" contained in the *Annual Report of the Secretary of the Navy* for 1882.

21. Jaques, 169.

22. Ibid., 171, from an appended report by F. M. Barber, "Torpedo-Boat Coast Defense," a report from the Naval Advisory Board dated October 1885.

23. Gray, 156.

24. See Buhl, 145–73, for this analysis.

25. Gray, 140–41.

26. See ibid., 113–14, for a brief description of this controversy. As for the notion that reports of the sinking were believed, see Charles Chabaud Arnault, "The Employment of Torpedoes in Steam Launches Against Men-of-War," 87. Arnault's article was originally published in France. The article gives no hint that Europeans, or Americans who later published it, entertained any doubts that a Whitehead torpedo had indeed claimed its first wartime victim.

27. In 1889 the British launched the 373-foot *Vulcan*, specially built for carrying six second-class TBs. The French also employed this type of mother vessel for its small torpedo boats. Neither country was ever able to prove the wartime worth of this piggyback concept, however, since by the time general European war broke out in 1914 it was out of vogue. The *Vulcan* was by then a submarine depot ship. From *Conway's All the World's Fighting Ships, 1860–1905*, 106.

28. Ibid., 105.

29. Ibid.

30. Tamara Moser Melia, *"Damn the Torpedoes": A Short History of U.S. Naval Mine Countermeasures, 1777–1991*, 19.

31. Harris, House Report No. 943, 2.

32. Arnault, 97–98.

33. Edward Simpson, "What Has Been Done for a New Navy," extract from an address delivered before the Washington Branch of the U.S. Naval Institute, 4 December 1885, Senate Reports 1-90, 49th Cong., 1st sess., 143 (serial set vol. no. 2355). The eventual result of the Naval Advisory Board's report was the famous ABCD ships, the nucleus of the "New American Navy."

34. Ibid., 144.

35. Jaques, 149.

36. Jaques, from an appended report by F. M. Barber, "Torpedo-Boat Coast Defense," a report from the Naval Advisory Board dated October 1885, 172–73.

37. Ibid., 173.

38. From *Dictionary of American Fighting Ships* 2:222, we see that William Cushing's namesake continued his legacy during the Spanish-American War.

On August 7 the *Cushing* "captured four small vessels and towed them to her anchorage at Piedras Cay. Four days later armed boats from *Cushing* and *Gwin* captured and burned a 20-ton schooner."

39. Ibid., 6:635.

40. *Conway's 1860–1905*, chart, 137. See also ship descriptions, 159–62.

41. The maximum attainable speed of a vessel with a true displacement hull is determined by its displacement speed, or "hull speed." To calculate, take the boat or ship's length at the waterline (LWL), in feet, and determine the square root. Then multiply the square root by 1.34. This is the vessel's approximate maximum speed in nautical miles per hour. It is a hydrodynamic fact that no matter how much power is applied to a vessel with a true displacement hull, it cannot exceed its hull speed. U.S. Coast Guard Auxiliary, *Sailing and Seamanship*, 1–4, 1–5.

Chapter Three: They Were Ignorable

1. Gordon Adamson and Douglas Van Patten, "Motor Torpedo Boats: A Technical Study," *U.S. Naval Institute Proceedings*, July 1940, 977.

2. Antony Preston, *Strike Craft*, 8.

3. *Conway's All the World's Fighting Ships, 1906–1921*, 321.

4. Frank A. Tredinnick and Harrison L. Bennett, "An Administrative History of PT's in World War II," 11. The description of Yarrow's boat is attributed to a sketch given by W. Kaemmerer before a meeting of the Verein Deutscher Ingenieure in 1906.

5. Tredinnick and Bennett, 2. Also Preston, 8.

6. Preston, 8.

7. Peter Kemp, *The History of Ships*, 190–91.

8. Gray, 178–79.

9. Preston, 9.

10. See *Conway's All the World's Fighting Ships, 1906–1921*, 281–86, for a breakdown of MAS boat types and characteristics.

11. Paul G. Halpern, *A Naval History of World War I*, 175.

12. A. E. Sokol, "Italian Attempts at Harbor Forcing During the Last War," *U.S. Naval Institute Proceedings*, January 1942, 38.

13. Adamson and Van Patten, 983.

14. *Conway's 1906–1921*, 100.

15. Halpern, 443–44.

16. Adamson and Van Patten, pp. 979–82.

17. Alfred Thayer Mahan, *The Influence of Sea Power upon History, 1660–1805*. This theme is explicit throughout the book.

18. Michael T. Corgan, "Mahan and Theodore Roosevelt: The Assessment of Influence," *Naval War College Review*, November–December 1980, 89–97.

19. Mahan, 66.

20. Harold Sprout and Margaret Sprout, *The Rise of American Naval Power, 1776–1918*, 324.

21. Preston, 8.

22. Captain H.A.V. Von Pflugk, "Torpedo Boats," *U.S. Naval Institute Proceedings*, August 1941, 1117–18.

23. Kenneth J. Hagan, *This People's Navy: The Making of American Sea Power*, 232.

24. Richard W. Turk, "Defending the New Empire, 1900–1914," in *In Peace and War: Interpretations of American Naval History, 1775–1984*, 187.

25. "Vedette Boat" proposal dated 27 June 1906, 2 pages plus blueprint, Record Group 80, Secretary of the Navy, General Board of the Navy Files, 420-14, National Archives, Washington, D.C.

26. Tredinnick and Bennett, 2.

27. General Board Files, 420-14, G.B. Serial No. 407.

28. Tredinnick and Bennett, 4–5.

29. Adamson and Van Patten, 983–84.

30. "Proposed design of submarine chaser," 26 March 1917, General Board Files, 420-14, G.B. Serial No. 681.

31. Tredinnick and Bennett, 7–8, quoting a report in *Shipping Illustrated*, 19 February 1916.

32. "Motor Torpedo Boats," dated 14 April 1937, General Board Files, 420–14, 4th Endorsement, G.B. Serial No. 1740, p. 2, para. 4. This is an invaluable document, one quoted extensively by Tredinnick and Bennett, and by Bulkley in *At Close Quarters*. The serial is the General Board's response to a request by the secretary of the navy to study the feasibility of MTBs. Before giving the board's recommendations, it includes a summary of MTB experimentation performed in the United States to that date, as well as the procession of administrative correspondence behind the current initiative. A paper on CMBs by J. E. Thornycroft is also included in Serial No. 1740, providing evidence of British influence in PT development even at this early stage in the administrative process.

33. See *Conway's 1906–1921*, 321, for description of Russian motorboats built in the United States; p. 101 for a description of the Elco MLs built for the British; and pp. 282–85 for various series of Elco-built Italian boats.

34. "Motor Torpedo Boats," dated 14 April 1937, General Board Files, 420-14, 4th Endorsement, G.B. Serial No. 1740, p. 2, para. 5.

35. Preston, 14.

36. Capt. Robert J. Bulkley, Jr., *At Close Quarters: PT Boats in the United States Navy*, 41.

37. Reference to bootlegger influence on PT development seems to have originated with Tredinnick and Bennett (p. 13), citing comments about CMBs laid up in East Coast ports. Bulkley in *At Close Quarters* augments this thesis with his observations concerning the conversion of Liberty engines and concerning navy technicians with past "rummie" experience to offer. These references are repeated by writers such as Bryan Cooper and William Breuer.

38. Letter from Rear Adm. F. C. Billard, USCG, to Bureau of Ordnance, 2 February 1924, Record Group 26, United States Coast Guard General Correspondence, 1910–41 (Box 1440), National Archives. This letter also provides a good indication of when British CMBs and other high-performance motorboats first appeared in rumrunning gangs on the East Coast.

39. Letter from Billard to the Chief of the Bureau of Navigation, 11 June 1924, United States Coast Guard General Correspondence 1910–41, Box 1440.

40. Letter from George Rappleyea, of Higgins Industries, Inc., to Congressman J. O. Fernandez, 11 December 1939, attached to letter from Fernandez to Charles Edison, 27 February 1940, Record Group 80, Secretary of the Navy Correspondence.

41. Tredinnick and Bennett, 13. Quoted from a conversation with Lt. (jg) Ralph A. Richardson of the Radio Experimental Laboratory at Anacostia, D.C.

42. Bulkley, 41–42

43. Tredinnick and Bennett, 13. For a description of this boat see a letter from the Chairman of the General Board to the Director of Naval Intelligence, 2 July 1935, General Board Files, 420-14.

44. Tredinnick and Bennett, 13. For a description of this boat see a letter from the Chairman of the General Board to the Secretary of the Navy, "Aluminum hulled vessels; proposals of the Aluminum Company of America," 14 May 1937, General Board Files, 420-14 (Serial No. 1738).

45. After World War II, aluminum replaced wood as the standard material for the postwar descendants of the PT. S. A. Peters, "The Motor Torpedo Boat," *Ordnance*, May–June 1954, 946.

46. Thomas C. Hone and Mark D. Mandeles, "Managerial Style in the Interwar Navy: A Reappraisal," *Naval War College Review*, September–October 1980, 97.

47. Thomas C. Hone, "Spending Patterns of the United States Navy," *Armed Forces and Society*, Spring 1982, 443–59. See also Rosen, "The Treaty Navy, 1919–1937," in *In Peace and War: Interpretations of American Naval History, 1775–1984*, 221–36.

48. John Major, "The Navy Plans for War, 1937–1941," in *In Peace and War: Interpretations of American Naval History, 1775–1984*, 238.

Chapter Four: "A Moderate Experimental Program"

1. See Emory S. Land, Biographical Files, Operational Archives, Naval Historical Center, Washington, D.C. Land's duties on this board (Inspection and Survey) are not spelled out. It is known that after the war broke out the next year, in the Third Naval District (New York), "some 350 pleasure craft adapted for conversion into war vessels were taken over." Lawrence Perry, *Our Navy in the War*, 241. This effort was greatly speeded up because of advance inspection by skilled naval architects such as Land.

2. John Major, "The Navy Plans for War, 1937–1941," in *In Peace and War: Interpretations of American Naval History*, 238.

3. Letter from the Bureau of Construction and Repair to the Chief of Naval Operations, dated 5 December 1936, General Board of the Navy Files, 420-14, G.B. Serial No. 1740, 18 April 1937.

4. Letter from Bureau of Engineering to CNO, dated 16 December 1936, General Board Files, Serial #1740.

5. Letter from CNO to SecNav, 5 January 1937. See also letter from SecNav to General Board, 5 January 1937, General Board Files, Serial #1740.

6. Douglas MacArthur, *Reminiscences*, 114.

7. "Notes of an Address by Field Marshal Douglas MacArthur Delivered to a Group of Officers Today, August 3, 1936," MacArthur Archives, MacArthur Memorial Museum, Norfolk, Va., Record Group 1, Military Advisor Records, Box 1, Folder 3, p. 2.

8. A secondary function of the boats was "to provide a valuable adjunct in law enforcement" during peacetime. "MacArthur's First Report on National Defense, 1936," MacArthur Archives, Record Group 1, Box 1, Folder 3, p. 27.

9. Ibid., 27–28.

10. Sidney Huff, *My Fifteen Years with General MacArthur*, 26–28.

11. MacArthur, 117.

12. The author searched through Admiral Stark's comparatively limited collection of pre–World War II papers and correspondence at the Operational Archives Branch, Naval Historical Center. Stark made no mention of the meeting with MacArthur in which MTBs were apparently discussed. Leahy diary excerpt courtesy of Robert J. Cressman, Naval Historical Center, Washington, D.C.

13. Letter from Chairman of the General Board to SecNav, dated 14 April 1937, on "Motor Torpedo Boats," General Board Files, 420-14, 4th Endorsement, G.B. Serial No. 1740, 18 April 1937.

14. After World War II, the round-bilge displacement hull became the dominant hull form of the United States' new PT boat, called the Fast Patrol Craft (PTF). The German E-boats of World War II, considered by many MTB analysts to be the best all-weather MTBs used during the war, were of this basic hull form.

15. Letter to Eisenhower from Ord in Washington, D.C., 27 July 1937, 2 pages, MacArthur Archives, Record Group 1, Box 1, Folder 6B, Ord-Eisenhower Correspondence.

16. Letter from Eisenhower to Ord, 13 August 1937, Folder 6D, p. 2, Ord-Eisenhower Correspondence. The allotted total for the Off-Shore Patrol program in calendar year 1938 was only 668,000 pesos.

17. Huff, 29.

18. Ibid.

19. See Ibid., 30, for MacArthur's description of these boats. MacArthur makes no mention of them in his autobiography. See Gordon Adamson and Douglas Van Patten, "Motor Torpedo Boats: A Technical Study," *U. S. Naval Institute Proceedings*, July 1940, 981, for a brief table description of the Q-boats. Huff, who provided the details for a Q-boat story appearing in the 10 March 1939 issue of *Bamboo Breezes*, differs with Adamson and Van Patten on the length. The article says they were 55 feet long (not 65), with an 11-foot beam. There are several excellent prewar photos of these boats in the 9 February 1942 issue of *Life* magazine.

20. See *New York Times*, 6 December 1938. See also *Bamboo Breezes*, 10 March 1939, describing the arrival of the first Q-boat in the Philippines.

21. Tredinnick and Bennett, 24.

22. Kenneth S. Davis, *FDR: Into the Storm, 1937–1940*, 155.

23. Allison W. Saville, "Charles Edison, 2 January 1940–24 June 1940," in *American Secretaries of the Navy* 2:669. Quoted from Elliot Roosevelt, ed., *F.D.R.: His Personal Letters*, 4 vols. (New York: Duell, Sloan, & Pearce, 1948–1950), 1:613.

24. John D. Venable, *Out of the Shadow: The Story of Charles Edison*, 25.

25. Ibid., 122.

26. Ibid., 123.

27. Ibid., 125–26.

28. John Major, "William Daniel Leahy," in *The Chiefs of Naval Operations*, 103.

29. Venable, 143.

30. W. S. Humphrey and W. C. Specht, "The Motor Torpedo Boat—Past, Present and Future: History, Development, Employment and Tactics; Accomplishments to 1 February 1943," see p. 1 under chapter heading "Development."

31. The author twice submitted detailed requests for documents related to FDR's involvement with PT boat development to archivists at the Roosevelt Library in Hyde Park, New York. They turned up no such documents.

32. Kenneth S. Davis, *FDR: The Beckoning of Destiny, 1882–1928*, 319–20.

33. Ibid., 686.

34. The text of Roosevelt's January 28 speech is included in House Report No. 1899, House Committee on Naval Affairs, 75th Congress, 3d sess., printed to accompany H.R. 9218, submitted to the House 4 March 1938 by Chairman Carl Vinson of Georgia.

35. Ibid., 1.

36. *New York Times*, 7 April 1938, 14.

37. For Roosevelt's opinion on the rigid-airship controversy see *New York Times*, 2 March 1938, 1. The Congressional Record, 75th Congress, 3d sess., contains the text of the debates on H.R. 9218 in March and April 1938.

38. From *House Journal*, 75th Congress, 3d sess., 467.

39. Second Deficiency Appropriation Bill, Fiscal Year 1938, House Committee on Appropriations, House Report No. 2614, 75th Congress, 3d sess., submitted 7 June 1938, 12.

Chapter Five: A Scandalous Birth

1. Saburo Ienaga, *The Pacific War, 1931–1945*, 81.

2. *Washington Daily News*, 9 June 1938, 16.

3. Ibid.

4. See Tredinnick and Bennett, 19–23 and 27–33, for the most detailed description of the contest and its immediate results. See also Bulkley, *At Close Quarters*, 44–45, for a good summation of the Tredinnick material.

5. Tredinnick and Bennett, 22.

6. Ibid., 29.

7. Ibid., 47–48.

8. Ibid., 35. Quoted from "The Story Behind the Expendables," by Irwin Chase.

9. Tredinnick and Bennett, 36.

10. Adamson and Van Patten, "Motor Torpedo Boats: A Technical Study," 990–91.

11. Ibid., 991–92.

12. Venable, 143.

13. Letter from SecNav to General Board, 13 January 1939, Record Group 80, Secretary of the Navy, General Board of the Navy Files, 420-14, National Archives.

14. Letter from General Board to SecNav, dated 16 January 1939, General Board Files, 420-14, G.B. Serial No. 1825(A). Scott-Paine's boat is not mentioned by name, though at the end of 1938 his was the only 70-foot boat under Admiralty consideration. Vosper came out with its own 70-footer in 1939.

15. Tredinnick and Bennett, 38–39.

16. Ibid., 40.

17. Ibid.

18. Ibid., 42. Quoted from a conversation with Sidney Peters, Bureau of Ships architect.

19. Ibid., 41.

20. Letter from Charles Edison to FDR, 3 October 1939, Record Group 80, Secretary of the Navy, SecNav Correspondence.

21. Bulkley, 47.

22. Letter from Lewis Compton to Carl Vinson, Chairman of the House Naval Affairs Committee, 20 June 1940, General Board Files, 420-14, G.B. Serial No. 1976-A, dated 10 July 1940. The *New York Times*, 10 December 1939, notes that Elco planned to increase its small-craft workforce from 300 to 900, as a result of the PT order for 23 boats of the Scott-Paine design.

23. *New York Times*, 10 December 1939.

24. Letter from Andrew Jackson Higgins to Comdr. Robert B. Carney, 28 December 1939, Secretary of the Navy, SecNav Correspondence. See Jerry E. Strahan, *Andrew Jackson Higgins and the Boats That Won World War II* (Baton Rouge, La: Louisiana State University Press, 1994), pp. 42–54, for a closer look at Higgins's struggle to get his PT designs accepted by the navy.

25. *St. Louis Globe-Democrat*, 31 December 1939.

26. Letter from J. O. Fernandez to Charles Edison, 27 February 1940, includes letter from George Rappleyea dated 11 December 1939, Record Group 80, Secretary of the Navy, SecNav Correspondence.

27. Letter from George Rappleyea to Charles Edison, 30 January 1940, Record Group 80, Secretary of the Navy, SecNav Correspondence.

28. *London Times*, 13 January 1936, p. 8.

29. Letter from Senator Alexander Wiley to Charles Edison on behalf of a constituent, H. C. Burger of Burger Boat Company, Manitowoc, Wis., 29 March 1940, Secretary of the Navy, Record Group 80, Secretary of the Navy,

SecNav Correspondence. The quote is from a typed enclosure, a copy of an article in *Motor Boat*, dated 13 March 1940.

30. Memorandum from Comdr. Robert B. Carney to Rear Adm. A. P. Fairfield, General Board Files, 420-14. Carney was responding to a paper submitted to Fairfield by a John T. Rowland, entitled "A Doctrine for the Employment of Small Craft in War." While the paper added nothing especially new to the navy's thinking, it does show the interest America's small-boat and yachting community continued to take in MTBs.

31. See SecNav Correspondence, PT/L4 Files, covering the period January to March 1940, for correspondence relating to the controversy over the Elco deal.

32. In June 1996 the author approached Electric Boat Company asking for any company records dealing with the purchase of the Scott-Paine boat and with Elco's subsequent manufacturing of PT boats during World War II. Mr. Neil Reunzel, director of public affairs, stated in response: "We have no archival material on Elco PT boats." This should not be construed as evidence that Elco has something to hide regarding its role in the Scott-Paine purchase or the manufacture of PT boats during the war. It does, however, tend to put a damper on further inquiry in this potentially sensitive area.

33. Venable, 142.

34. Ibid.

35. Letter from General Board to Lewis Compton, 28 June 1940, General Board Files, 420-14, G.B. Serial No. 1976-A, dated 10 July 1940.

36. Letter from the Chairman of the General Board to Secretary of the Navy, General Board Files, 420-14, G.B. Serial No. 1976-A, dated 10 July 1940. See also same Serial No., letter from the Chief of the Bureau of Ordnance to the Assistant Secretary of the Navy, 11 July 1940.

37. Tredinnick and Bennett, 58.

38. Ibid.

39. Ibid., 59.

40. Ibid., 65.

41. Ibid., 85.

42. Ibid., 88.

43. Bulkley, 56–57.

44. Venable, 145.

Chapter Six: To the Firing Line

1. Tredinnick and Bennett, 64.

2. Ibid., 54.

3. For details regarding these early prewar squadrons, see Tredinnick and Bennett, 54–61, and Bulkley, 48–51.

4. Bulkley, 52.

5. *New York Times*, 10 December 1939.

6. Letter from Kimmel to Stark, 18 February 1941, *Hearings Before the Joint Committee on the Investigation of the Pearl Harbor Attack, Congress of the United States, Seventy-ninth Congress* (Washington, D.C., 1946), Part 16, 2228 (cited hereafter as *PHA*).

7. Letter from Stark to Kimmel, 22 March 1941, *PHA*, Part 16, 2157.

8. Draft of a letter from Stark to Kimmel, repeating excerpts from a letter from Kimmel to Stark, 19 August 1941, *PHA*, Part 16, 2190.

9. Stark to Kimmel, 2 August 1941, *PHA*, Part 16, 2175.

10. Bulkley, 57–58.

11. Kimmel to Stark, 22 October 1941, *PHA*, Part 16, 2249.

12. Stark to Hart, 1 November 1941, *PHA*, Part 16, 2452.

13. Ronald H. Spector, *Eagle Against the Sun*, 56.

14. D. Clayton James, *The Years of MacArthur*, 1:474.

15. Ibid., 594–96.

16. Samuel Eliot Morison, *The Rising Sun in the Pacific*, vol. 3 of *History of United States Naval Operations in World War II*, 152.

17. William Breuer, *Sea Wolf: A Biography of John D. Bulkeley, USN*, 20.

18. Ibid., 23. Per Comdr. Henry J. Brantingham, USN (Ret.).

19. Bulkley, 2–3.

20. Gordon W. Prange, *At Dawn We Slept*, 582.

Chapter Seven: Philippine Tragedy

1. See William H. Bartsch, "Philippine Air Debacle," *Air Power History*, Summer 1997, for an excellent analysis of the destruction of MacArthur's air force.

2. Morison, *The Rising Sun in the Pacific*, 198.

3. James, *The Years of MacArthur*, 2:27–37.

4. Bulkley, *At Close Quarters*, 5.

5. Ibid., 6.

6. Huff, *My Fifteen Years with General MacArthur*, 37.

7. Bulkley, 8.

8. Lieutenant Bulkeley report of 18 January 1942 reconnaissance to Commandant, Sixteenth Naval District, dated 18 February 1942, Sixteenth Naval District War Diary, covering period from 8 December 1941 to 19 February 1942, Motor Torpedo Boat Materials, Box XX, Operational Archives, Naval Historical Center, Washington, D.C.

9. Sixteenth Naval District War Diary entry for 18 January 1942.

10. Lieutenant Bulkeley report of attack on enemy vessels in Port Binanga, 19 January 1942, to Commandant, Sixteenth Naval District, dated 20 January 1942, Sixteenth Naval District War Diary.

11. Lieutenant DeLong report on loss of PT-31 to Commander, Motor Torpedo Boat Squadron Three, dated 23 January 1942, Sixteenth Naval District War Diary.

12. PT Claims, No. 1 (of 5), Motor Torpedo Boat Materials, Box 13, Operational Archives, Naval Historical Center, Washington, D.C.

13. Rockwell to Hart, 25 January 1942, Sixteenth Naval District War Diary.

14. Sixteenth Naval District War Diary entry for 21 January 1942.

15. Ibid., entry for 23 January 1942. See also Bulkley, p. 13.

16. Morison, *Rising Sun*, 201.

17. Lieutenant Bulkeley report on operations of PT-41, night of 24 January 1942, to Commandant, Sixteenth Naval District, dated 26 January 1942, Sixteenth Naval District War Diary. See also PT Claims, No. 2.

18. Lieutenant DeLong report of attack of PT-32 on enemy cruiser during night of 1 February 1942, to Commandant, Sixteenth Naval District, dated 3 February 1942, Sixteenth Naval District War Diary. See also PT Claims, No. 3.

19. Lieutenant Bulkeley report of night operations of PT-35 and 41 off Subic Bay, 17–18 February 1942, to Commandant, Sixteenth Naval District, dated 17 February 1942, Sixteenth Naval District War Diary. See also PT Claims, No. 4.

20. Rockwell to Hart, 25 January 1942, Sixteenth Naval District War Diary.

21. Sixteenth Naval District War Diary entry for 25 December 1941.

22. Ibid., entry for 27 January 1942.

23. W. L. White, *They Were Expendable*, 62.

24. Clark Lee, *They Call It Pacific*, 200.

25. Ibid., 201–2

26. White, 62–64, 92.

27. Ibid., 95.

28. James, 2:98; MacArthur to Marshall, 24 February 1942, Record Group 4, USAFFE #1-87, 7 December 1941 to 16 March 1942, Box 15, Folder 1, MacArthur Archives, MacArthur Memorial Museum, Norfolk, Va.

29. Marshall to MacArthur, dated 25 February 1942, and reply from MacArthur to Marshall, 26 February 1942, Record Group 2, MacArthur's Personal File, 23 January 1942 to 11 April 1942, Box 2, Folder 4, MacArthur Archives.

30. See Record Group 4, USAFFE #1-87, MacArthur Archives for transcripts of these dispatches; see also Clay Blair, Jr., *Silent Victory: The U.S. Submarine War Against Japan* 1:170.

31. William Breuer, 53, quoting *Saga* magazine, August 1958, 86.

32. Huff, 52–53.

33. Breuer, 54.

34. Huff, 51–52.

35. Ibid., 54.

36. Operation Order from Commandant, Sixteenth Naval District, to Commander, MTB Squadron Three, 10 March 1942, Record Group 30, Papers of R. K. Sutherland, Box 1, Folder 9, 8 pages, MacArthur Archives.

37. Morison, *Rising Sun*, 203; Bulkley, 16.

38. Rockwell Report, Narrative of Naval Activities in Luzon Area, December 1, 1941, to March 19, 1942, p. 20. Report courtesy of Robert Cressman, Naval Historical Center.

39. Huff, 52.

40. Operation Order from Commandant, Sixteenth Naval District, to Commander, MTB Squadron Three, 10 March 1942. See p. 4 and Annex "D." For the dispatch ordering the *Permit* to rendezvous with the PTs on March 13, see Record Group 4, USAFFE #1-87, 7 December 1941 to 16 March 1942, Box 15, Folder 1, MacArthur Archives.

41. Rockwell Report, 20.

42. Operation Order from Commandant, Sixteenth Naval District, to Commander, MTB Squadron Three, 10 March 1942. See Annex "B": Alternate Plans.

43. Breuer, 55–56; see also William Manchester, *American Caesar*, 254.

44. Douglas MacArthur, *Reminiscences*, 157.

45. PT Claims, No. 5.

46. White, 104.

47. See Carlos P. Romulo, *I Saw the Fall of the Philippines*, 228; Huff, 51–52.

48. Huff, 51–52. Having speculated that claustrophobia might be the reason MacArthur chose PT boats over submarines, Huff adds that the general probably "wanted room to move about and to see what the enemy was doing; and most of all he needed to feel that he could fight back if necessary even if he had only a pistol with which to fight." It should be noted that the fear of loss of control is a prime psychological component of phobias. If, however, we take MacArthur's perceived need to fight back at face value, what better platform than a modern fleet boat?

49. MacArthur, 154.

50. Blair 1:146–47.

51. Breuer, 54.

52. Blair 1:170–71. When he reached Corregidor, Chapple sent eight PT-32 survivors ashore, keeping seven. When Chapple departed, he was ordered to conduct offensive patrols south of Manila Bay. He did so despite having 36 valuable codebreakers aboard, unsuccessfully attacking three Japanese destroyers. They in turn depth-charged him, but he managed to escape and reach Australia unharmed. It is doubtful Chapple would have attacked with MacArthur aboard, had the general chosen that route. This episode demonstrates that despite the fact the Japanese were supposedly expecting MacArthur to leave by submarine during that period, the *Permit* was able to get in and out of Corregidor without being damaged or sunk.

53. White, 107.

54. Rear Adm. John Bulkeley to Col. L. H. Hammond, Jr., 11 May 1982, Contribution of J. D. Bulkeley, Record Group 15, Box 32, Folder 4, page 2, MacArthur Archives.

55. Bulkley, 26.

Chapter Eight: Great Expectations

1. Robert J. Cressman et al., *"A Glorious Page in Our History": The Battle of Midway, 4–6 June 1942*, 34.

2. Ibid., 41.

3. Ibid., 142–43, 165. See also Bulkley, 79–81.

4. Bulkley, 82.

5. See "Oral Conversation between Cominch and ComPtron 3, 14 May 1942," 21 May 1942, Record Group 15, Papers of R. K. Sutherland, Box 8, Folder 7, 1 page, MacArthur Archives. See also Bulkley, 27–28.

6. Nigel Hamilton, *JFK, Reckless Youth*, 500–503.

7. Ernest B. King, *U.S. Navy at War 1941–1945: Official Reports to the Secretary of the Navy*, 20.

8. Bulkley, 86.

9. Bern Keating, *The Mosquito Fleet*, 26.

10. Bulkley, 92–93.

11. Ibid., 96.

12. Ibid., 97–105. See also Samuel Eliot Morison, *The Struggle for Guadalcanal*, vol. 5 of *History of United States Naval Operations in World War II*, 368–69, quoting a Japanese report about PT operations, "Battle Lessons Learned in Greater East Asia War (Torpedoes)." For a more recent (1990), highly authoritative look at the Guadalcanal campaign, see Richard B. Frank, *Guadalcanal*.

Chapter Nine: Transformation

1. Bulkley, *At Close Quarters*, 173–75.

2. See Spector, *Eagle Against the Sun*, 216; Samuel Eliot Morison, *Breaking the Bismarcks Barrier*, vol. 6 of *History of United States Naval Operations in World War II*, 48–49; Bulkley, 191.

3. See Spector, 226–28; Bulkley, 180–81.

4. Spector, 224–25; E. B. Potter, *Sea Power: A Naval History*, 317–18.

5. Bulkley, 192–93.

6. Ibid., 114–15.

7. Dick Keresey, *PT-105*, 90.

8. Nigel Hamilton, *JFK, Reckless Youth*, 545–92.

9. See Warfield's official report, "PT Operations night 1–2 August 1943," dated 5 August 1943, presented as Enclosure A of a report "Loss of PT 109—Information Concerning," submitted by E. J. Moran, Commander, MTB Squadrons, South Pacific Force, to Commander-in-Chief, United States Fleet, dated 13 January 1944. Report courtesy of the Naval Historical Center, Washington, D.C.

10. See the official report, "Sinking of PT 109 and subsequent rescue of survivors," prepared 22 August 1943 by Lt. (jg) J. C. McClure, USNR, and Lt. (jg) Byron R. White, USNR, MTB Flotilla One intelligence officers, available from the Naval Historical Center, Washington, D.C. Note that this is the same Byron "Whizzer" White President Kennedy appointed to the Supreme Court in 1962.

11. For a more detailed, more balanced account of Kennedy's wartime experiences, see Hamilton, 497–633. It should be noted that Hamilton does not fault Kennedy for the loss of PT-109, despite his work's title.

12. Bulkley, Introduction by Rear Adm. E. M. Eller, p. x.

13. See Hamilton, 567–70; see also Michael Isenberg, *Shield of the Republic*, 750–51, quoting a passage from Lt. Comdr. Patrick Monroe, "Luck of the Toss," *American Heritage* 43, n.6 (October 1992): 32–33.

14. See Hamilton, 570–71; Keresey, 71–81; see also the official report, "Sinking of PT 109 and subsequent rescue of survivors," prepared 22 August 1943.

15. Keresey, 93.
16. Hamilton, 570–79; Keresey, 93.
17. Ibid., 605–33.
18. Bulkley, 129–30.
19. Morison, *Breaking the Bismarcks Barrier*, 208. Quoted from a SoPac Combat Intelligence Center Bulletin, "Japanese Barges," January 1944.
20. See Bulkley, 131.
21. Ibid., 131.
22. Ibid., 132–33.
23. Ibid., 152.
24. Ibid., 128–29.
25. Ibid., 151.
26. Ibid., 259.
27. For a detailed operational account of barge-hunting and other functions performed by PTs in New Guinea, see Bulkley, 191–259. One reason the PTs had such good hunting was the failure of the Japanese to employ MTB-type craft to oppose them. The Japanese did have some MTBs, but this program suffered from a severe shortage of gasoline engines.

Chapter Ten: From Lend-Lease to Leyte Gulf

1. Keating, *The Mosquito Fleet*, 125–26. See also Bulkley, 277–79, for details of the arrival of MTB Squadron Fifteen in the Mediterranean.
2. Samuel Eliot Morison, *Operations in North African Waters*, vol. 2 of *History of United States Naval Operations in World War II*, 265–66. See pp. 261–65, for Morison's account of the origins of the PT and the initial operations of Squadron Fifteen. Morison relies heavily on Gordon Adamson and Douglas Van Patten, "Motor Torpedo Boats: A Technical Study," also used as a source in this work.
3. Letter from John Bulkeley to Commander L. K. Scott, Office of the Chief of Naval Operations, 13 May 1945, Record Group 15, Papers of R. K. Sutherland, Box 8, Folder 7, MacArthur Archives.
4. Bulkley, 288.
5. For the official history of PT operations in the Mediterranean, see Bulkley, 277–346. See also Keating, 125–69.
6. Bulkley, 346.
7. Ibid., 339.
8. Peter Scott, *The Battle of the Narrow Seas: A History of the Light Coastal Forces in the Channel and North Sea, 1939–1945*, 222–23.
9. Bulkley, 349–65; Keating, 170–80.
10. There are numerous, often voluminous, accounts of the Leyte Gulf action. This work relied on Morison's account in *Leyte*, vol. 12 of his *History of United States Naval Operations in World War II*; Ronald H. Spector, *Eagle Against the Sun*; and an even more recent (1994) arrival to the roster, Thomas J. Cutler, *The Battle of Leyte Gulf: 23–26 October 1944*. Cutler, on p. 188, rightly calls the PTs' torpedo attacks in Surigao Strait "frustratingly impotent."

11. Morison, *Leyte*, 208.

12. Ibid., 209.

13. See Bulkley, 376–90, for the official history of the PT battle. Bulkley reports that a second torpedo found its mark that morning in Surigao Strait, one fired by PT-323, commanded by Lt. (jg.) Herbert Stadler, against the stern of the Japanese destroyer *Asagumo*. Neither Morison nor Cutler gives credit for this attack, possibly because the *Asagumo* was already badly damaged and dead in the water. Gunfire from American cruisers and destroyers finished *Asagumo* off shortly afterward.

14. Morison, *Leyte*, 204.

15. Bulkley, 390.

16. "The Man JFK Picked to Play His Wartime Role," *Look*, 18 June 1963, 50. As of this writing, two nonfloating PT boats, one Higgins-78 and one Elco-80, are on display at the PT Museum at Battleship Cove, Fall River, Massachusetts. Two other PT boats are in the process of being restored, PT-658 in Oregon and PT-309 in Texas.

17. Admiral King's comments may be found in Ernest B. King, *U.S. Navy at War, 1941–1945: Official Reports to the Secretary of the Navy*, 58 and 114. Admiral Nimitz gave a good summation of his feelings about PTs, including their technical limitations, in the foreword to Chandler Whipple, *Lt. John F. Kennedy—Expendable!* See William D. Leahy, *I Was There*, 180.

18. See the foreword to Bulkley, for Kennedy's comments about PTs.

Epilogue: The PT as Torpedo Boat: An Assessment of Value

1. Samuel Eliot Morison, *New Guinea and the Marianas*, vol. 8 of *History of United States Naval Operations in World War II*, 56–57.

2. Keresey, *PT-105*, p. 23.

3. Torpedo chart compiled from Bulkley. Bulkley was kind enough to provide the total from the Mediterranean; remaining figures were tallied up by the author from the operational details given. Bulkley makes clear he did not include every single PT operation that took place, for reasons of space and clarity. One can be reasonably certain of his torpedo figures, however; firing a torpedo at an enemy ship was not an everyday occurrence, especially in the Pacific.

❖

Selected Bibliography

Primary Sources

Most Congressional and archival citations are contained in the notes. There are, however, several primary sources of special significance:

Bradford, R. B. *Notes on Movable Torpedoes*. Published by the U.S. Torpedo Station, Newport, R. I., 1882.

King, Ernest B. *U.S. Navy at War 1941–1945: Official Reports to the Secretary of the Navy*. Published by the United States Navy Department, Washington, D.C., 1946.

Record Group 1, Military Advisor Records. MacArthur Archives, MacArthur Memorial Museum, Norfolk, Va.

Record Group 80. Secretary of the Navy. General Board of the Navy Files, 420-14 and 420-09. National Archives, Washington, D.C.

U.S. Naval War Records Office. Series 1, vol. 10 and 11, Series 2, vol. 1, of *Official Records of the Union and Confederate Navies in the War of the Rebellion*. 31 vols. Washington, D.C.: Government Printing Office, 1894–1922.

Books

Blair, Clay, Jr. *Silent Victory: The U.S. Submarine War Against Japan*. 2 vols. Philadelphia and New York: Lippincott, 1975.

Breuer, William. *Sea Wolf: A Biography of John D. Bulkeley, USN*. Novato, Calif.: Presidio Press, 1989.

Buhl, Lance C. "Maintaining 'An American Navy,' 1865–1889." In *In Peace and War: Interpretations of American Naval History, 1775–1984*, ed. Kenneth J. Hagan, 237–62. Westport, Conn.: Greenwood Press, 1984.

Bulkley, Capt. Robert J., Jr. *At Close Quarters: PT Boats in the United States Navy*. Washington, D.C.: Government Printing Office, 1962.

Cave, Hugh B. *Long Were the Nights: The Saga of a PT boat Squadron in World War II*. Washington, D.C.: Zenger, 1943.

Conway's All the World's Fighting Ships, 1860–1905. Naval Institute Press Edition. New York: Mayflower Books, 1979.

Conway's All the World's Fighting Ships, 1906–1921. Naval Institute Press Edition. New York: Mayflower Books, 1979.

Cooper, Bryan. *PT Boats*. New York: Ballantine, 1970.

———. *The Battle of the Torpedo Boats*. New York: Stein & Day, 1970.

Cressman, Robert J., et al. *"A Glorious Page in Our History": The Battle of Midway, 4–6 June 1942."* Missoula, Mont.: Pictorial Histories, 1990.

Crowley, R. O. "The Confederate Torpedo Service." In *Secret Missions of the Civil War*, ed. Philip Van Doren Stern, 207–18. New York: Rand McNally, 1959.

Cutler, Thomas J. *The Battle of Leyte Gulf: 23–26 October 1944*. New York: HarperCollins, 1994.

Davis, Kenneth S. *FDR: The Beckoning of Destiny, 1882–1928*. New York: Random House, 1971.

———. *FDR: Into the Storm, 1937–1940*. New York: Random House, 1993.

Dictionary of American Naval Fighting Ships. 8 vols. Washington, D.C.: Government Printing Office, 1968.

Donovan, Robert J. *PT 109: John F. Kennedy in World War II*. New York: McGraw-Hill, 1961.

Ferrell, Bob, and Al Ross. *Early Elco PT Boats*. Memphis, Tenn.: PT Boat Museum and Library, 1980.

Frank, Richard B. *Guadalcanal*. New York: Random House, 1990.

Friedman, Norman. *U.S. Naval Weapons: Every Gun, Missile, Mine and Torpedo Used by the U.S. Navy from 1883 to the Present*. Annapolis, Md.: Naval Institute Press, 1984.

Gray, Edwyn. *The Devil's Device: Robert Whitehead and the History of the Torpedo*. Annapolis, Md.: Naval Institute Press, 1991.

Hagan, Kenneth J. *This People's Navy: The Making of American Sea Power*. New York: Free Press, 1991.

Halpern, Paul G. *A Naval History of World War I*. Annapolis, Md.: Naval Institute Press, 1994.

Hamilton, Nigel. *JFK, Reckless Youth*. New York: Random House, 1992.

Huff, Sidney. *My Fifteen Years with General MacArthur*. 1951. Reprint. New York: Paperback Library, 1964.

Ienaga, Saburo. *The Pacific War, 1931–1945*. New York: Pantheon, 1978.

Isenberg, Michael T. *Shield of the Republic: The United States Navy in an Era of Cold War and Violent Peace*. Vol. 1, *1945–1962*. New York: St. Martin's Press, 1993.

James, D. Clayton. *The Years of MacArthur*. Vol. 1, *1880–1941*. Boston: Houghton Mifflin, 1970. Vol. 2, *1941–1945*. Boston: Houghton Mifflin, 1975.

Johnson, Frank D. *United States PT-Boats of World War II*. Dorset, UK: Blandford Press, 1980.

Johnson, Robert Underwood, and Clarence C. Buel, eds. *Retreat with Honor*. Vol. 4 of *Battles and Leaders of the Civil War*. 4 vols. Reprint. Secaucus, N.J.: Castle, 1983.

Karnow, Stanley. *In Our Image: America's Empire in the Philippines*. New York: Ballantine, 1990.

Keating, Bern. *The Mosquito Fleet*. New York: Scholastic Book Services, 1963.

Kemp, Peter. *The History of Ships*. Stamford, Conn.: Longmeadow Press, 1988.

Keresey, Dick. *PT-105*. Annapolis, Md.: Naval Institute Press, 1996.

Leahy, William D. *I Was There*. London: Victor Gollancz, 1950.

Lee, Clark. *They Call It Pacific*. New York: Viking, 1943.

MacArthur, Douglas. *Reminiscences*. New York: Fawcett/Crest Books, 1965.

Macksey, Kenneth. *The Penguin Encyclopedia of Weapons and Military Technology*. London: Penguin, 1993.

Mahan, Alfred Thayer. *The Influence of Sea Power upon History, 1660–1805*. Novato, Calif.: Presidio Press, 1980.

Major, John. "The Navy Plans for War, 1937–1941." In *In Peace and War: Interpretations of American Naval History, 1775–1984*, ed. Kenneth J. Hagan, 237–62. Westport, Conn.: Greenwood Press, 1984.

———. "William Daniel Leahy, 2 January 1937–1 August 1939." In *The Chiefs of Naval Operations*, ed. Robert William Love, Jr. Annapolis, Md.: Naval Institute Press, 1980.

Manchester, William. *American Caesar*. Boston: Little, Brown, 1978.

Melia, Tamara Moser. *"Damn the Torpedoes": A Short History of U.S. Naval Mine Countermeasures, 1777–1991*. Washington, D.C.: Department of the Navy, Navy Historical Center, 1991.

Morison, Samuel Eliot. *History of United States Naval Operations in World War II*. 15 vols. Boston: Little, Brown, 1947–62. Volumes consulted: vol. 2, *Operations in North African Waters*; vol. 3, *The Rising Sun in the Pacific*; vol. 5, *The Struggle for Guadalcanal*; vol. 6, *Breaking the Bismarcks Barrier*; vol. 8, *New Guinea and the Marianas*; vol. 9, *Sicily–Salerno–Anzio*; vol. 12, *Leyte*.

———. *The Two Ocean War: A Short History of the United States Navy in the Second World War*. Boston: Little, Brown, 1963.

Perry, Milton F. *Infernal Machines: The Story of Confederate Submarine and Mine Warfare*. Baton Rouge: Louisiana State University Press, 1985.

Potter, E. B. *Sea Power: A Naval History*. 2nd ed. Annapolis, Md.: Naval Institute Press, 1981.

Prange, Gordon W. *At Dawn We Slept: The Untold Story of Pearl Harbor*. 1981. Reprint. New York: Viking Penguin, 1991.

Preston, Antony. *Strike Craft*. Greenwich, Conn.: Bison Books, 1982.

Romulo, Carlos P. *I Saw the Fall of the Philippines*. New York: Doubleday, Doran, 1943.

Rosen, Philip. "The Treaty Navy, 1919–1937." In *In Peace and War: Interpretations of American Naval History, 1775–1984*, ed. Kenneth J. Hagan, 221–36. Westport, Conn.: Greenwood Press, 1984.

Roske, Ralph J., and Charles Van Doren. *Lincoln's Commando: The Biography of Commander William B. Cushing, U.S.N.* New York: Harper & Brothers, 1957.

Saville, Allison W. "Charles Edison, 2 January 1940–24 June 1940." In *American Secretaries of the Navy*, vol. 2, 1913–1972, ed. Paolo E. Coletta. Annapolis, Md.: Naval Institute Press, 1980.

Scott, Peter. *The Battle of the Narrow Seas: A History of the Light Coastal Forces in the Channel and North Sea, 1939–1945*. New York: Charles Scribner's Sons, 1946.

Shulman, Mark Russell. *Navalism and the Emergence of American Sea Power, 1882–1893*. Annapolis, Md.: Naval Institute Press, 1995.

Spector, Ronald H. *Eagle Against the Sun*. New York: Vintage Books, 1985.

Sprout, Harold, and Margaret Sprout. *The Rise of American Naval Power, 1776–1918*. 1939. Reprint. Annapolis, Md.: Naval Institute Press, 1966.

Tregaskis, Richard. *John F. Kennedy: War Hero*. New York: Dell, 1962.

Turk, Richard W. "Defending the New Empire, 1900–1914." In *In Peace and War: Interpretations of American Naval History, 1775–1984*, ed. Kenneth J. Hagan, 186–204. Westport, Conn.: Greenwood Press, 1984.

U.S. Coast Guard Auxiliary. *Sailing and Seamanship*. 4th ed. Washington, D.C.: Coast Guard Auxiliary National Board, 1983.

Venable, John D. *Out of the Shadow: The Story of Charles Edison*. East Orange, N. J.: Charles Edison Fund, 1978.

Whipple, Chandler. *Lt. John F. Kennedy—Expendable!* New York: Nova Books, 1964.

White, W. L. *They Were Expendable*. New York: Harcourt, Brace, 1942.

Wolfert, Ira. *American Guerrilla in the Philippines*. New York: Simon & Schuster, 1945.

Articles

Adamson, Gordon, and Douglas Van Patten. "Motor Torpedo Boats: A Technical Study." *U.S. Naval Institute Proceedings*, July 1940, 976–96.

Arnault, Charles Chabaud. "The Employment of Torpedoes in Steam Launches Against Men-of-War." *U.S. Naval Institute Proceedings* 6, no. 11 (1880). Originally published in France in *Revue Maritime et Coloniale* 62, no. 214.

Bartsch, William H. "Philippine Air Debacle." *Air Power History*, Summer 1997.

Corgan, Michael T. "Mahan and Theodore Roosevelt: The Assessment of Influence." *Naval War College Review*, November–December 1980, 89–97.

Hone, Thomas C. "Spending Patterns of the United States Navy." *Armed Forces and Society*, Spring 1982, 443–62.

Hone, Thomas C., and Mark D. Mandeles. "Managerial Style in the Interwar Navy: A Reappraisal." *Naval War College Review*, September–October 1980, 88–101.

Peters, S. A. "The Motor Torpedo Boat." *Ordnance*, May–June 1954, 943–46.

Sokol, A. E. "Italian Attempts at Harbor Forcing During the Last War." *U.S. Naval Institute Proceedings*, January 1942, 37–41.

Von Pflugk, Captain H.A.V. "Torpedo Boats." *U.S. Naval Institute Proceedings*, August 1941, 1115–20.

Periodical

"The Man JFK Picked to Play His Wartime Role." *Look*. 18 June 1963, 48–54.

Unpublished Sources

Humphrey, W. S., and W. C. Specht. "The Motor Torpedo Boat—Past, Present and Future: History, Development, Employment and Tactics; Accomplishments to 1 February 1943." Paper first delivered to the Naval War College 17 March 1943. Administrative Histories Appendices. Box 13, Motor Torpedo Boat Materials. Operational Archives. Naval Historical Center, Washington, D.C.

Tredinnick, Frank A., Jr., and Harrison L. Bennett. "An Administrative History of PT's in World War II." U.S. Naval Administration in World War II Series, No. 171. Washington, D.C.: Office of Naval History, 1946. Rare books collection, Navy Department Library. Naval Historical Center, Washington, D.C.

Index

Page numbers in italics refer to maps or illustrations.

240 ❖ Index

❖

About the Author

Curtis L. Nelson graduated in 1978 from the University of Minnesota, Duluth, with a degree in sociology. Currently he is a distance-learning graduate student in naval warfare studies at American Military University in Manassas Park, Virginia. He lives in Eden Prairie, Minnesota, with his wife and two daughters. This is his first book.